# EXPLORING IRELAND

# EXPLORING IRELAND

## Paddy Dillon

Photographs by the author

WARD LOCK

A WARD LOCK BOOK

First published in the UK 1998
by Ward Lock
Wellington House
125 Strand
London
WC2R 0BB

A Cassell Imprint

Copyright © Paddy Dillon 1998

The maps in this book were prepared from out-of-copyright
Ordnance Survey material.

A British Library Cataloguing in Publication Data block for this book may
be obtained from the British Library.

ISBN 1-85079-352-2

Printed and bound in Slovenia by DELO tiskarna d.d.
by arrangement with Korotan-Ljubljana

# Contents

# Preface

Welcome to walking in Ireland, and in particular to walking in the east, south and west of the country. The purpose of this book is to guide your steps around a selection of classic walks across Ireland, as well as to reveal a few lesser-known areas for you to enjoy. In addition, there are notes explaining how you can shorten or extend the majority of these walks, plus brief notes detailing the availability of long-distance waymarked trails.

You will be able to wander the bleak and rugged moorland of the Wicklow Mountains, visit the Comeragh, Knockmealdown and Galty Mountains, or enjoy hills of lesser stature such as Brandon Hill and the Slieve Bloom. You can climb Ireland's highest mountains by scaling Carrauntoohil and MacGillycuddy's Reeks, or ascend revered Brandon at the end of the Dingle Peninsula. The Cliffs of Moher, The Burren, and the mountains of Connemara and Co Mayo are amazingly varied, and long walks such as the Tóchar Phádraig and Bangor Trail provide excellent cross-country routes. Then there are the glens of Sligo and Leitrim, which display bright flanks of limestone and offer a series of intricate, interesting walks.

The walks have been chosen to inspire you through their sheer variety – including mountains, moorlands, cliff coastlines, lakes, forest parks and national parks. The information is as detailed as you will need, provided that you supplement this book with the necessary maps, a compass, and the skills to use them all together. There are also lists of further contacts, so that you can smooth your travelling arrangements and be assured of a bed and a meal each night. How you travel is largely up to you, but all the walks start from a parking place, and many of them are easily accessed using public transport. Read the text carefully and choose routes which are suited your own particular ability, so that you can enjoy this selection of walks both safely and comfortably.

## Acknowledgements

There are many people throughout Ireland to whom I owe a debt of thanks for their help and advice over the years. My correspondence with the late J.B. Malone, 'The Walking Encyclopaedia', was very brief, but valuable. Both Jimmy Murphy and Frank Fahy of Cospoir have kept me up to date on waymarked trail developments. Frank Greally had the vision to launch *Walking World Ireland*, a magazine dedicated to covering walks in all parts of Ireland.

Help and assistance has been gratefully received from representatives of the Ordnance Survey of Ireland, the Office of Public Works, Midlands East Tourism, Nire Valley Failte, Glen of Aherlow Failte, Ballyhoura Failte, Kenmare Walking Club, Joyce Country Tourism, Mayo County Council, Castlebar International Four-Day Walks committee, the North Leitrim Glens Association and North West Tourism, and many small community associations striving to improve access and facilities for walkers have been generous with their time.

Accommodation providers have often gone out of their way to welcome me and help me with extra services, while local visitor centres and information points have provided me with an abundance of extra facts. You are benefiting from their enthusiasm and expertise as you follow the routes in this book, and I apologize for not being able to mention everyone who has been of assistance to me in my research.

*Looking down on the lovely Upper Lake from the rugged prow of Lugduff Spink.*

# Using the Book

In brief, this book covers the whole of the south of Ireland, taking in some of the best mountain walks in the country, as well as a handful of low-level ones. The selection includes both well-known and less frequented walking areas. Proceeding northwards into Ulster, the companion guide, *Exploring the North of Ireland*, offers further scenic and interesting walks.

## Arrangement

The layout of this book is basically quite simple. There are 36 walking routes which are arranged roughly in a clockwise direction from Co Louth to Co Leitrim. Starting with routes on the east coast and in the Wicklow Mountains, coverage extends through the south-east and south of Ireland to reach the mountainous regions of West Cork and Kerry. Many of Ireland's highest mountains are included in the walks in these areas. Hugging the coast of Co Clare, there are walks exploring The Burren before heading for Connemara and Co Mayo. Linear walks such as the ancient Tóchar Phádraig and Bangor Trail are included. The limestone glens and rugged uplands of Sligo and Leitrim are becoming better known, and routes are included there, too. In total, the walks cover over 690km (430 miles), while the cumulative ascent over the 36 routes is around 30,000m (98,500 ft) – or three-and-a-half times the height of Everest!

## Summary tables

The relevant statistics for each walk are provided in a summary table at the start of the description of the route. The information provided includes:

- time to allow for the walk
- starting and finishing locations, with details of maps, available car parking and public transport
- an overview of the route and features of interest
- details on the state of footpaths
- distance covered
- total height gained
- principal heights scaled

## Alternative routes

For each walk, details of alternative routes are provided. These are divided into 'escapes', which allow you to shorten the route for whatever reason, and 'extensions', which provide fit walkers with the option of a longer route.

## Abbreviations

The minimum of abbreviations has been used, and only to avoid constant repetition. These are listed below.

| | |
|---|---|
| N | north |
| NNE | north north-east |
| NE | north-east |
| ENE | east north-east |
| E | east |
| ESE | east south-east |
| SE | south-east |
| SSE | south south-east |
| S | south |
| SSW | south south-west |
| SW | south-west |
| WSW | west south-west |
| W | west |

| | |
|---|---|
| WNW | west north-west |
| NW | north-west |
| NNW | north north-west |
| M | metre(s) |
| FT | foot/feet |
| KM | kilometre(s) |
| GR | grid reference |
| OSNI | Ordnance Survey of Northern Ireland |
| OSI | Ordnance Survey of Ireland |

## Photographs

Walkers who like to take photographs are very much at the mercy of the weather in Ireland. Clouds roll in from the Atlantic and cover the whole country, bringing rain and mist on the high ground. Persevere. It often clears wonderfully in between times, and the air can be crystal clear after frequent rain washing, so that colours are especially vibrant. Ireland has a reputation for being '40 shades of green', which is unfortunate for anyone wanting contrasting colours, but sometimes you get a blue sky, shadowed crags, autumnal trees – and someone obligingly wearing a startlingly red jacket posing in the right place! The photographs in this guidebook are a mixed bag which illustrate the changeable nature of the weather, and the varied nature of the terrain which is crossed on the walks.

## Maps

The outline map provided for each walk is marked with the following information:

- start and finish locations
- line of the route, with directional arrows
- relevant place names and features

The standard scale of mapping which is available across Ireland is 1:50,000, although there are a couple of useful maps at 1:25,000. The maps you should use are quoted in the introduction and statistics relating to each of the walks.

Maps are published by the Ordnance Survey of Ireland, based in Dublin. Walkers who are used to

using maps will have no difficulty with these, but anyone new to map reading should proceed cautiously. The maps are numbered as part of an all-Ireland series, in co-operation with the Ordnance Survey of Northern Ireland.

The Ordnance Survey Holiday Maps of Ireland – East, South and West, are produced at a scale of 1:250,000 and are therefore useful travelling maps and good for overall planning. These small-scale maps also show many of the longer waymarked trails.

## Place names

The place names throughout this guidebook are taken from Ordnance Survey maps, unless there is a very strong case to be made for spelling to be at variance. The chapter headings are fairly arbitrary, and may not appear as such on the maps, but within the body of each route description the recorded map place names are used. Bear in mind that when talking to local people they may use different spellings and pronunciations than you might expect, or may even be accustomed to using wildly different names which simply aren't on your map – and there is always the possibility that they have never heard of the names on your map either.

Place names are half the fun of exploring an area, and those which come from a Gaelic root are often highly descriptive. However, it is important to remember that although they may have been accurately descriptive 2,000 years ago, they may not be so apt today!

## Heights

There are two methods used to indicate heights in the text. One is to give the full figure for the height of a mountain or hill, taken from the map. These are displayed in both metres and feet. Anyone converting one to another, or vice versa, will find that the values often do not match exactly. This is because the newer metric maps are drawn from a different Ordnance Datum than the previous imperial maps. The older maps were drawn from a low-water Ordnance Datum, while the newer maps are based upon a mean sea-level Ordnance Datum. The practical upshot of this is that the metric heights may appear 'shorter' than the imperial values given, if you try to convert them. However, the metric heights are given as they are taken from metric maps – and these are the ones you should be using. The imperial values are taken from the older maps and their height information is presented unchanged.

The other way of expressing heights is to give them in a rounded-up form – eg 100m (300ft) – which, while not being an exact conversion, is near enough for the purposes of presenting approximate values.

## Transport

While the car is undoubtedly the most convenient way of accessing these walks, there may not always be large car parks available. The provision of car parks is indeed indicated in the introduction to each walk, and the routes are often structured to take advantage of these; however, in some areas there may only be small parking spaces capable of holding one, two or three cars. If these prove to be full, you will need to park elsewhere.

Some of the routes are fairly well served by public transport. Rail transport is not particularly useful, but some bus services are quite good. Generally, the further away from Dublin you progress, the sparser the bus services become. Bus Eireann operates the vast majority of services around Ireland, and these are mentioned where appropriate. Note that the 'table numbers' from the timetables are given, and these may not always be the same as the service numbers. St Kevin's Bus is the only one offering good access to the Wicklow Mountains, and you may discover other small, local operators in some areas.

## Accommodation

Almost any Tourist Information Office can handle enquiries about local accommodation, and should be able to book you into an establishment. The larger offices can book you into accommodation on an all-Ireland basis, so you do not necessarily have to contact Bord Failte (the Irish Tourist Board) to sort out places to stay. In the peak summer season, advance booking is strongly recommended and some areas have been known to run out of accommodation at busy times. If you book through a Tourist Information Office or a travel agency, then you will almost certainly be booked into 'approved' accommodation which meets certain standards. If you simply travel in hope and sort out your accommodation at the last minute, then you may have to settle for 'unapproved' addresses, where you may be unable to check facilities or standards with reference to an accommodation guide.

The range of accommodation varies from campsites to hostels, self-catering, bed & breakfast, guest houses and hotels. Some places are particularly good for walkers and you should make a habit of searching them out in all the best walking areas. Bord Failte produce general accommodation guides, and there are also specific groupings of accommodation providers who produce their own listings.

## Safety

Safety is largely a matter of common sense. If you are going walking, then you need to wear appropriate walking gear, which means warm or cool clothes depending on the weather, and comfortable boots, with waterproofs readily available. You will need to carry a rucksack containing your food and drink for the day, plus a little extra to cope with unexpected emergencies; a small comprehensive first aid kit and the knowledge to use it; and possibly a change of clothing – do bear in mind that the weather can change rapidly and unexpectedly at all times of year. Your map and compass should be easily accessible, and you must have the necessary skills to use them effectively.

Safety is about being ready for any eventuality by being aware of what can go wrong and making sure that it doesn't have the chance to do so. However, accidents can happen and people may become lost, injured, or caught out in darkness. When things go badly wrong and you are alone, then you are in trouble, especially as many of the walks in this book are in remote and unfrequented countryside. If you have more than one companion, then some can stay with you and others can go for help. There are Mountain Rescue Teams ready to help, and you alert them by getting to a telephone, dialling 999 and asking for Mountain Rescue. The actual call-out may be co-ordinated by the Gardai (Police). Decisions will be based on the information you can supply, so make sure you can give details of any injury or illness, the timing of the accident and first aid given, the map reference of the spot and any distinctive land features there. All this will help the co-ordinators decide whether additional equipment or a helicopter is required. Once you have made contact, do as you are told and leave the rest to the experts. Better still – avoid getting into difficulty in the first instance. Aim to enjoy the walks in safety.

*Walkers leave Carrauntoohil's summit in the direction of the Devil's Ladder.*

# Route 1: CARLINGFORD MOUNTAIN

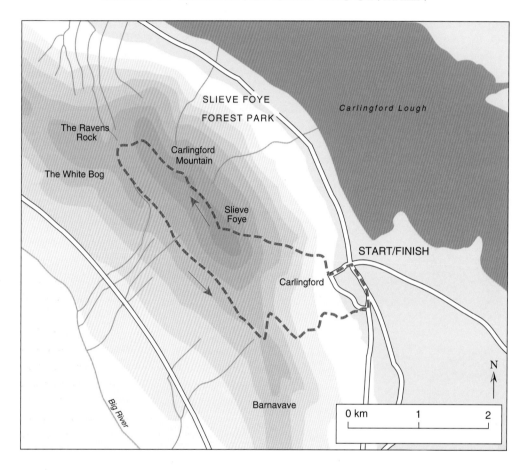

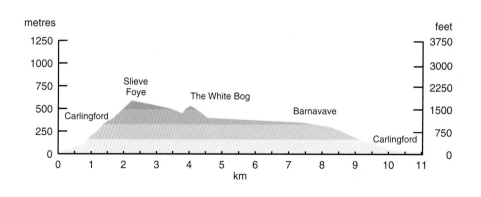

# 1

# EAST COAST

## Route 1: Carlingford Mountain

TIME ALLOWANCE 4 hours.

STARTING/FINISHING LOCATION
Carlingford.
OSNI Discoverer 29 or 36A: GR188116.
Large car park in the village.
Bus Eireann table 161.

OVERVIEW/INTEREST
Ruined buildings around Carlingford.
Highest mountain in Co Louth, rich in history
  and legend.
Features a rugged, rocky ridge and includes part
  of the waymarked Tain Way.
Fine views of near and distant mountains.

FOOTPATHS
Low-level paths and tracks are clear.
Paths on the ridge of the mountain can be vague.
The Tain Way on the mountain is waymarked.

STATISTICS
| | |
|---|---|
| WALKING DISTANCE | 12km (7½ miles) |
| TOTAL HEIGHT GAINED | 600m (1,970ft) |
| PRINCIPAL HEIGHT | |
| Slieve Foye | 589m (1,935ft) |

### The way to Slieve Foye       *Allow 1½ hours*

Carlingford is an interesting medieval village,
dominated by the steep and rocky flanks of
Carlingford Mountain. Features of interest around
Carlingford include the ruins of the Tholsel, Mint,
King John's Castle, Taafe's Castle and a Dominican
priory. There is still a portion of the original town
wall remaining, and the central parts of Carlingford
retain their narrow, poky streets.

The route starts from the middle of the village
and climbs straight up to the summit of the
mountain, returning by contouring around the
slopes before descending back into the village. The
Tain Way, which is encountered at the beginning
and end of this walk, is named after the earliest
Irish epic tale, *Táin Bó Cuailgne* – The Cattle Raid of
Cooley. Several features of the landscape have been
attributed to violent acts carried out during this
raid, when Ulster was besieged by a vast army
intent on carrying off their famous brown bull.

Start in the middle of Carlingford at McKevitt's
Village Inn and follow the narrow road which
climbs straight uphill. At the top of this road take a
turning to the right, where another road and track
head straight towards Slieve Foye Forest. You will
also notice the waymark arrows of the Tain Way,
which follow the track into the forest. Do not
actually enter the forest, but turn left and follow
the forest fence uphill. The ground is steep and
rugged underfoot, and after leaving the top side of
the forest fence it becomes even more so. You will
need to outflank the rocky outcrops, and there are
plenty of options for doing this all the way up the
slope. Views back across Carlingford Lough towards
the Mountains of Mourne open up wonderfully as
you climb, so there are plenty of excuses to pause
for breath. Eventually, on the topmost rock of
Slieve Foye, you will gain the summit trig point at

an altitude of 589m (1,935ft). In clear weather the views are remarkably extensive and can include:

N       Belfast Hills, Antrim Mountains
NNE   Slieve Martin, Eagle Mountain, Slieve Muck, Slieve Bearnagh
NE     Slieve Binnian, Slieve Donard
E        Cranfield, Kilkeel, Isle of Man
S        Howth Peninsula, Wicklow Mountains
SE      Slievenaglogh, Slieve Bloom Mountains
NW    Clermont, Slieve Gullion
NNW  Sperrin Mountains

## The way back to Carlingford
*Allow 2½ hours*

Although a direct descent could be made back towards Carlingford, it is worth walking along the rugged crest of Carlingford Mountain and returning by a more circuitous route. The mountain is composed from a rock called gabbro, which is noted for producing a rough and rugged landscape, and it occurs only very rarely in Ireland. The crest of the mountain runs roughly north-westwards, but it has so many humps and bumps that you could walk in almost any direction while trying to cross it. It is completely up to you whether or not to include every rugged top: you can steer a course around any obstacles, trying not to gain or lose height.

The trend is now gradually downwards at first, but then there is a steep and rough descent towards the gap where the White Bog is located. If you wanted to continue over to the Windy Gap you could do so, but that would mean ending up on the road with no satisfactory way to close the walk. Instead, make a pronounced turn south-east at the White Bog, to follow the line of a rugged shelf of moorland between two steep slopes of the mountain. This shelf can be boggy underfoot in places, but it is a fairly definite feature which allows you to contour across the slopes of the mountain without gaining or losing too much height. Expect a few ups and downs, and in mist the course could be difficult to maintain. By keeping the steepest slopes above you at all times, with a gentler slope falling down to your right towards the Big River,

*Walking towards Barnavave – or Maeve's Gap – to join the waymarked Táin Way.*

you will be able to contour around the mountain until you reach a shoulder bearing a reasonable path. Turning around, you will see that the summit of Slieve Foye is now directly above you, more or less to the north. Follow the path roughly south-east along the broad shoulder of the mountain, heading towards what appears to be a low hill with a notch cut into its summit. This is Barnavave, or Maeve's Gap, which according to legend was cut by the armies of Ireland in three days to leave a mark to shame Ulster. You can walk all the way to the gap if you wish, or you can begin the final descent towards Carlingford earlier.

Look out for a point where the waymarked Táin Way crosses the shoulder of the mountain. This is the clearest path crossing the shoulder and you should turn left to start following it down the rugged slope. The track makes sweeping zigzags across the slope, with occasional yellow marker

arrows confirming that you are still on course. There should be no problem following the path down to a minor road, where you turn left. The road quickly leads down into Carlingford, where all manner of shops, pubs and restaurants are on hand to serve the needs of weary walkers.

## Alternative routes

ESCAPES

Although the slopes of Carlingford Mountain seem exceptionally rugged, there are all sorts of weaknesses in their flanks. There are indeed some cliffs which should not be approached too closely, but most of the outcrops have easy ways around them. It is possible to descend from many points, but what may bring progress to a halt on the eastern flanks are masses of gorse and the conifers of Slieve Foye Forest. To the west, a descent to the Windy Gap is possible, but other descents may lead into farmland where fences and walls will need to be hurdled. On the ascent described, the easiest

escape is to turn around and walk back down. Once on the summit, however, a course south-east down a rugged ridge, to link with the Tain Way, would be preferable. Carlingford village crouches at the foot of the mountain, so in case of serious need help is close at hand.

EXTENSIONS

As already mentioned, the route could be extended to the Windy Gap, where four roads meet. Unfortunately, this leaves you with little choice but to follow one of them. A recent re-routing of the course of the Tain Way offers a return around the northern slopes of the mountain which is fine at first, but then the final stretches are confined to the conifers of Slieve Foye Forest. Anyone who is prepared to cross the Windy Gap and organize a pick-up far away from Carlingford could enjoy a greatly extended walk by crossing Carnawaddy, Clermont and possibly even Anglesey Mountain, descending then towards Flagstaff, overlooking the Narrow Water.

# Route 2: HOWTH HEAD

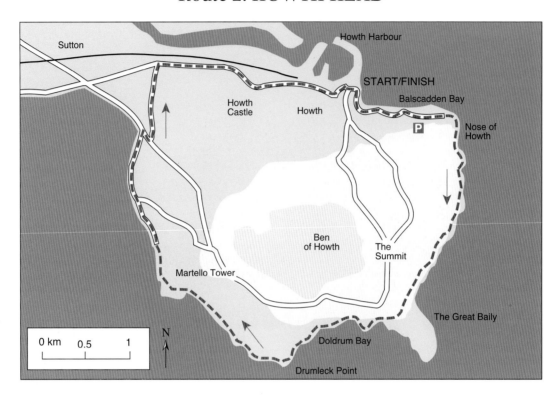

Sutton

Howth Harbour

START/FINISH

Balscadden Bay

Howth
Castle

Howth

P

Nose of
Howth

Ben
of Howth

The
Summit

Martello Tower

The Great Baily

0 km    0.5    1

N

Doldrum Bay

Drumleck Point

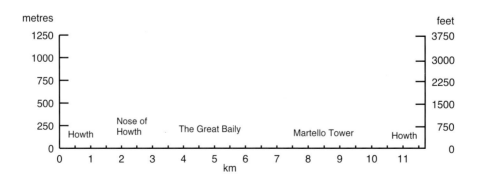

metres

feet

1250

3750

1000

3000

750

2250

500

1500

250

750

Howth

Nose of
Howth

The Great Baily

Martello Tower

Howth

0

0

0    1    2    3    4    5    6    7    8    9    10    11

km

# Route 2: Howth Head

TIME ALLOWANCE 4 hours.

STARTING/FINISHING LOCATION
Howth Harbour.
OSI Discovery 50: GR288393.
Large car park near the harbour.
Dublin Bus numbers 31 and 31B.
DART rail service from Dublin.

OVERVIEW/INTEREST
Interesting harbour at Howth.
Classic coastal walking in sight of Dublin, offering
a complete circuit of the peninsula.
Suitable for children.
Fine views from Wicklow to the Mountains of
Mourne.

FOOTPATHS
Clear, well-trodden cliff paths throughout.
One short section is on steep rock.
Includes road walking towards the end.
Mostly firm and dry underfoot.

STATISTICS
| | |
|---|---|
| WALKING DISTANCE | 13km (8 miles) |
| TOTAL HEIGHT GAINED | 150m (490ft) |
| PRINCIPAL HEIGHT | |
| The Summit | 100m (325ft) |

*Following a rocky stretch of the cliff path towards a Martello tower.*

## The way to the Great Baily

*Allow 1½ hours*

Howth Head dominates the northern side of Dublin Bay. The abrupt headland, crowned by a heathery hill, stands watch over the bay and naturally draws the eye. Despite this being connected to the mainland only by a narrow neck of land, the city of Dublin has spread on to the headland, creating a suburb out of Howth village.

The village and harbour make a good starting point for a coastal walk which encircles the entire rugged peninsula. There are steep cliffs, hidden coves, a lighthouse, Martello towers, colonies of birds, exotic plants, and more.

DART trains and Dublin Bus services reach Howth. If you are arriving by train, leave the station and turn left to follow the road to the harbour. Buses run all the way along Harbour Road; there are also car parks beside it. Follow the road to the East Pier, then turn right and follow Balscadden Road uphill. This road is perched on a rugged cliff overlooking Balscadden Bay, but views extend back to the rugged island of Ireland's Eye and in clear weather may take in the distant Mountains of Mourne. A Martello tower is perched at a higher level overlooking both the bay and the harbour.

Follow the road marked as a cul-de-sac. Look out for Balscadden House, which bears a plaque recording that the poet W. B. Yeats lived there from 1880–3. 'I have spread my dreams under your feet,' he wrote, 'Tread softly because you tread on my dreams.' Follow the road to its end, where there is a car-parking space and a few buildings. Keep to the right of the buildings to follow a very well-trodden path beyond a set of bollards. This track climbs gently as it proceeds around the Nose of Howth, and becomes a well-surfaced cliff path. Stay on the path, because there

*Looking from the Ben of Howth to the narrow neck of land at Sutton, near Dublin.*

are steep and rugged slopes both above and below it, where it is easy to get into difficulty. After turning around the point, there are fine views towards the Wicklow Mountains, Killiney, Bray Head and Wicklow Head.

The Baily Lighthouse is situated at the end of a rocky point, and once it has been spotted the cliff path starts to decend gradually down towards it. This is not a direct descent as the way twists and turns, and it is important not to take any paths leading inland. The track runs down to the access road for the lighthouse; cross over this and you will find another path which leads between dense bushes, although it is still well trodden.

## The way back to Howth Harbour

*Allow 2½ hours*

The bushes flanking the path look like garden escapees and add an exotic flavour to the walk. At one point there is an open view around the steep and rugged Doldrum Bay, with the Baily Lighthouse to the left and a white cottage perched on the cliff to the right. The path runs behind the cottage and reaches a junction with another path. Turn right and note the small metal plaque set at ground level, which reads: 'Right of way – Please do not throw stones over cliffs'.

The way is broad and clear, but remember to avoid paths leading through gates to right and left. Turn left at a junction of paths beside a short stretch of lapboard fencing, and continue to follow the path gradually downhill. It leaves the hedging behind and runs across more open slopes. After turning around Drumleck Point the views of the Baily Lighthouse are lost, but there are wider prospects around Dublin Bay. Further on there are short flights of steps, and the path follows a stout wall whith stones bonded using a rough seashell mortar. The wall is lost later as the path crosses a steep and rocky slope. Look carefully ahead to spot its course, and keep children and dogs under close control. Hands may be required as your feet move steadily across the slope. An easier path then continues towards a Martello tower, beyond which a clear track leads to a road. Turn left to follow

Strand Road, which has a bus service, and later a shop. Where it joins Carrickbrack Road, turn right, and later, left along the road called Offington Park. This is a pleasant, leafy, suburban road, and at its end a right turn leads on to the busy Howth Road. This has a bus service, and the DART railway runs alongside; the station is reached before the village and harbour at Howth. There are shops, pubs and restaurants around the harbour, and anyone staying for a while longer might enjoy an evening stroll along either the West or East Pier. At busy times there may be ferries to the rocky Ireland's Eye, which is in view offshore.

## Alternative routes

ESCAPES
This is basically a low-level route on well-trodden cliff paths. The distance is not great and there should be no need for escape routes. However, if the route is attempted in wet weather, with gale-force winds, you might regret having started the walk. Under these circumstances, either turn around and retrace your steps, or continue towards the Baily Lighthouse, and then cut inland and uphill, to link with the Dublin Bus service on Carrickbrack and Thormanby Road.

EXTENSIONS
The route makes a complete circuit around the Howth Peninsula, and walkers may assume that there is no way of extending the walk. In fact, it is also possible to climb on to the Ben of Howth – a rugged, rocky, heathery upland reaching an altitude of 171m (560ft). Unfortunately, this highest summit is spoiled by its tall transmitter masts, but other summits nearby are quite pleasant. Views stretch in all directions, perhaps embracing the mountains of Snowdonia in North Wales in conditions of crystal clarity. The Ben of Howth can be approached either from the road leaving the Baily Lighthouse, or by climbing above the access road to the Deer Park Golf Course from Howth Castle. The castle also houses a Transport Museum which is an interesting distraction.

# Route 3: DJOUCE MOUNTAIN

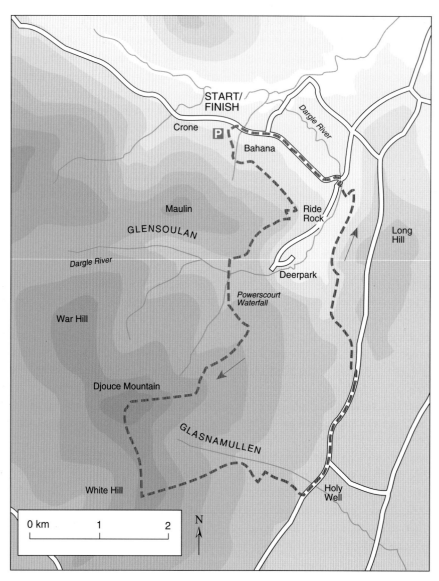

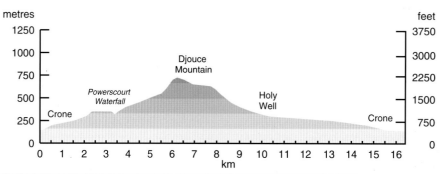

# 2
# WICKLOW MOUNTAINS

## Route 3: Djouce Mountain

TIME ALLOWANCE 6 hours.

STARTING/FINISHING LOCATION
Crone Wood, Glencree.
OSI Discovery 56: GR194143.
Forest car park at the start.
Dublin Bus 44 serves nearby Enniskerry.
St Kevin's Bus serves nearby Rocky Valley.

OVERVIEW/INTEREST
Splendid views from the summit.
Within part of the Wicklow Mountains National
    Park, and follows part of the Wicklow Way.
Can include Powerscourt Waterfall and Coolakay
    House Agricultural Heritage Centre.

FOOTPATHS
Forest tracks are generally firm and dry.
Some paths on Djouce are badly eroded.
Part of the descent is pathless.

STATISTICS
| | |
|---|---|
| WALKING DISTANCE | 20km (12½ miles) |
| TOTAL HEIGHT GAINED | 700m (2,300ft) |
| PRINCIPAL HEIGHT | |
| Djouce Mountain | 725m (2,385ft) |

### The way to Djouce Mountain

*Allow 3 hours*

The start of this walk is at Crone Wood in Glencree, in an area served by a network of minor roads. Although buses do not run into Glencree, they do run to places such as Enniskerry and the Rocky Valley, bringing you within an hour's walk of the route. In fact, if you are using St Kevin's Bus you would do well to restructure the walk and start near Calary, where a minor road departs from the R755 to lead walkers on to the route around Glasnamullen.

Motorists can navigate along minor roads signposted for Powerscourt Waterfall, or simply Waterfall, and then head for the forest car park at Crone Wood. Some walkers are in the habit of climbing Djouce Mountain from Powerscourt Waterfall, but the Powerscourt Estate would prefer that they didn't. Entrance to Powerscourt Waterfall and the Deerpark is subject to payment, and limited to specific opening times. Anyone parking there and heading off for a long walk could risk having their car locked in when the place closes in the evening.

The forest car park at Crone Wood is easily identified nearby as it has a sign at its entrance, and there is also a signpost indicating the course of the Wicklow Way to distant Glendalough. Park in the car park, which also has a couple of picnic tables nearby. Walk past a barrier and follow a forest track for a short way. Take the turning off to the left, which is indicated by a Wicklow Way marker post. This track later swings to the right, after which there is another waymarked turning to the left.

The Wicklow Way follows a forest track gradually uphill and there are occasional peeps out between the trees to fields around Bahana. Later on the forest track zigzags more steeply uphill, and then reaches something of a surprise viewpoint at Ride Rock. A deep, wooded glen suddenly opens up,

with a patchwork of grassy areas threaded by paths. The eye is immediately drawn to the head of the glen, where Powerscourt Waterfall slides down a rockface. When the water is in spate it hits a ledge and spurts upwards, before cascading down and spraying outwards from the foot of the fall. Also in view, beyond the head of the glen, is Djouce Mountain. Across the glen is the pyramidal peak of the Great Sugar Loaf.

Following the track onwards from Ride Rock, the way is flanked by growths of bilberry. You then enter a stretch of mixed woodland, but the route emerges for another view of the waterfall. From this position, only the lower half of the fall can be seen. The path crosses boulders and passes beneath an overhang of rock, which can offer shelter when bad weather obliges by coming from the right direction. The Wicklow Way now enters a dense patch of forestry and it is important to look for a couple of markers which keep you on paths heading to the right. You also need to watch where you place your feet, as there are tree roots, boulders and patches of mud waiting to trap the unwary. The path soon reaches the edge of the forest, where there is a view of Djouce Mountain across Glensoulan.

Turn left to walk downhill on a well-trodden path alongside the forest. There is a footbridge spanning the Dargle River, where the water is already hurrying briskly towards its powerful leap at Powerscourt. Continue walking uphill alongside the wall running parallel to the edge of the forest, and you will notice that the grass and bracken give way to a uniform covering of heather. On the shoulder of the mountain, a Wicklow Way marker points to the right, where a clear path heads across the heathery slopes.

The path climbs easily, but gradually steepens. Look out for a number of marker posts indicating where the Wicklow Way bears left across the shoulder of the mountain. The path becomes quite stony, cutting a clear line across the heathery slope. The Wicklow Way actually pursues a course south-westwards across the flanks of Djouce Mountain, but to make a summit bid you need to take a path

*The powerful plunge of Powerscourt Waterfall can be visited by a short detour.*

heading eastwards. There should be no mistaking the path you require, as it heads off uphill to the right and is quite clear. At the junction with the Wicklow Way there is a small cairn, which usually bears a Wicklow Way marker post. Unfortunately, this post is loose and sometimes gets knocked over or goes missing.

The path climbs straight uphill and is mostly firm and stony, although some of its upper and lower sections can be muddy. Try to keep erosion under control by walking on the stony sections, rather than on the worn heather and peat to either side of the path. As the path climbs, it becomes steeper. The summit trig point cannot be seen until the last minute, and stands perched on a jagged spike of rock at 725m (2,385ft). Views in clear weather can be remarkably extensive, stretching even to Wales, and certainly embracing all that is best in the Wicklow Mountains. Try to spot the following near and distant features:

| | |
|---|---|
| N | Maulin, Prince William's Seat |
| NNE | Dublin Bay, Howth Head |
| NE | Great Sugar Loaf |
| E | Downs Hill, Greystones, Snowdonia |
| S | White Hill, Trooperstown Hill |
| SSW | Scarr, Mullacor |
| SW | Fancy Mountain, Tonelagee, Camaderry, Lugnaquillia |
| WSW | Mullaghcleevaun |
| W | Carrigvore |
| NW | War Hill, Kippure |
| NNW | Tonduff |

## The way back to Crone Wood
*Allow 3 hours*

There are a number of spikes of rock leading back from the trig point on top of Djouce. A path accompanies them and gradually swings to the left, until it is running roughly southwards down the slopes of the mountain. Note the occasional metal posts of an old boundary fence, and beware of stumps of metal protruding from the ground. The path is badly eroded in places, and runs across bare rock for a short while at a point where it follows a blunt ridge. You will pass a Wicklow Way marker post, where the waymarked trail comes in from the left.

The route continues southwards to cross a broad and boggy gap, followed by a slight ascent on to the broad crest of White Hill. Follow the Wicklow Way no further than the summit of the hill, which is marked by a small cairn, an outcrop of rock and a metal post. The altitude is 630m (2,075ft). You may wonder why this hump of bog, heather and grass is called White Hill: if you descend roughly north-west you will pass a scattering of huge white quartz boulders, and this may be how the hill acquired its name. Heading in this direction, you will first cross tussocky grass and then have to forge

through deep, pathless heather as you head towards the top side of a forest near Glasnamullen.

Keep to the left side of the forest, crossing two firebreak tracks and looking for the end of an access track in a clear-felled part of the forest. Join this track and let it lead you on a zigzag course down to a small parking space beside a minor road. Turn left to follow the road. As you cross a small river, there is access to a small holy well. Beyond a road junction, look out for a VR postbox, and pass the attractive house called Grouse Lodge.

Follow the minor road until it climbs uphill alongside a forest. On the left is a small forest car park, which you should enter. Out of sight at the end of the car park is a path leading downhill to a

gateway. Swing sharply to the right at the gateway and follow a level track alongside a couple of disused dams in a forested valley. Avoid any junctions to left and right, and follow this clear track gradually downhill across a forested slope. You may have a brief glimpse of Powerscourt Waterfall through the trees on the way.

At the bottom of this broad forest track there is an intersection with other, lesser tracks. Head slightly to the left, to follow a track passing between two wooden gateposts. This track continues gently downhill, ending with a series of graded zigzags. There is a barrier at the end of the track, where you should turn right along a minor road. The road leads out through a pair of iron gates also on the right, although if you turned left towards a cottage you could obtain a ticket to visit Powerscourt Waterfall and approach it from the base.

To bring the walk to a close, however, go through the gates and turn left. Follow the road across Waterfall Bridge and continue uphill through Bahana. Once you have passed a junction with another minor road, you will see the sign for Crone Wood and the Wicklow Way signpost which points towards the forest car park where the walk started.

## Alternative routes

ESCAPES

Although many people do climb up and down alongside Powerscourt Waterfall, these paths can be steep and slippery in places, especially after bad weather. Accidents have occurred in the area. If an escape is needed on the way towards Djouce Mountain, the best course of action is to retrace your steps to Crone Wood. Once you have crossed the summit of Djouce or, more particularly, reached the summit of White Hill, the course of the Wicklow Way could be used to reach the R759 road at Luggala. This does, unfortunately, leave you on the wrong side of Djouce, but aid might be more easily summoned from a passing motorist.

EXTENSIONS

The walk along the Wicklow Way from Crone Wood to Luggala can be very pleasant after a dry spell has made the boggy parts firmer underfoot. This is also a very popular stretch of the Wicklow Way, but to complete it requires transport at both ends. The circular walk can be extended by following a path up Glensoulan and then climbing War Hill. A longer and tougher extension could include Maulin, Tonduff and War Hill. The shapely peak of the Great Sugar Loaf might also beckon, but its inclusion would entail a lot of road walking. Save an ascent of the Sugar Loaf for some other time: it only needs an hour or so for a there-and-back walk from a minor road on Glencap Common.

*Powerscourt Waterfall and Djouce Mountain seen from Ride Rock.*

25

# Route 4: MULLAGHCLEEVAUN

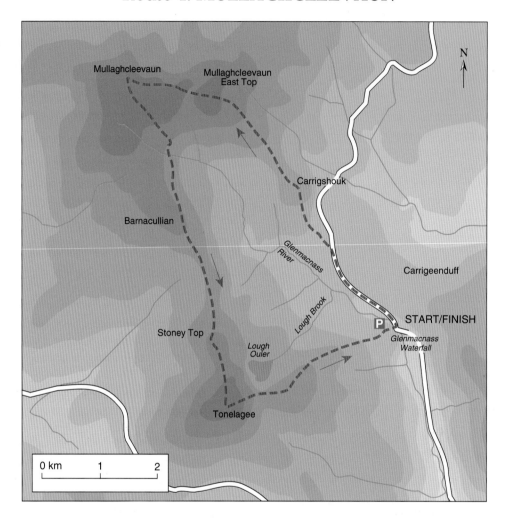

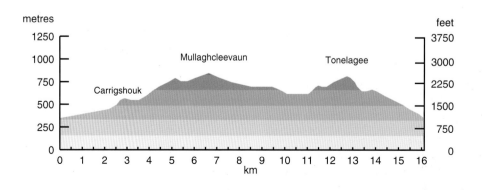

# Route 4: Mullaghcleevaun

TIME ALLOWANCE 6 hours.

STARTING/FINISHING LOCATION
Glenmacnass Waterfall.
OSI Discovery 56: GR114030.
Car park at the top of the waterfall.
St Kevin's Bus serves nearby Laragh.

OVERVIEW/INTEREST
Circuit in the heart of the Wicklow wilderness,
    starting on the Military Road.
Includes Glenmacnass Waterfall and part of the
    Wicklow Mountains National Park.
Wide-ranging views from the summits.

FOOTPATHS
The Military Road is the only road used.
Paths on high ground tend to be vague.
Some parts of the route cross rugged bogs.

STATISTICS
| | |
|---|---|
| WALKING DISTANCE | 16km (10 miles) |
| TOTAL HEIGHT GAINED | 850m (2,790ft) |
| PRINCIPAL HEIGHTS | |
| Mullaghcleevaun | 849m (2,788ft) |
| Tonelagee | 817m (2,686ft) |

## The way to Mullaghcleevaun

*Allow 2½ hours*

This walk is in the middle of the Wicklow Mountains, in an area devoid of real paths and tracks, and served only by the Military Road. This route was pushed through the Wicklow wilderness by the British Army following the 1798 Rebellion, and it is signposted all the way through the Wicklow Mountains. As it is one of the highest roads in Ireland, it naturally offers good access to the uplands and allows walkers to start high-level walks with greater ease. Another feature of note on this particular stretch of the Military Road is

Glenmacnass Waterfall. As the route starts and finishes at the top of the waterfall, you will have opportunities to view it on arrival and departure.

There is a car park at the top of Glenmacnass Waterfall. To the left, look out for a footbridge which you may wish to use at the end of the day. Leave the car park and follow the Military Road gradually uphill. It rises across a bleak and rugged heather moorland and you follow it until it reaches a crest and begins to descend towards a forest. You should notice a sheep pen to the left, and after passing this you can leave the road and head diagonally left across the rugged moorland.

Aim for a corner of a young forest, where you will find a gate in a fence. Go through the gate and continue straight uphill on the slopes of Carrigshouk. The short ascent crosses deep heather and a vague path passes a few boulders. There is a small cairn marking the summit at 571m (1,877ft). A path can be traced where the bog has been worn from the bedrock, beyond which the line is less obvious. However, the direction to follow is roughly north-westwards towards Mullaghcleevaun.

You now cross a broad and boggy gap and then a fence, shortly after the next ascent begins. The ground supports rough grass and heather, and is scattered with occasional boulders. As you gain height, there are opportunities to walk on grassy or stony surfaces where the blanket bog has been eroded away. Then, as the gradient eases, the summit area is gained among a scattering of huge boulders. There is also a cairn on Mullaghcleevaun East Top at 795m (2,615ft). The views are beginning to develop nicely, but the bulk of Mullaghcleevaun still obstructs the western prospect.

Descend roughly westwards for a short way to land on a broad gap. This gap is completely covered in black peat, bearing hardly a blade of grass. It is much less deep than it once was and should not prove difficult to cross, but much of it can be outflanked by keeping well to the right. Once across the gap, follow a firm slope of grass on to the broad summit of Mullaghcleevaun. There is a trig point encased in a bouldery cairn at 849m (2,788ft). Attached to a large boulder nearby is a memorial plaque recording the drowning of three Wicklow hikers at Clogher Head. The views take in most of the Wicklow Mountains, a large expanse of the Blessington Lakes, and stretch well across the plains. Look out for:

| | |
|---|---|
| N | Seefin, Seefingan |
| NNE | Kippure |
| NE | Duff Hill, Gravale, Tonduff |
| ENE | War Hill, Djouce |
| E | Mullaghcleevaun East Top, Luggala |
| SE | Scarr, Trooperstown Hill |
| SSE | Tonelagee, Brockagh, Derrybawn |
| S | Turlough Hill, Lugduff |
| SSW | Conavalla, Lugnaquillia |
| SW | Lobawn, Keadeen Mountain |
| WSW | Silsean, Church Mountain |
| W | Moanbane, Slieve Bloom Mountains |
| NNW | Sorrel Hill |

### The way to Tonelagee

*Allow 2½ hours*

Tonelagee lies almost due south of Mullaghcleevaun, but to suggest walking in that direction seems ridiculous. Stretching away to Barnacullian is a broad, black crest of eroded blanket bog, which is either bereft of vegetation or cut into a maze of peat hags and groughs. It looks incredibly difficult terrain, and make no mistake that it is, but it can be avoided by using the Green Road. This is the name given by some walkers to the grassy strip between the eastern edge of the blanket bog and the steep slopes falling towards Glenmacnass. The line is easy to spot and follow on a clear day, but could just as easily be missed in poor visibility. The choice is yours, but the route description assumes you will opt for the Green Road to get away from Mullaghcleevaun.

Leave the summit of Mullaghcleevaun roughly south-eastwards, as if heading straight towards the distant Glenmacnass Waterfall. Keep scanning the slope falling before you, aiming to follow the firm and grassy stretches. When you reach the first few patches of blanket bog, look out for a grassy, stony channel which charts a winding course on towards the head of the glen. You should emerge dry-shod from the blanket bog at the top of a steep slope, where a right turn will lead you across a small stream full of little waterfalls. Beyond this stream is a fence which you cross using a small stile.

To continue, simply follow the firm, grassy strip between the blanket bog and the steep slope falling eastwards. If you notice any completely separate patches of blanket bog, you could wander behind them and view the more desolate parts of the Barnacullian ridge. At the end of this long, black ridge, the ground is covered with grass and heather,

*Glenmacnass Waterfall tumbles into Glenmacnass at the end of the walk.*

is more rugged underfoot, and falls a short way to a broad and boggy gap. There is a path which you might be lucky to pick up on the way downhill, but it is not essential that you use it.

There is no real path across the broad and boggy gap, but the softest parts and the majority of peat hags can be avoided by keeping just to the west of the crest. There is even a firm, stony patch encountered in this direction. Looking beyond the gap, a path can be seen climbing up the grass and heather slopes of Stoney Top. Follow this up to the summit, which is indeed bare and stony.

The path now drops a short way to cross a gap of bare, black peat and stones. It then rises up a heathery slope studded with boulders to reach a shoulder of Tonelagee. There is a view of the heart-shaped Lough Ouler, and then the path crosses stones, peat and grass to reach the summit trig point at 817m (2,686ft). The trig point has been planted on top of a bouldery cairn. The views are essentially the same as from Mullaghcleevaun, but there are differences: from this point you may be able to see the water in the reservoir on top of Turlough Hill, while views of Blessington Lake have vanished.

## The way back to Glenmacnass
*Allow 1 hour*

The descent from Tonelagee is basically quite simple, but the broad slopes could be confusing in mist, when a compass bearing would be recommended. In clear weather, walk along a vague path which becomes much more obvious as it descends a steep slope to the south of Lough Ouler. The path twists and turns and eventually lands on a stony gap. There are good views of Lough Ouler below the eastern cliff face of Tonelagee.

Continue eastwards on to a slight hump of grassy bog, then descend more to the north-east for a while. There is grass, heather and some boggy patches on the slope, and only vague traces of a path, which is a bit more obvious at a lower level. The final part of the slope is steeper, wetter, bouldery and roughly vegetated. Keep well to the left of a forest to drop down to Glenmacnass River and cross at a point where there are boulders to use as stepping stones.

Alternatively, you can use the footbridge. The car park is beside the road.

If you have not seen Glenmacnass Waterfall there are two ways of doing so. One is from a viewing point near the car park, where signs warn you not to proceed beyond a wall – people have fallen here and been killed or injured. Alternatively, the full length of the falls can be seen from points further down the Military Road in Glenmacnass.

## Alternative routes

### ESCAPES

Once this route has been started and completed as far as Mullaghcleevaun, the logical escape route is to retreat the same way. Continuing from Mullaghcleevaun, take care to locate the course of the Green Road across Barnacullian, otherwise time and energy could be lost thrashing around in the black bogs on the crest of the ridge. If an escape is needed from the boggy gap between Barnacullian and Stoney Top, you could cross the rugged moorland slopes and head eastwards to find the Glenmacnass River, which can then be followed downstream towards the waterfall. Once Tonelagee's summit has been gained, it makes more sense to continue with the route. However, the nearest road to the summit of Tonelagee is on the Wicklow Gap, and this is reached easily by walking south-westwards. It may leave you on the wrong side of the mountain, but would bring you more quickly to a passing motorist if aid were needed urgently.

### EXTENSIONS

This is a rough and wild but basically straight-forward circuit. It could be extended in any number of ways. Starting from Laragh, you could climb Paddock Hill and Scarr before heading for Carrigshouk and Mullaghcleevaun. After leaving Tonelagee, the route could be continued across Brockagh Mountain to return to Laragh. A fine high-level, linear walk could be enjoyed all the way from the Sally Gap to Laragh, and much of this route is included in the gruelling Lug Walk, which stretches from Kippure to Lugnaquillia and embraces the wildest and boggiest of the Wicklow Mountains.

# Route 5: GLENDALOUGH

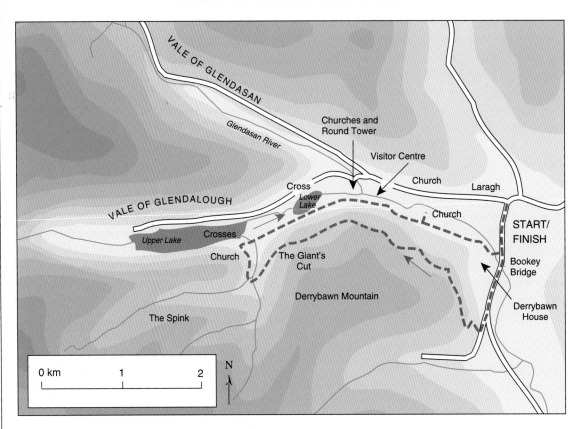

VALE OF GLENDASAN

Glendasan River

Churches and
Round Tower

Visitor Centre

Cross

VALE OF GLENDALOUGH

Lower
Lake

Church

Laragh

Church

Upper Lake

Crosses

START/
FINISH

Church

The Giant's
Cut

Bookey
Bridge

Derrybawn Mountain

Derrybawn
House

The Spink

0 km          1          2          N

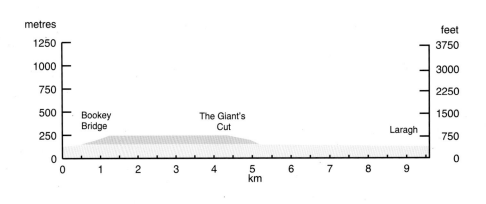

| metres | | | feet |
| --- | --- | --- | --- |
| 1250 | | | 3750 |
| 1000 | | | 3000 |
| 750 | | | 2250 |
| 500 | Bookey | The Giant's | 1500 |
| | Bridge | Cut | |
| 250 | | | Laragh |
| | | | 750 |
| 0 | | | 0 |

0    1    2    3    4    5    6    7    8    9
km

# Route 5: Glendalough

TIME ALLOWANCE 4 hours.

STARTING/FINISHING LOCATION
Laragh.
OSI Discovery 56: GR143966. Also 1:25,000 map
of Glendalough.
Car parking around the village.
St Kevin's Bus service to and from Dublin.

OVERVIEW/INTEREST
Pleasant walk around a scenic glen with lovely
views, in the Wicklow Mountains National
Park.
Suitable for children.
Plenty of heritage features to study, including an
impressive range of ruined monastic buildings.
Runs close to the informative Glendalough Visitor
Centre.

FOOTPATHS
Paths and tracks are clear and firm throughout.
Some parts use the waymarked Wicklow Way.

STATISTICS
WALKING DISTANCE    11km (7miles)
TOTAL HEIGHT GAINED    200m (650ft)

## The way to the Upper Lake

*Allow 2½ hours*

Glendalough is forever associated with St Kevin, who lived in a cave overlooking the Upper Lake. It is said that when he waded into the cold waters of the lake to pray with outstretched arms, a bird made a nest and laid her eggs in the palm of his hand. The good saint duly waited until the eggs were hatched and the fledglings flown before he emerged from the lake. It is also said that he was tempted by the Devil in the guise of a beautiful woman, whom he pushed over the cliff into the lake! Of such men are legends born, and a small rural monastery grew in Glendalough. The ruins of the celebrated Seven Churches can be seen on this walk, as well as a ruined cathedral, St Kevin's Kitchen and a round tower. Plenty of background information is available from the Glendalough Visitor Centre, which also supplies a detailed 1:25,000 map of the area.

Starting from the village of Laragh, follow the R755 southwards. This is the road known as the Military Road, constructed by the British Army through the Wicklow Mountains after the 1798 Rebellion. After crossing Glendasan River, branch off to the right along the minor road for Glenmalure, which is also part of the Military Road. As you follow this road uphill, look out for a turning on the right, where a grassy track zigzags uphill on the wooded slope. There is a sign pointing out that you are entering a National Nature Reserve.

When you reach a forest track at a higher level, turn right to follow it gently uphill and then downhill. Bear left at the next prominent junction, climbing gently uphill before contouring around the forested slopes of Derrybawn Mountain. The track roughly marks the junction between well-established oakwoods and later coniferous plantations, and there is a bird's-eye view over the oakwoods to the ancient monastic enclosure and modern Visitor Centre. Further on there is a wooden bench beside the track where a splendid view looks across the waters of the Upper Lake, which are framed by rugged, mountainous slopes hemming in a view towards the remote head of the glen. Spend time here to make the most of the view.

The track now descends and you should keep walking downhill to reach a bridge crossing Lugduff Brook. A selection of rocks and minerals featured in this area have been set into a block beside the bridge. The brook flows steeply down through a

31

rocky gorge, and by turning right down a path after crossing the bridge, you will be able to enjoy a view of the lovely little Poulanass Waterfall. The path later rejoins the broader track, and as the ground levels out you can bear left and walk towards the foot of the Upper Lake. On still days the water reflects the surrounding steep walls of the glen perfectly, but in windy conditions there may be waves breaking all along the sandy beach. St Kevin's Bed is in a cave high up on the cliff to the left but an approach is not particularly recommended, as the way can be steep and slippery. Someone takes a bad fall or is killed there every year.

## The way back to Laragh          *Allow 1½ hours*

There are all sorts of odd little features to be discovered on the way back to Laragh, and you could easily spend all day searching for them. Close to the head of the Upper Lake are the ruins of Reefert Church, one of the celebrated Seven Churches. There are also little stone crosses waiting to be discovered. A small Information Office may be open, where some details can be gathered in advance of reaching the main Visitor Centre. To continue the walk, stay on the broad and clear track at the foot of the wooded slope, passing the Information Office on the way from the Upper Lake to the Lower Lake.

like in its heyday, and an audio-visual presentation looks at the development of Irish rural monasticism with reference to Glendalough.

When the ruins have been explored, walk back across the bridge to join the course of the Wicklow Way again and turn left. The wooded track leads onwards, with occasional glimpses of Glendasan River. Later on, when the river has veered away from the track, there is a signposted access route to St Saviour's Church, the ruins of which lie in a wooded setting close to the river. Retrace your steps after visiting this site and continue along the track. Next, enter a courtyard that is not far from Derrybawn House, where an old mill offers hostel accommodation on the Wicklow Way. Leaving the mill, the access road crosses the river to reach the R755 road. Simply turn left to follow this road back into Laragh, where tea shops, pubs, restaurants and accommodation are available.

## Alternative routes

ESCAPES

This walk is so easy and straightforward that escape routes are hardly necessary. If it is attempted in exceptionally bad weather, you might wish to pop into the Glendalough Hotel or the Glendalough Visitor Centre at the half-way mark and abandon the walk, but normally there would be no problem completing the whole route.

EXTENSIONS

This route is intended to be a low-level, easy walk which gives the interested visitor time to appreciate the history, heritage and natural beauty of Glendalough. It could be extended by tying it in with the course of the Glendalough Horseshoe walk, which would drastically reduce the amount of time available to spend around the monastic ruins. You might like to sample the walk a number of times, bearing in mind that according to an old tradition, seven pilgrimages to Glendalough were reckoned to equal one pilgrimage to Rome!

This clear track is part of the waymarked Wicklow Way, and it runs close to the Visitor Centre. Access to the centre lies across a bridge, but few people get there without being distracted. Immediately across an earlier bridge is a curious stonework structure known as St Kevin's Kitchen, which looks like a combination of an ancient church and a miniature round tower. A short walk up through a graveyard leads to the ruins of the cathedral, and a lofty round tower also catches the eye just off to the left. The original stone gatehouse is still in use as an access point from near the Glendalough Hotel. The Glendalough Visitor Centre contains a model of what the monastic enclosure would have looked

# Route 6: GLENDALOUGH HORSESHOE

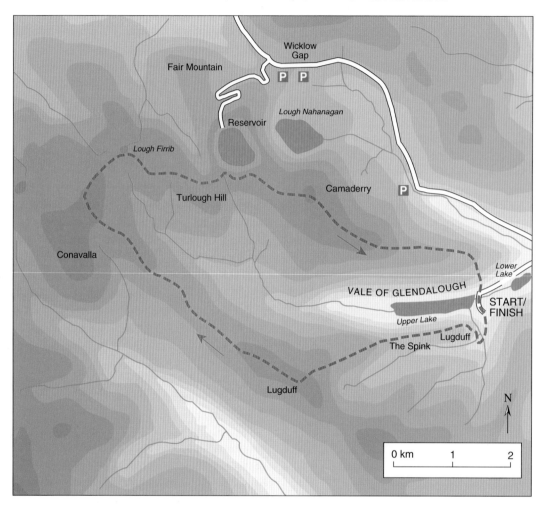

Fair Mountain

Wicklow Gap

P P

Lough Nahanagan

Reservoir

Lough Firrib

Turlough Hill

Camaderry

P

Conavalla

Lower Lake

VALE OF GLENDALOUGH

START/ FINISH

Upper Lake

Lugduff

The Spink

Lugduff

N

0 km 1 2

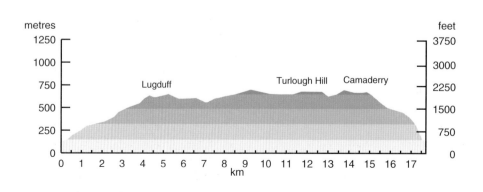

metres | feet

1250 — 3750

1000 — 3000

Lugduff    Turlough Hill  Camaderry

750 — 2250

500 — 1500

250 — 750

0 — 0

0 1 2 3 4 5 6 7 8 9 10 11 12 13 14 15 16 17

km

# Route 6: Glendalough Horseshoe

TIME ALLOWANCE 6 hours.

STARTING/FINISHING LOCATION
Upper Lake, Glendalough.
OSI Discovery 56: GR111964.
Large car park at the Upper Lake.
St Kevin's Bus serves Glendalough.

OVERVIEW/INTEREST
Popular circuit of the mountains above
  Glendalough.
Fine views of the Upper and Lower Lakes, and the
  surrounding Wicklow Mountains.
Includes parts of the Wicklow Mountains National
  Park.
Close to the monastic ruins and Seven Churches.

FOOTPATHS
A fairly continuous path is available.
Paths can be vague and some are overtrodden.
Starts with a stretch of the Wicklow Way.

STATISTICS

| STATISTICS | |
|---|---|
| WALKING DISTANCE | 18km (11 miles) |
| TOTAL HEIGHT GAINED | 780m (2,560ft) |
| PRINCIPAL HEIGHTS | |
| Lugduff | 652m (2,154ft) |
| Conavalla (north-eastern summit) | 702m (2,310ft) |
| Turlough Hill | 681m (2,228ft) |
| Camaderry | 698m (2,296ft) |

## The way to Lugduff
*Allow 1½ hours*

The road signposted for Glendalough ends at a car park beside the Upper Lake. Views along the length of the lake take in a rugged, wooded cliff-line, a bouldery glen-head and a distant view of bleak moorland heights. This walk makes a complete circuit around the rolling summits surrounding Glendalough, and the scenery varies from sheer cliffs to bleak bogs, with both forestry and heather moorlands. The circuit is popular enough for some of the paths to be badly eroded, but in other parts locating the line can prove quite difficult.

Leaving the car park beside the Upper Lake, follow a narrow tarmac road towards the nearby Information Office. There is a wide wooden bridge spanning a river, with a signpost indicating Poulanass Waterfall. Although a track can be followed onwards, you should climb a flight of steps and follow a path climbing uphill alongside the waterfall. There is a fence flanking the edge of a deep gorge through which the water pours. When you reach the top of the path, turn left to follow a forest track, which is waymarked as part of the Wicklow Way. At the next junction of tracks, however, turn sharply to the right and then follow the track uphill for a short way until it bends to the left. Cross a stile on the right to leave the track.

A sign fixed to the stile warns 'Danger – Cliffs', and a path runs up a slope planted with young trees. At a higher level, there are more mature trees to the left. After a steep ascent you cross another stile and continue uphill on a strip of ground between the forest and the cliffs dropping into the Upper Lake. The path can be rough and muddy underfoot, and it is quite overtrodden on top of Lugduff Spink. Look out for little spur paths, which generally lead to precarious viewpoints much favoured by photographers.

The blunt ridge of Lugduff Spink is clothed with grass, heather and bracken. It also has a broad dip along its length, and walkers following the path may encounter deer or goats. There are also a couple of deep and precipitous gullies which appear with very little warning: enjoy the scenery, but tread with care. You will find that the path steepens again beyond a stile, and as you climb you need to watch for a gradual parting of the way. By keeping to the right you will be drawn further along the top

of the cliffs, but away from the summit of Lugduff. By keeping to the left, however, you can follow the forest fence towards Lugduff.

The fence is actually some distance away from the top edge of the forest, but is accompanied by a firebreak track which is pleasant and easy to trace. It is flanked by rugged heather moorlands which would be quite difficult to cross without the aid of a path. Follow the forest fence uphill until it turns to the left. At this point you should head off to the right along a narrower path, which climbs on to a broad shoulder of Lugduff. There is a fairly well-trodden path along the crest of the mountain which you follow downhill for a short distance before it leads to the summit of Lugduff. The path skilfully avoids patches of blanket bog, crossing grass and heather to reach a bouldery cairn on the 652m (2,154ft) summit of Lugduff. From this vantage point there is a clear view all the way around the route.

### The way to Turlough Hill    *Allow 2½ hours*

The route now runs roughly north-westwards along a broad crest beyond the summit of Lugduff. There is a slight descent, then the path runs out across a bouldery shoulder where it is harder to trace. On the next descent you will reach a broad and boggy gap, where the path needs to be followed with greater care as it is easily lost among peat hags. When you climb on to the next rugged shoulder, you will be able to look along the broad crest to spot an area of relatively undecayed blanket bog. Climb towards this, because it offers a fairly good footing for a while.

You next reach a very broad and bouldery area to the north-east of Conavalla, rising to 702m (2,310ft). There are some patches of black bog which often bear many footprints and the broad crest is obviously walked quite frequently. There is a sort of ditch cut straight along part of the crest, and most walkers tend to follow this line. You will cross a desolate tract of rock and bog on the way

*The Upper Lake in early morning mirrors the rugged Glendalough Horseshoe.*

to the little Lough Firrib. In clear weather, you will be able to see the huge hump of Tonelagee rising beyond the lough; in poor visibility, the lough is a useful feature to aim towards.

Here a change of direction is needed. Walk roughly south-eastwards along a broad, bouldery and boggy moorland crest, then aim more eastwards across a rugged little gap. Rock outcrops are passed on a slight ascent, and there are monstrous boulders perched on the next part of the rugged crest. In clear weather you will have noticed a little hut with an aerial earlier in the route, and this stands on a summit at 681m (2,228ft), which has been disturbed. There is also a quarry surrounded by a fence. You now join a gravel track which leads towards Turlough Hill.

Turlough Hill is an intrusion into the Wicklow wilderness and has the strange appearance of a volcanic cone. In fact, the summit of the hill bears an artificial circular dam holding a reservoir. Water flows down from the reservoir into Lough Nahanagan, turning turbines to produce electricity during the day. At night-time, when a surplus of electricity is available, water is pumped back from Lough Nahanagan into the reservoir on Turlough Hill so that it can be used to produce more power the next day. There are occasional minibus tours around the reservoir on top of Turlough Hill, but most walkers will be happy to leave the huge dam behind and continue the walk.

## The way back to the
## Upper Lake
*Allow 2 hours*

Turn right to walk around the foot of the dam on Turlough Hill, following the perimeter fence for a while. There is a vague path leaving the fence and heading across a broad and boggy gap. Try to follow this path faithfully, as it makes use of stony and peaty channels through the blanket bog. Once across the gap, the path rises on the broad, heathery slopes of Camaderry to reach a rash of boulders on the summit at 698m (2,296ft). As this is quite a prominent height on the circuit, it is worth spending some time sampling the view, which is largely restricted to the surrounding

Wicklow Mountains. Look around to spot some of the following features:

| | |
|---|---|
| N | Tonelagee, Mullaghcleevaun, Kippure |
| NE | Scarr, Luggala, Djouce Mountain |
| ENE | Brockagh Mountain |
| ESE | Trooperstown Hill |
| SSE | Mullacor, Croaghanmoira, Croaghan Mountain |
| SSW | Lugduff, Clohernagh |
| SW | Lugnaquillia |
| WSW | Conavalla, Camenabologue |
| WNW | Turlough Hill |
| NW | Silsean, Moanbane |

The path now heads south-eastwards along the broad crest of Camaderry, crossing a broad gap and rising slightly to a subsidiary summit bearing a cairn. Continuing more eastwards, it descends a steep and rugged slope for a while, and then runs out on to a gentler slope of uniform heather. You cross a fence and the path continues onward, later dropping downhill again on to a grassy, bracken-covered slope. You then pass a few gnarled pines and larches and the path begins to swing to the right.

There is a steep descent down the final slopes of Camaderry, which becomes quite knee-jarring as the forested slope runs even more steeply downhill. You should follow the path faithfully; after crossing a forest track it drops straight downhill on to a minor road, close to the entrance to the car park beside the Upper Lake. At popular times, there is a snack van serving food and drinks in the car park; otherwise you will have to make your way to the Glendalough Hotel and Laragh in search of refreshments.

## Alternative routes

ESCAPES
The high summits around Glendalough are often rough and boggy underfoot, but the gradients from summit to summit are fairly gentle. The ascent and descent paths are quite steep in places, and it is essential that these are used to avoid excessively steep slopes and cliffs. It is usually possible to descend into the glen at any point from Lugduff to

Turlough Hill. The ground may be rough underfoot, but there are no serious cliffs and any outcrops of rock are easily passed. However, if you make an early descent into Glendalough be sure to walk downstream on the northern bank of the river. This allows you to pick up the former miner's path, which in turn leads on to a fine lakeshore track running back to the car park. The sheer cliffs on the southern shore of the Upper Lake must be avoided at all costs.

A quick descent is also available from Turlough Hill. Simply follow the tarmac access road away from the reservoir dam. It zigzags down to the Wicklow Gap, where the road can be followed through Glendasan to return to Glendalough.

EXTENSIONS

This route includes all the high ground around the head of Glendalough, and the only logical extension is to include the summit of Derrybawn. However, this would be at the expense of Lugduff Spink and its marvellous views. Tough walkers might like to exchange an ascent of Camaderry for one of Tonelagee, returning to Glendalough over Brockagh Mountain. It is also possible to combine the circuit around the mountains above Glendalough with the shorter heritage walk around Glendalough (Route 5).

*The reservoir on top of Turlough Hill as seen from nearby Camaderry.*

# Route 7: LUGNAQUILLIA

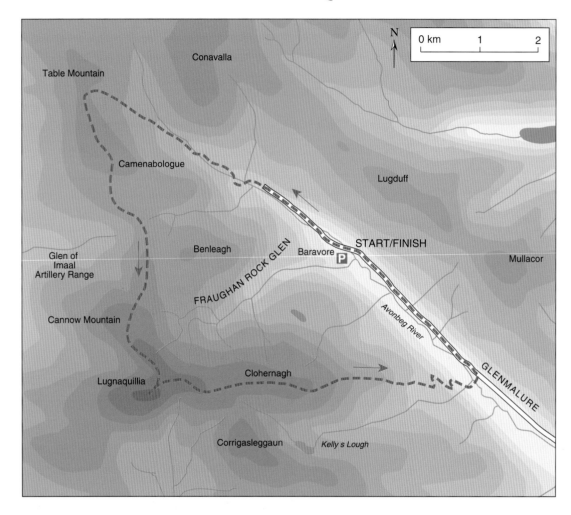

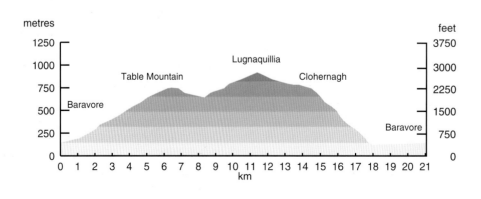

# Route 7: Lugnaquillia

TIME ALLOWANCE 7 hours.

STARTING/FINISHING LOCATION
Baravore, Glenmalure.
OSI Discovery 56: GR066943.
Car park beside the river.
No public transport.

OVERVIEW/INTEREST
One of the highest mountains in Ireland, with
  extensive views from the summit.
Includes part of the Wicklow Mountains National
  Park.
Features a well-graded ascent.
Echoes of the 1798 Rebellion in Glenmalure.

FOOTPATHS
Clear tracks are used on the ascent and descent.
Paths on the ridges are sometimes eroded and can
  be vague.

STATISTICS

| | |
|---|---|
| WALKING DISTANCE | 22km (13½ miles) |
| TOTAL HEIGHT GAINED | 950m (3,115ft) |
| PRINCIPAL HEIGHTS | |
| Camenabologue | 758m (2,495ft) |
| Lugnaquillia | 925m (3,039ft) |
| Clohernagh | 800m (2,623ft) |

## The way to Table Mountain    *Allow 2 hours*

There are three roads which can be used to reach
the Glenmalure Lodge, where a fourth road runs
from the hotel towards the rugged head of the glen.
The minor roads reaching Glenmalure from Laragh
and Aughavannagh were both part of the Military
Road built through the Wicklow Mountains by the
British following the 1798 Rebellion. The minor
road running towards the head of Glenmalure from
the Glenmalure Lodge serves a few farmhouses and
a youth hostel. There is a gravel car park at

Baravore, where the road crosses the Avonbeg
River by means of a large concrete slab.

Park at Baravore and cross the river. If the water
is running high, there is a footbridge a short way
upstream. Either way, the road leads onwards
towards the Glenmalure Youth Hostel. This will
usually be closed, and even when it is open the
facilities are basic and it is used mainly by groups.
There is a Department of Defence information
board fixed to the wall of the hostel and a map is
enclosed which shows the extent of an artillery
range on the western slopes of Lugnaquillia and
advises dates and times when shelling may be in
progress. The route described below follows the
edge of the range boundary along the crest of the
mountains but does not enter the impact area. Bear
in mind that descents westwards from this walk
could be dangerous.

The road loses its tarmac surface beyond the
hostel and a clear gravel track runs between the
edge of the forest and the river. This is known as
the Table Track. The unforested slopes are
exceedingly steep and bouldery, but the course
taken by the track is a pleasant and gradual ascent.
When the track begins to climb more steeply, it
crosses a log bridge and has forest trees on both
sides, so that views of the rugged glen are
restricted. As the track climbs, avoid any turnings
to the left. There is a sharp turning to the right,
where a waterfall can be viewed from a little
further on. At a higher level a forest track runs
parallel to the Table Track, but do not be tempted
to follow it.

The Table Track quickly gains a grassy surface
and is flanked by heather, boulders and forestry.
Although a forest track slices across the Table Track
a couple of times, make sure you pick up the line of
the grassy track immediately after each
interruption. After crossing a stream, the Table
Track is flanked by rugged heather moorlands and
the forest trees are much further away. A line of
rotting fenceposts and a small stream run parallel to

the track on the left, and it must be admitted that without the track to follow, walkers would have a hard time.

The Table Track finally reaches a broad moorland gap where a Department of Defence notice again reminds walkers of the artillery range in the Glen of Imaal. To the right is Table Mountain – a boggy expanse of moorland from which the Table Track takes its name. Just beyond the noticeboard is a crude stone shelter, and a path heads off to the left on its way to distant Lugnaquillia. For the moment it is worth taking in the view, which has been largely restricted to Glenmalure throughout the ascent. The altitude is already around 700m (2,300ft) – and the crest of the range has only just been gained.

*Glenmalure Youth Hostel in the forested glen at the start of the walk.*

## The way to Lugnaquillia

*Allow 2½ hours*

A trodden path runs roughly southwards from the top of the Table Track, climbing gently up the slopes of Camenabologue. On this slope the blanket bog has been eroded to leave only isolated peat hags, so that walkers cross grassy or stony surfaces. Even when there is a larger patch of blanket bog, the path steps neatly through a gap to continue towards the summit of the mountain. This is a broad, bouldery top, but it is easy to cross. What may appear to be the summit cairn is not actually on the highest point: the height of Camenabologue is 758m (2,495ft) and views are getting better.

The path which you are following becomes rather vague on the descent. If you can trace it, follow it south-eastwards before swinging more to the south-west. The idea is to avoid a boggy patch on the way

down to a rugged gap. Crossing the gap can prove awkward, but if you aim to stay high on the rugged crest you can make use of boulders and outcrops of rock, limiting your involvement with soft patches of bog. Aim to cross a slight grassy rise, before descending past another noticeboard on the way down to the lower part of the gap at around 620m (2,035ft). This area is firmer and easier to cross.

On the next ascent there are the mangled remains of former Department of Defence notices, but there is also a much clearer path to follow. This climbs up a bouldery, heathery slope, passing small outcrops on the way up to a minor summit at 712m (2,344ft). The slight descent beyond this is hardly noticeable, but the break of slope helps you fix your position on the map. Another point to note is that the heather cover gives way to grass on the next ascent, although boulders remain embedded in the ground.

The path is fairly clear as it climbs, but despite crossing only short grass and moss later on, it could prove difficult to trace in poor visibility. The gradient is gentle, and by walking ever upwards the summit of Lugnaquillia will eventually be gained in a broad area of short grass and moss. There is a trig point at 925m (3,039ft) which is perched on top of a huge, square cairn. This cairn is all the more remarkable because the stones used for its construction would not have been readily available on the top of the mountain. Also to hand, courtesy of An Oige, is a view indicator giving a detailed round-up of mountains, hills and other features of interest. Some of the main ones include:

| | |
|---|---|
| N | Camenabologue, Silsean, Moanbane |
| NNE | Mullaghcleevaun, Kippure, Tonelagee |
| NE | Lugduff, Scarr, Djouce, Great Sugar Loaf |
| ENE | Mullacor, Trooperstown Hill |
| E | Clohernagh, Kirikee Mountain, Snowdonia |
| SE | Croaghanmoira |
| SSE | Croaghan Mountain |
| SSW | Mount Leinster, Blackstairs Mountain, Brandon Hill |
| SW | Comeragh Mountains, Galty Mountains |
| WSW | Keadeen Mountain |
| W | Slieve Bloom Mountains |
| NW | Great Sugar Loaf, Lobawn |

## The way back to Glenmalure
*Allow 2½ hours*

To leave the summit of Lugnaquillia, retrace your steps slightly, heading north-east for a short distance before swinging more to the east. There is a fairly clear path, but in poor visibility you should note that the cliffs of the North Prison and South Prison fall away abruptly from the grassy summit plateau. Once you have located the faint path running roughly eastwards towards Clohernagh, there should be no problem following it along the broad, grassy ridge. Blanket bog has almost completely disappeared from this high-level crest, leaving a surface of grass and stones. The descent is gradual and in clear weather the views remain good for some time. The slight hump of Clohernagh rises to an altitude of 800m (2,623ft), with a bouldery cairn just off the highest point and overlooking Glenmalure.

The path onwards is very poorly trodden and the ground is steeper, more heathery, and quite rugged in some parts. However, if you aim to follow the top of a steep slope overlooking Glenmalure you will find a much clearer path to follow. In fact, this path is becoming overtrodden and badly eroded in places. After a steep descent, the path passes a prominent rocky outcrop and runs through a gateway in a fence.

Further downhill you join a clear track, which zigzags at a good gradient down a slope that would otherwise prove steep and rocky. Take all the zigzags in turn and do not be tempted to short cut down the slope. The surface varies from boggy to grassy to stony. The track passes through a farmyard in a stand of tall trees, after which there are two rivers to cross. The usual way across the Carrawaystick Brook is to use stepping stones, while a footbridge spans the Avonbeg River. Look back towards the steep slope of the glen to see the fine waterfalls on Carrawaystick Brook.

Follow a short track up to a minor road and turn left. The road runs along the floor of Glenmalure – you drove along it earlier in the day on the way to the car park at Baravore. In places the road features views along the glen, while at other times it is flanked by forestry. You will pass a forest car park before reaching the car park at Baravore. The nearest point of refreshment is back along the road at the Glenmalure Lodge.

## Alternative routes

ESCAPES

The existence of an artillery range in the Glen of Imaal has already been mentioned, and up-to-date Ordnance Survey maps show its full extent. Walkers on the Table Track or Camenabologue who need an escape route are advised to retrace their steps to Glenmalure Youth Hostel and Baravore. The easiest escape from Lugnaquillia to Glenmalure is by the route described for the descent. However, when there is no firing on the artillery range, descents via the Table Track to the Glen of Imaal, or from Lugnaquillia via Camarahill to the Glen of Imaal could be considered. If you need a telephone or mountain rescue, head for the Army Information and Advice Centre. If there is firing on the ranges, such descents must not be used. Information on firing times can be obtained in advance by phoning the Warden Service on 045 404653.

EXTENSIONS

The classic full-day walk over Lugnaquillia is actually a complete circuit around the Glen of Imaal. This can be structured to run from Ballineddan Mountain to the Great Sugar Loaf, avoiding the artillery ranges at all times. When there is no firing on the ranges, an ascent by way of Camarahill is a possibility. Those preferring to walk from Glenmalure could also consider an extended high-level walk, by omitting the Table Track and following the crest of Lugduff and Conavalla to reach Table Mountain, then continuing towards Lugnaquillia and Clohernagh. Even this route could be extended further to start and finish at Glenmalure Lodge, using forestry tracks at either end of the walk. Make no mistake – you will need all the services offered by the hotel at the end of such a walk.

*The summit cairn and trig point on Lugnaquillia plastered with spring snow.*

# Route 8: MOUNT LEINSTER

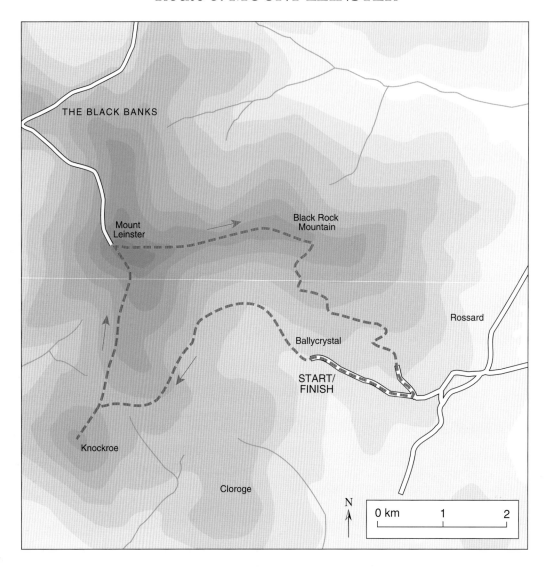

THE BLACK BANKS

Mount Leinster

Black Rock Mountain

Rossard

Ballycrystal

START/ FINISH

Knockroe

Cloroge

N

0 km        1        2

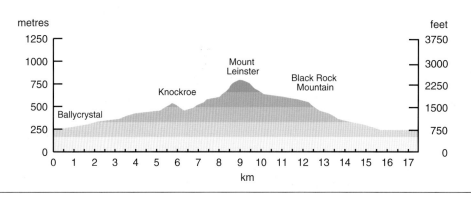

metres

1250

1000

750

500

250

0

feet

3750

3000

2250

1500

750

0

Mount Leinster

Knockroe

Black Rock Mountain

Ballycrystal

0   1   2   3   4   5   6   7   8   9   10  11  12  13  14  15  16  17

km

# 3

# SOUTH-EAST

## Route 8: Mount Leinster

TIME ALLOWANCE 5 hours.

STARTING/FINISHING LOCATION
Ballycrystal.
OSI Discovery 61: GR861508.
Car parking is very tight beside the road.
No public transport nearer than Bunclody.

OVERVIEW/INTEREST
Fine circuit around Mount Leinster, the highest
    mountain in Co Wexford and Co Carlow.
Wide-ranging views from the summit.
Includes an unfrequented glen, and Ireland's
    highest motor road.

FOOTPATHS
A good road and track are used at the start, and a
    good track leaves the mountain at the end.
There are some old paths on the mountain.
Some parts are untrodden or have vague paths.

STATISTICS
| | |
|---|---|
| WALKING DISTANCE | 18km (11 miles) |
| TOTAL HEIGHT GAINED | 670m (2,200ft) |
| PRINCIPAL HEIGHTS | |
| Knockroe | 540m (1,777ft) |
| Mount Leinster | 795m (2,610ft) |

## The way to Mount Leinster    *Allow 3 hours*

The lazy mountaineer can drive to the summit of
Mount Leinster – and this is the highest point that
can be reached by car in Ireland. Many walkers
use the easy access offered by the road to the
summit TV mast, climbing up the Black Banks
from the Nine Stones on the Mount Leinster
Scenic Drive. Hang gliders are also in the habit of
driving high before launching themselves into the
thermals. For those walkers who are looking for a
route which is largely free of cars and roads, the
circuit around the glen at Ballycrystal is perhaps
the best choice.

Ballycrystal is in between Bunclody and Kiltealy,
but the glen is off the beaten track and is not
adequately signposted from the R746 road. Parking
spaces are extremely limited, but if you head for
the road junction located at the grid reference given
for the start, then you will find a patch of gravel
which will accommodate a couple of cars. There is
a corrugated tin shelter at the junction, which helps
to mark it on the approach.

Start the walk by following the narrow road
towards the head of the glen. It runs through forest
and if you look carefully you can see the remains of
former fields, gateways and other signs of an
agricultural past. The road emerges from the forest
to pass a couple of farmhouses, and then the
tarmac gives way to a gravel surface as you enter
the last stand of forestry. On leaving this forest
there is one final hill farm, before the track passes
through a gate to reach the open mountainside.

The rugged track passes through fields which
have been reclaimed by the moorland, and you
then reach a ruined farmstead beside three
prominent beech trees. Beyond this point the track
splits and you should bear right and walk gradually

*A pleasant view across the glen at Ballycrystal at the start of the walk.*

Although you will be able to see the remains of old paths and tracks on the southern slopes of Mount Leinster, these are overgrown and are not easy to follow. From the gap, it is best simply to climb straight uphill on the slopes of heather and boulders. The initial steep slope levels out on to a bouldery shoulder which bears a small cairn. A recent heather burn has reduced the depth of heather and made the underlying boulders easier to see. Continue up the final steep slope, heading for the obvious landmark of the TV mast. Weave a way around the massive anchorage points to find the summit cairn and trig point at 795m (2,610ft). The trig point actually stands inside a huge, hollowed-out cairn. Views from here are naturally extensive, as Mount Leinster is such an isolated height – even though it is part of the Blackstairs Mountains. Look around for the following features, which are mostly quite distant:

| | |
|---|---|
| NNE | Lugnaquillia, Wicklow Mountains |
| NE | Croaghan Mountain |
| E | Black Rock Mountain |
| SSE | Forth Mountain |
| SSW | Knockroe, Blackstairs Mountain |
| SW | Brandon Hill, Comeraghs, Knockmealdowns |
| WSW | Slievenamon, Galty Mountains |
| W | Keeper Hill, Slieve Felim, Silvermine Mountains |
| WNW | Devilsbit Mountain |
| NW | Slieve Bloom Mountains |

### The way back to Ballycrystal

*Allow 2 hours*

Leave the summit of Mount Leinster by heading roughly eastwards. There is some boggy ground to cover at first, but a channel later offers a firmer footing on to drier heather. There are some boulders along the broad crest, and a couple of bouldery steps to be negotiated on the way downhill. There is a vague path along the heather and grass ridge, and two broad humps along the ridge which are both crowned by rocky outcrops.

By keeping to the ridge, you will not miss a useful feature: a stout stone building whose

uphill to continue. The old track is becoming quite overgrown with heather, but it can be traced easily around the southern slopes of Mount Leinster, contouring at around 400m (1,300ft). Once the gap in between Mount Leinster and Knockroe comes into view, simply head straight for it and avoid being drawn off-course by other trodden paths and tracks.

The summit TV mast on Mount Leinster will have been in view many times already if the day is clear, and you could have made a beeline for it from a number of points. However, the mountain has broad shoulders and it is worth exploring these as part of a longer route. Admittedly, Knockroe is more of a subsidiary summit than a shoulder. It is worth climbing directly from the gap, but you will have to return to the same gap afterwards. Its slopes are set at a reasonable gradient and its heather and boulder covering is fairly easy to negotiate. The 540m (1,777ft) summit bears a cairn and the ruin of a small two-roomed building, and the views are already quite extensive, although Mount Leinster's bulk hides the whole of the Wicklow Mountains.

window-holes look towards the Wicklow Mountains. This hut is an old turf-cutter's shelter, and as it has been left open it offers shelter for any walkers passing this way in bad weather. You could continue a short way along the ridge to gain the nearby summit of Black Rock Mountain, but you should return to the stone hut afterwards to start the descent from the high ground.

A clear track leaves the stone hut and runs down the southern slopes of Black Rock Mountain. Follow this faithfully downhill, no matter how much it may change direction. The track leads to a forest and passes through a gate on to a clear-felled slope. Keep to the right at a junction and follow the stony track downhill as it makes a large, sweeping zigzag on the forested slope. Later on it runs straight out of the forest, passing through another gate, and is flanked by gorse bushes as it passes lower fields. When you reach a minor tarmac road, simply turn right to follow this back to the junction used at the start of the walk, where the little parking space is located.

*Mount Leinster and its summit mast as seen from the heathery slopes of Knockroe.*

## Alternative routes

ESCAPES
On this route, the old track used on the southern slopes of Mount Leinster is always available as an escape route if required. The route is rather novel in that it possesses a means of easy escape even at its highest point. The road serving the TV mast is often used by cars, so that aid may be readily available in an emergency; there may even be people in the buildings at the foot of the mast. Unfortunately, walking off the mountain by way of the access road leaves you on the opposite side of the mountain to Ballycrystal.

EXTENSIONS
Mount Leinster and the Blackstairs Mountains form a long ridge of high ground and natural circuits are rather difficult to construct. It is difficult to extend the walk around Ballycrystal further, and in any case this would involve more time spent in forests or on roads. For those who can organize effective transport, the circuit could be reversed and then extended across the Scullogue Gap to cover the whole of the Blackstairs ridge.

# Route 9: BRANDON HILL

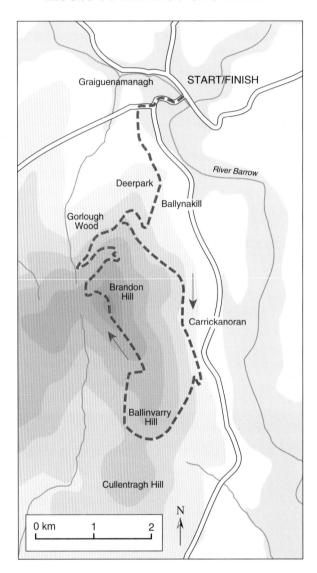

Graiguenamanagh  START/FINISH

River Barrow

Deerpark

Ballynakill

Gorlough
Wood

Brandon
Hill

Carrickanoran

Ballinvarry
Hill

Cullentragh Hill

N

0 km    1    2

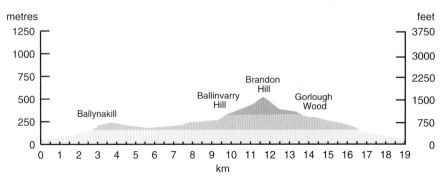

metres                                                      feet
1250                                                        3750

1000                                                        3000

750                          Brandon                        2250
                              Hill
500               Ballinvarry        Gorlough               1500
                     Hill             Wood
250    Ballynakill                                           750

0                                                            0
   0 1 2 3 4 5 6 7 8 9 10 11 12 13 14 15 16 17 18 19
                          km

# Route 9: Brandon Hill

TIME ALLOWANCE 6 hours.

STARTING/FINISHING LOCATION
Graiguenamanagh.
OSI Discovery 68: GR710435.
Parking spaces around town.
No public transport.

OVERVIEW/INTEREST
Fine hill rising above the River Barrow, with good views – the highest point in Co Kilkenny.
Pleasant waymarked Brandon Way circuit is suitable for children.
Includes part of the South Leinster Way.
Fine abbey and bridge at Graiguenamanagh.

FOOTPATHS
Circuit is marked by stone waymark plinths.
Firm forest tracks are used most of the way.
Route over the open hill is vague.

STATISTICS
| | |
|---|---|
| WALKING DISTANCE | 20km (12½ miles) |
| TOTAL HEIGHT GAINED | 580m (1,900ft) |
| PRINCIPAL HEIGHT | |
| Brandon Hill | 519m (1,703ft) |

## The way to Brandon Hill

*Allow 4 hours*

Graiguenamanagh grew up around the site of Duiske Abbey, which was itself founded in 1204. Although the abbey fell into ruins after the Dissolution, the abbey church was restored and remains as the centrepiece of the town; it is still used for worship and is beautifully floodlit at night. The lovely arched stone bridge which spans the River Barrow is floodlit at night, while during the day it is a foreground to views of Brandon Hill.

In recent years the summit of Brandon Hill has sprouted a tall metal cross, and this is a prominent feature even when seen from a distance at Graiguenamanagh. The hill does not dominate the town to excess, yet gently beckons the walker to make an ascent. The waymarked South Leinster Way was blazed across its forested flanks many years ago, and more recently a circular route around the slopes and over the top has also been developed. This is known as the Brandon Way, and is the route followed in the description below.

Starting in Graiguenamanagh's narrow Main Street, with its lovely traditional shop fronts, follow the R705 which is signposted for New Ross. This road climbs steeply, and you then turn right along the minor road which runs towards Inistioge. There are views back across the town towards the Blackstairs Mountains, which appear almost as a rock wall. Turn left along a narrow farm road, which is marked by a South Leinster Way signpost and a BW marker for the Brandon Way.

Follow the farm road to its end, keeping to the right of the last dwelling, and follow a track onwards to reach the forested flanks of the hill. The track curves to the right as it climbs, and you then reach a junction of forest tracks where a Brandon Way marker stone bears an arrow pointing to the left, accompanied by the word GO. Take note of the style of these stone plinths, as they mark the entire circuit.

The forest track which you are following basically contours around the eastern slopes of Brandon Hill, but generally drifts downhill as it proceeds. You pass a fairly young plantation which was established with American aid. It is unfortunate that so much of the hill has been turned over to forestry, as in the past it was a notable game reserve, with rich pickings for both the gentry and local poachers. An incident known as The Brandon Shootings occurred in 1888, when an argument between gamekeepers and poachers led to shots being fired, with one death on each side.

There are gates along the track, before a right turn leads uphill in a series of zigzags. The track gradient gradually eases and the Brandon Way passes over a broad, forested gap between Ballinvarry Hill and Cullentragh Hill, both of which are really only little outliers of Brandon Hill. A Brandon Way marker stands at the next junction, but the arrow is rather ambiguous. You actually need to turn right and follow a rough track steeply uphill. This reaches the edge of the forest, where you turn right.

Follow the edge of the forest to the crest of the hill, then turn left to start walking up the broad moorland slopes towards the summit. In mist, unwary walkers could go astray unless they look carefully for posts which indicate the way. The moorland underfoot can be difficult, but the slope is set at a reasonable gradient. The summit of Brandon Hill is crowned by a large burial cairn and a rather squat trig point at 519m (1,703ft). The cross, which appears to be on the summit when seen from Graiguenamanagh, is actually off to one side and has been planted for effect when seen from the town.

This summit is the last great upthrust of Wicklow granite, even though the Wicklow Mountains are some distance away. Heading further westwards, the hills are much lower for some distance. The view is quite pleasant and takes in the following features:

| | |
|---|---|
| N | Upstream along the River Barrow |
| NE | Mount Leinster, Wicklow Mountains |
| ENE | Blackstairs Mountain |
| E | Ballybaun |
| S | Towards the sea at Waterford |
| SW | Mount Alto, Comeragh Mountains |
| WSW | Slievenamon, Galty Mountains |
| NW | Coppanagh |

## The way back to Graiguenamanagh          *Allow 2 hours*

The descent from the top of Brandon Hill is relatively simple, although there are opportunities to go astray at junctions on the forested slope. A stony track zigzags downhill from the summit, and continues zigzagging down through the forest too. Look out for the Brandon Way markers and watch

in particular for a forest track heading off to the right. You will reach a Brandon Way marker which has the word FINISH inscribed upon it, even though you are still deep in the forest!

The next forest track off to the left is one which you used earlier in the day, and it soon leaves the forest and joins the narrow farm access road. Continue to retrace your steps, turning right and left by road to return to the centre of Graiguenamanagh. With the Brandon Way, the South Leinster Way and the Barrow Way all available, you might expect the place to be crowded with walkers, but surprisingly that is not the case.

## Alternative routes

This circuit uses mainly firm and clear forest tracks, so escapes are hardly necessary. The taller stands of forest give some protection against bad weather. The summit of Brandon Hill can appear to be broad and featureless in mist, but a compass bearing should be all that is necessary to cross it in poor visibility. Walkers who do go astray on Brandon Hill may find themselves inconvenienced for a while but are unlikely to become seriously lost, and any forest track will bail them out.

Brandon Hill is a solitary hill surrounded on most sides by forestry. Easy connections with the neighbouring Blackstairs Mountains are not possible. It is possible to incorporate a stretch of riverside walking along the towpath of the Barrow, but this is unfortunately on the opposite side of the river to Brandon Hill, and in the absence of a bridge downstream from Graiguenamanagh, you would need to organise a ferry across at St Mullins.

*Brandon Hill swells gently above the countryside near Graiguenamanagh.*

# Route 10: GLENBARROW AND RIDGE OF CAPARD

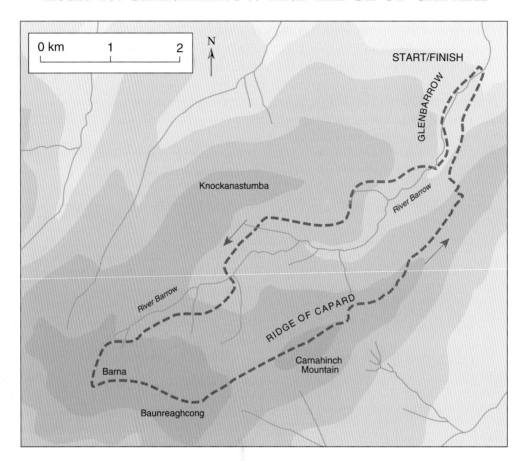

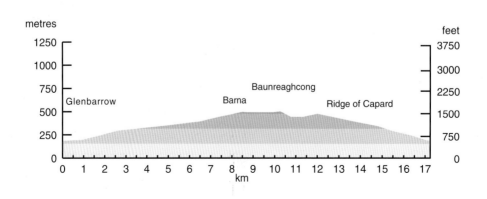

# 4

# SLIEVE BLOOM

## Route 10: Glenbarrow and Ridge of Capard

TIME ALLOWANCE 6 hours.

STARTING/FINISHING LOCATION
Glenbarrow, near Rosenallis.
OSI Discovery 54: GR367082.
Car park in Glenbarrow.
No bus services nearer than Mountmellick.

OVERVIEW/INTEREST
Walk to the source of a major Irish river.
Includes part of the Slieve Bloom Way and lies
    within the Slieve Bloom Environment Park.
Features a splendid series of little waterfalls and
    extensive moorlands on the Ridge of Capard.
Includes the legendary Well of Slieve Bloom.

FOOTPATHS
Forest tracks and paths are used at a low level.
Higher moorlands are largely untrodden, and
    some moorland paths are becoming eroded.

STATISTICS
| | |
|---|---|
| WALKING DISTANCE | 18km (11 miles) |
| TOTAL HEIGHT GAINED | 430m (1,410ft) |
| PRINCIPAL HEIGHTS | |
| Baunreaghcong | 509m (1,677ft) |
| Carnahinch Mountain | 483m (1,589ft) |

### The way to Barna
*Allow 3 hours*

The Slieve Bloom are the most centrally located uplands in Ireland. Although they are of modest height and extensively forested, they are also quite wild in places. On the moorland slopes of Barna is the legendary Well of Slieve Bloom, also known in ancient times as Conle's Well. There were seven secret streams of knowledge flowing from this well, including the Three Sisters of Ireland – the rivers Barrow, Suir and Nore – which began to flow on the night that Conn of the Hundred Battles was born. It is also related that Sinann, a beautiful princess, yearned for the knowledge contained in the well. Unfortunately it erupted in a fury, sweeping her away in a deluge which flooded the plains and left a river which bears her name to this day – the mighty River Shannon.

This walk dares to approach the mysterious Well of Slieve Bloom, but you could have a problem locating it on the bleak, high moorland slopes of Barna. Perhaps this is all for the good, as you would not want to be swept away by another violent flood. By way of consolation, the walk includes a lovely stretch of the River Barrow, complete with charming waterfalls, wandering easily up the forested glen and then offering walkers a broad, heathery crest ending with a descent along the Ridge of Capard to return to Glenbarrow.

Glenbarrow is well signposted from the R422 between Rosenallis and Clonaslee. Minor roads lead into the mouth of the glen and there is a car park in a lovely wooded setting. A large mapboard illustrates the Slieve Bloom Environment Park and the course of the Slieve Bloom Way. There are two tracks leaving the car park, both of which are used by the waymarked Slieve Bloom Way. Take the one to the right, which is signposted for Tinnahinch and

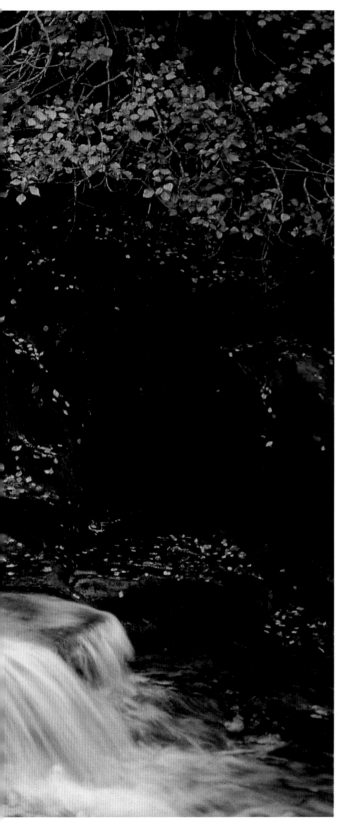

also twice for the nearby waterfalls. The track runs downhill and turns left, and then proceeds across a forested slope until it reaches a wooden shelter beside a clearing.

The River Barrow slides across slabs of rock which look natural but were actually left behind by quarrying. A vast slope of glacial debris lies across the river, and the slopes feature a mixture of deciduous and coniferous trees. Continue following the riverside path upstream. A kind of rocky stairway climbs up alongside a series of fine waterfalls. Follow the path onwards across the steep, forested slope above the river, then look out for a waymark post which indicates a right turn on the Slieve Bloom Way. A path descends to the River Barrow and crosses it using a footbridge.

Turn left to continue following the path. It rises away from the river through mixed woodland and then follows a dark line in the shade of conifers. Turn left again along a rather squelchy path, where moss has filled a grooved pathway. In wet weather it might be better to walk alongside this. When you reach a firm forest track turn left to follow it, even though a Slieve Bloom Way marker points to the right. The forest track is quite clear, and either climbs or falls gently, or simply contours around the slopes of Glenbarrow. It is generally a good step away from the River Barrow, and views across the glen take in the Ridge of Capard, which you will walk later in the day.

Follow the forest track faithfully until you reach a junction with another track. Turn left to follow this other track downhill and then cross the River Barrow. Climb uphill for a short way and then turn right along another forest track. This track proceeds along a clear line, but may be muddy, boggy or roughly vegetated in places. The forest through which it passes is generally well back from the track, so there is a sense of spaciousness and a good view along the length of Glenbarrow. The track eventually reaches the edge of the forest, beyond which lie the heathery slopes of Barna.

Turn right and walk parallel to the edge of the forest until you enter a fold in the heather

*One of a handful of pleasant little waterfalls passed on the way through Glenbarrow.*

moorland. The infant River Barrow may or may not be nestling in this fold, depending on the state of the weather. Walk uphill anyway, and you should find little pools of water and a green ribbon of soggy sphagnum moss. The Well of Slieve Bloom is elusive, and no visitor in recent years has managed to discover a convincing site.

Eventually, you will have to abandon your search for the sacred spring and head instead for the summit of Barna. As you climb up the heather and grass slopes a vast, open expanse of moorland spreads in all directions. In mist this can be a tricky area, but on a clear day you should head for what appears to be a little hump of grass at 504m (1,659ft). In fact, sods have been cut and piled into a heap here, no doubt because there were no stones for a cairn. A couple of saplings and a bramble have taken root, and it will be interesting to see if they thrive over the years.

## The way back to Glenbarrow
*Allow 3 hours*

Barna is not the highest point in the Slieve Bloom. That distinction belongs to Arderin, which was once believed to be the highest mountain in Ireland! Nor is Barna the highest point gained on this particular walk, as it is slightly overshadowed by a moorland rise to the east called Baun-reaghcong. In mist, care will need to be exercised when walking from Barna to Baunreaghcong, but on a clear day the broad, grassy, heathery crest should present no problem. Baunreaghcong features a summit hump of grass at 509m (1,677ft), and this was apparently cut from a hole alongside which is now filled with water. There is also a small, solitary conifer nearby. The views can be extensive but are not spectacular, and embrace the following:

E    Wicklow Mountains
SE   Stradbally Hills
S    Slievenamon, Comeragh Mountains
SSW  Galty Mountains
SW   Keeper Hill, Slieve Felim, Silvermines

A grooved arrangement of ditches and mounds runs roughly north-eastwards along the crest of the moorland towards a couple of little conifers overlooking a broad gap. From these two little trees you can look across the gap to Carnahinch Mountain, and the ditches and mounds run all the way between the two summits.

On the way down towards the gap you will pass a few boulders on a short, steep stretch, and then the lowest part of the gap can be a bit boggy. At this point, the rotting posts of an old fence accompany the line of the ditch uphill. There is also a line of small trees alongside which stand well away from the nearest forest. At the top of the slope there are the ruins of small radio masts next to a small tin hut. The undistinguished summit of Carnahinch Mountain is just beyond, close to where the line of old fenceposts is left behind. The altitude is 483m (1,589ft).

The moorland crest leading onwards is tough underfoot and has no trodden path. You will need to take care if you are following it in mist, but on a clear day you can look ahead and spot the prominent cairn known as the Stony Man. This was in ruins in recent years, but was completely rebuilt by local people and is a prominent landmark on this part of the Ridge of Capard. There is a small quarry alongside, which appears rather suddenly.

On leaving the Stony Man, bear a little to the left to spot a couple of Slieve Bloom Way marker posts. A path leads down to a clearer track, which itself proceeds through a gateway in a fence. Follow the track onwards across the moor, but take care to turn left along a rather squelchy, grassy track indicated by another marker post. Look ahead to spot a series of tall poles which were planted to aid walkers following the Slieve Bloom Way along the broad, heathery, grassy Ridge of Capard. There is now a path trodden from one pole to the next, and in some parts this is becoming badly overtrodden.

You now join a track and follow it to the right for only a short way, and then continue along another path heading off to the left. The final stretch of path along the Ridge of Capard eventually drops down to a car park, picnic benches and sundry signposts. A transmitter mast perched on a moorland hump further away is known as the Metal Man – no doubt after its neighbour the Stony Man on the Ridge of

Capard. A Slieve Bloom Way marker points to the left along the narrow tarmac road, but almost immediately there is a turning to the right along a gravel track. Only a short way along the track there is another marker post indicating a left turn across a muddy patch to enter a forest.

Follow a path downhill in between young and older stands of forest. Keep walking downhill until a marker post indicates a right turn along a rather muddy path. This short path runs out on to a forest track, which leads gradually downhill. There is a large, clear-felled area where views stretch out across the plains towards Kildare. Leave the forest through a gate and then follow the track onwards downhill between high hedges from a house, to return to the car park where you started the walk.

## Alternative routes

### ESCAPES

This walk starts with an easy series of paths and forest tracks, before heading for bleak and barren moorlands. At any point on the way to the summit of Barna the easiest escape is to turn around and

*Pausing to sample the view from the Stony Man on the Ridge of Capard.*

retrace your steps through Glenbarrow. It is also possible to forge across the moors beyond the summit of Barna and reach the road known as The Cut, which crosses the crest of the Slieve Bloom. Once committed to following the moorland crest from Baunreaghcong to the Ridge of Capard, escapes are limited and it is better to continue along the route described above to return to Glenbarrow.

### EXTENSIONS

This circuit could be extended simply by incorporating more forest tracks, but that would not make the most of the area's merits. Bringing more of the rugged moorland crest into the route is rather difficult, although strong walkers might like to consider a walk all the way from one end to the other along the crest of the Slieve Bloom. To accomplish this successfully would require the aid of back-up transport. The waymarked circular Slieve Bloom Way is a much longer option, which usually takes three days to complete.

59

# Route 11: SLIEVENAMON

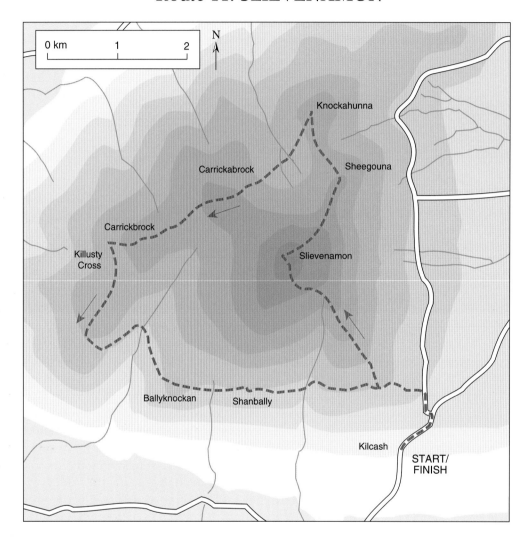

0 km 1 2

N

Knockahunna

Carrickabrock

Sheegouna

Carrickbrock

Killusty
Cross

Slievenamon

Ballyknockan Shanbally

Kilcash

START/
FINISH

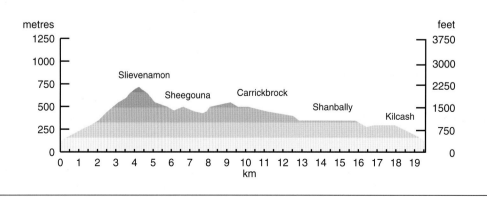

metres | feet

1250 — 3750

1000 — 3000

750 — 2250

Slievenamon

500 — 1500

Sheegouna

Carrickbrock

Shanbally

Kilcash

250 — 750

0 — 0

0 1 2 3 4 5 6 7 8 9 10 11 12 13 14 15 16 17 18 19
km

# 5

# SOUTH

## Route 11: Slievenamon

TIME ALLOWANCE 6 hours.

STARTING/FINISHING LOCATION
Kilcash.
OSI Discovery 67 and 75: GR315281.
Car park in the village.
Bus Eireann table numbers 7 and 385 run near
  Kilcash.

OVERVIEW/INTEREST
Little known circuit over mostly dry, short
  heather cover.
A mountain of legends, with splendid views.
Ancient cairns on some summits, including the
  legendary entrance to the Celtic Underworld.
Features an annual hill race.

FOOTPATHS
A clear track climbs all the way to the summit.
Most of the circuit is over untrodden heather.
A forest firebreak track is used near the end.

STATISTICS
WALKING DISTANCE       20km (12½ miles)
TOTAL HEIGHT GAINED    850m (2,790ft)
PRINCIPAL HEIGHT
Slievenamon    721m (2,368ft)

### The way to Slievenamon       *Allow 1½ hours*

Many walkers imagine that Slievenamon is a
solitary mountain which could not possibly support
a decent circular route. There is a clear track

leading all the way to the summit and most people
who use it return the same way. However, there is
an entertaining circuit which can be made over and
around the mountain, travelling along heathery
ridges which spread their sprawling shoulders
outwards from the huge, domed summit. Some of
the lower parts of Slievenamon have been forested,
but this circuit does not actually enter any of these
areas. The open parts of the hill form a vast sheep-
grazing range which is periodically burned to keep
the heather short and improve the pasture. As a
result, conditions underfoot are often easy and dry.
There are no great cliffs on the mountain.

According to legend, the hoary old warrior Fionn
MacCumhail once sat on the summit of the
mountain while women raced uphill to claim his
hand in marriage. Fionn secretly fancied Grainne,
the daughter of the High King of Ireland, and he
advised her on tactics so that she could win the
race. Not that they lived happily ever after, as
Grainne was soon running off again with one of
Fionn's warriors called Diarmuid. It all ended rather
tragically, but the name of the mountain is thought
to commemorate the original race undertaken by
the women, and hence Slievenamon is the
Mountain of the Women. In shape, it resembles a
huge breast and the summit cairn forms a nipple,
which suggests that the mountain has long been
regarded as a symbol of fertility.

Parking is available in the village of Kilcash in
front of Kehoe's Pub. The steep road rising up from
the village is signposted for Slievenamon Summit,
and a road leading off to the left later is also

signposted the same way. This road continues climbing and bears right, and then a final Slievenamon Summit sign points to the left along an enclosed track. At the end of the track is a gate and a set of sheep pens, beyond which are the open slopes of the mountain. Follow the track on to the mountain and turn right to start climbing uphill. A stony track cuts an obvious line up the heathery slopes of Slievenamon and runs roughly parallel to a forest, although at some distance from the trees. At a higher level, the track climbs above the top corner of the forest and forges onwards up the heathery slope. On the broad dome of the summit the track is covered in larger stones, and the summit area is also quite bouldery in places. A spur from the track heads off to the left to reach a small building bearing an aerial, while the main track itself expires only a short distance further away.

There are three features of interest on top of Slievenamon. There is a trig point at an altitude of 721m (2,368ft), a curious pillar of granite crowned by a coppery artichoke, and a huge burial cairn. The pillar was erected by a Cork sculptor, while the burial cairn is redolent with legend. It was thought to be an entrance to the Celtic Underworld, while a hollow in the underlying rock on one side of it is believed to have been used as a seat by the warrior Fionn MacCumhail. The views from this solitary summit are naturally distant, but there are many fine mountain ranges featured, including the following:

N     Slieveardagh Hills, Slieve Bloom Mountains
NE    Wicklow Mountains
ENE   Brandon Hill, Mount Leinster, Blackstairs Mountains
SE    Waterford Harbour
S     Knockanaffrin, Comeragh Mountains
SSW   Laghtnafrankee
SW    Knockmealdown Mountains
WSW   Galty Mountains
W     Slievenamuck
NW    Keeper Hill, Slieve Felim, Silvermine Mountains

*Sheegouna and Knockahunna lie on a heathery crest extending from Slievenamon.*

## The way to Killusty Cross   *Allow 2 hours*

Despite Slievenamon appearing in many views as a solitary, heathery hump, closer inspection reveals that there are several satellite summits arranged on two broad heathery ridges branching away from the main summit. Walking along these ridges allows you to extend the route, giving you a view of Slievenamon from all sides. To leave the main summit and gain the first of these lower ridges, walk roughly north-westwards down a heathery, bouldery slope. There is no path, but regular burning of the heather has resulted in a short cover, which is easy to walk across. On the descent, start to swing gradually northwards and follow the broad crest towards the hump of Sheegouna.

Although Sheegouna is only a minor summit, it bears a large ancient cairn. This has been disturbed over the years and now features crude drystone shelters. Keep walking along the broad crest heading downhill for a short way, roughly northwards, and crossing the lines of overgrown paths once used for drawing turf off long-expired bogs. You should pass a young fir tree which looks as if it has 'escaped' from a nearby forest. Climb straight up a short, steep, heathery and bouldery slope to reach the top of Knockahunna. This summit bears the tangled wreckage of former masts, which are an eyesore.

Turn left and walk along a firebreak track between the open hillside and the forest. Walk straight downhill to a lower corner of the forest, where you cross a stream. Continue straight onwards across deep heather, crossing another little stream beside a gnarled thorn. Continue on across the heather of the rugged moorland, walking uphill more steeply and passing boulders in some places. There is a bouldery cairn on top of Carrickabrock. Views of the Comeragh, Knockmealdown and Galty Mountains, which have been missing for a while, are now restored and in clear weather will feature for quite a while onwards.

As you continue along the broad, stony, heathery crest, heading roughly south-westwards, you should pick up the line of an old heathery path. This is no more than a vague groove along the crest and is almost absent in some places, but it can be traced towards the white form of Killusty Cross, which was erected during the Holy Year of 1950. It overlooks the patchwork agricultural acres surrounding Fethard. It also lies some way downhill from the main moorland crest you were following, and some walkers might prefer not to include the detour to the cross and stay high on the crest.

## The way back to Kilcash          *Allow 2½ hours*

Walk back up on to the moorland crest from Killusty Cross, heading for a rather rugged and bouldery rise of ground. Continuing roughly south-westwards, cross a short slope of boulders where there is long heather, long grass and a good spread of bilberry. Continue across a more uniform, broad heathery gap to reach a large, bouldery cairn which has been fashioned into a shelter. There is a chance to take in the last good views of the surrounding mountains before heading back towards Kilcash. From now on, the mountains will generally be seen above a stand of forest trees.

Walk straight down the heathery slope towards the forest, then turn left to walk steeply downhill along a stony firebreak track alongside the forest. This track runs at a gentler gradient, and then crosses a river where a row of oak and birch trees are surrounded by forest trees. The oaks may be a remnant of the famous oakwoods of Kilcash, which were felled long ago. Keep following the firebreak track; as there are two parallel lines, use the one furthest away from the forest to enjoy more of the open hillside. The track rises to cross a shoulder, then descends gently. There is a little dip to cross, and then later the firebreak makes a sudden right and left turn to continue across the slope well above the forest.

*The white form of Killusty Cross is a landmark on the slopes of Slievenamon.*

When the track drops down for a short way to cross a small river in The Glen, turn left and walk uphill a short way after crossing the water. This move makes sure that you follow a clear track at a high level around the slopes of Slievenamon. Later you will reach a junction with another track, where you turn right to walk downhill for a short way, and then turn left to follow a track contouring across the heathery slope again. This track joins the main track which was used at the start of the day's walk, taking you towards the gate beside the sheep pens. Pass through the gate and follow the enclosed track down to a minor road. Turn right to walk down the road, which later turns left. Another right turn at a junction leads back down to Kilcash and straight through the door of Kehoe's Pub.

## Alternative routes

ESCAPES

Slievenamon is almost uniformly covered in heather, which is mostly short but sometimes long. There may be areas of boulders, but there are no cliffs. The lower parts of the mountain feature small fields or extensive forest. The only clear track on the mountain is the one used for the ascent, and this is so clear that it could be used with confidence in mist or even darkness. Descending in almost any other direction from this walk is unlikely to lead on to dangerous ground, but could take you towards fields or forestry which .will prove less easy to negotiate. Some of the forest tracks on the southern slopes could be used to return to Kilcash, while a descent from Killusty Cross to Killusty village simply results in a long road walk back to Kilcash.

EXTENSIONS

As Slievenamon is essentially a huge, solitary dome of a mountain with minor satellite summits, it is difficult to extend this walk any further, as it already embraces most of the surrounding summits. Extensions which meander across the moorland slopes or through the surrounding forest simply add extra distance for the sake of it. The circuit described is about the longest walk, making the most of the mountain.

# Route 12: COMERAGH MOUNTAINS

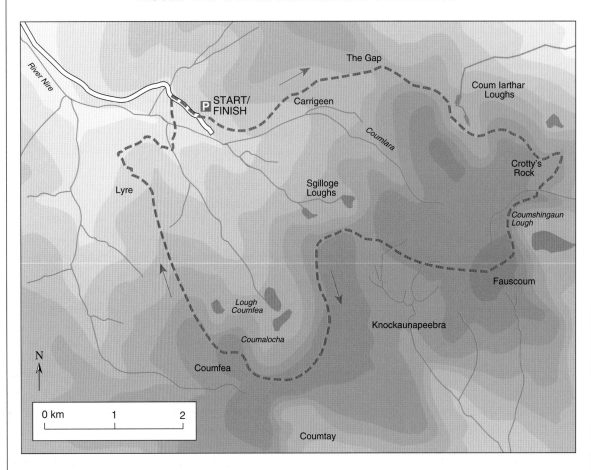

River Nire

The Gap

Coum Iarthar
Loughs

START/
FINISH

Carrigeen

Coumlara

Crotty's
Rock

Lyre

Sgilloge
Loughs

Coumshingaun
Lough

Fauscoum

Lough
Coumfea

Coumalocha

Knockaunapeebra

N

Coumfea

0 km          1          2

Coumtay

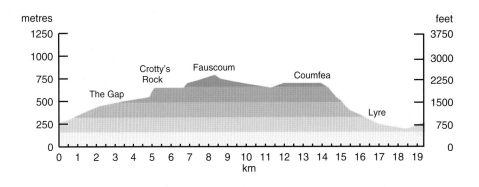

metres                                                    feet
1250                                                      3750

1000                                                      3000

                    Crotty's      Fauscoum
                    Rock
750                                         Coumfea       2250

              The Gap                                     1500
500

                                                   Lyre
250                                                       750

0                                                         0
   0  1  2  3  4  5  6  7  8  9 10 11 12 13 14 15 16 17 18 19
                          km

# Route 12: Comeragh Mountains

TIME ALLOWANCE 7 hours.

STARTING/FINISHING LOCATION
Head of the Nire Valley.
OSI Discovery 75: GR276128. Also 1:25,000
    Comeragh Mountains map.
Car park near the head of the Nire Valley.
No public transport.

OVERVIEW/INTEREST
Circuit taking in many rocky coums.
Features several enchanting loughs and a broad,
    bleak, boggy plateau.
Good views of surrounding moutain ranges.

FOOTPATHS
A waymarked path leads to The Gap.
Sheep paths are used in some places, while some
    parts are completely untrodden.
Rough tracks are used towards the end.

STATISTICS
WALKING DISTANCE        22km (13½ miles)
TOTAL HEIGHT GAINED     830m (2,725ft)
PRINCIPAL HEIGHT
Fauscoum                792m (2,597ft)

## The way to Coumshingaun

*Allow 3 hours*

A network of roads leads into the Nire Valley, and one of these leads beyond Nire Church to a car park near the head of the valley. There are routes leading into the Comeragh Mountains from this point, where all sorts of walks are possible. Keen hillwalkers might be tempted to head for the heights, but the bleak upland plateau is desperately boggy and should not be approached during or immediately after a spell of very wet weather. In fact, the highest parts of the Comeragh Mountains offer only arduous bog trots, and the best walks are actually found around the fringes of the range. A series of exceptionally rugged coums bite into the edges of the plateau and it is here

that the best scenery is to be found. A circuit taking in a handful of fine coums can also be structured to take in the highest part of the Comeragh Mountains.

Leave the car park near the head of the Nire Valley and follow the path which is signposted for The Gap. White marker posts show the way up a heathery slope to reach a gate. Pass through the gate and continue along the path, looking ahead to spot the marker posts when they become more widely spaced. The path crosses ground which is heathery, boggy and sometimes bouldery. As the path approaches The Gap it becomes fairly level, firm and stony. Two stout wooden stiles flank a gateway in a fence. Cross over one of these to stand at the head of The Gap at 466m (1,525ft). The Knockanaffrin ridge lies off to your left, while to the right the rocky prow of Carrigshaneun is a formidable obstacle barring a direct ascent to the Comeragh plateau.

Care is needed over route-finding to locate Coum Iarthar. You need to walk south-eastwards, climbing gently up a heathery slope and contouring across a bouldery one, hoping to pick up a fairly prominent sheep path now used by walkers. This leads around the mountainside and actually passes beneath an overhanging outcrop of conglomerate rock, which is home to many unusual plants safely out of the reach of sheep. The surroundings become awesomely rugged as you descend and pick up another path, which passes large boulders and enters Coum Iarthar. The coum is vast and fringed with cliffs, but only a couple of small, shallow loughs fill its floor. One of the loughs reflects the neighbouring hump of Slievenamon very well when the water is smooth.

To leave Coum Iarthar, first spot the rugged peak of rock which dominates the eastern side of the coum. You will have to climb a steep and bouldery slope in order to reach this rock, but once some of the height has been gained the ground becomes more gently graded and grassy for a while. A final bouldery slope leads towards the rocky peak. There is no need to scale the topmost rocks – simply walk across the little gap between the crown of the rock and the edge of the bleak Comeragh plateau. Continue walking by contouring around the edge of the plateau tracing the 650m (2,130ft) contour, where the ground is not too steep and rocky. Take care later on, as you will suddenly reach the edge of a coum flanked by sheer cliffs.

It is wise to step well back from the edge of the cliff and peer into the depths of the coum from safer positions further around. Crotty's Lough lies far below, named after a notorious robber. If you walk around the rim of the coum you will reach Crotty's Rock, which is a rugged boss of rock from which Crotty's wife is supposed to have jumped to her death. Some people believe that Crotty's stolen booty is hidden in the dark waters of the lough.

Walk southwards and aim to pick up another sheep path, again roughly on the 650m (2,130ft) contour. If you locate the correct path you should pass a small, tumbledown, circular sheepfold before crossing the bouldery watercourse of Iske Sullas. A path cuts across a slope to land above a little gap, where there is a sudden view into Coumshingaun. This immense coum is one of the most dramatic in Ireland, with a headwall of sheer rock and a lough which is embraced by two rocky arms. There is a path which completely encircles Coumshingaun, and by turning right you can follow its course up a steep and heathery spur to reach the edge of the Comeragh plateau. When the gradient eases there is a jumble of slabs and boulders, which looks strangely like a collapsed dolmen. Follow the narrow path which runs around the upper rim of Coumshingaun to reach the highest point overlooking the sheer headwall.

## The way to the Sgilloge Loughs
*Allow 1½ hours*

The whole character of the walk changes with the next move. Walk away from the head of Coumshingaun, heading on to the broad, bleak, boggy Comeragh plateau. There is only a very little height to climb and it may be necessary to outflank a couple of patches of black bog, although there are some firm, stony areas too. Aim for a fairly prominent cairn which sits on a broad expanse of grass. This is the highest point in the Comeragh Mountains, and although it is often referred to as Fauscoum it does not actually have a name. Its height is 792m (2,597ft). Looking around at other parts of the plateau, even the most ardent summit-bagger would have to admit that the Comeragh Mountains are entirely lacking in summits. All around is rolling bogland, cut into ribbons, often too soft to support a walker, and a most confusing place to navigate through in mist or darkness. Have no fear, however, for this walk will bypass the worst parts of the morass and lead you safely onwards to the next scenic delights. In the meantime, as this is the highest part of the range it is worth sampling the view, which includes the following features:

| | |
|---|---|
| N | Slievenamon |
| NE | Brandon Hill, Blackstairs Mountains, Wicklow Mountains |
| E | Croughaun Hill |
| SSW | Coumaraglin Mountain |
| SW | Seefin |
| W | Knockmealdown Mountains |
| WNW | Galty Mountains |
| NNW | Knockanaffrin |

The broad expanse of the summit area tends to mitigate against this point as a viewpoint, and by walking some distance around the area the quality of the view is enhanced a little. It has already been said that the best scenery in the Comeragh Mountains is around the flanks of the plateau rather than on the top: you will now believe this to be true, and may wish to find more of those splendid coums to walk around.

Leave the summit cairn by walking westwards down a moorland slope of heather and grass, which can be a bit squelchy in some places but is mostly firm. There are no paths to follow, but in clear weather you should be able to see the peaks of the Knockmealdown Mountains apparently

*Looking down on Sgilloge Lough and across to Knockanaffrin and Slievenamon.*

sitting on a broad moorland gap to the west. The gradual descent leads to a river, which you can ford easily where it breaks into small waterfalls. On the other side of the river, continue walking across the hillside, tracing the 700m (2,300ft) contour, which will cause you to head more to the north-west. You will actually be following a sort of natural shelf on the moorland slope, where the ground is generally firm and dry. In some parts there may be small outcrops of rock or more grass than heather, so the line is a good one to trace. You will spot a couple of cairns later on, and these give you your direction to reach a broad and boggy gap. Once on the gap, the views take in Knockanaffrin and Slievenamon, and you should then turn to the left to contour across a steep slope overlooking the Sgilloge Loughs.

## The way back to the Nire Valley

*Allow 2½ hours*

The Sgilloge Loughs actually occupy two neighbouring coums, and you will see the larger eastern lough before spotting the smaller western one. Keep above a series of cliffs and narrow gullies, following a narrow sheep path across the slopes of Curraghduff. By contouring around 650m (2,130ft) you will be drawn along a southwards course, looking into the vast hollow of Coumfea. You will need to start ascending by degrees to keep above the steeper slopes, so that most of the rim of the coum is traversed at over 700m (2,300ft). There are some fine views down narrow, rocky gullies towards the handful of little pools on the dimpled heather moorland at Coumalocha. The route describes a complete semi-circle around the rim of the coum, and you could end by climbing to a summit bearing a small cairn on a grassy bog at 711m (2,340ft).

Lough Coumfea lies in a separate coum, and it can be viewed closely as you begin the descent from the Comeragh plateau. Although there is no clear path, it is possible to walk straight towards a prominent track which runs through a series of fields and leads eventually to Lyre. The latter parts of this track twist and turn before you land on a narrow tarmac road. Turn right to follow the road to its very end, continuing down a gravel track. Turn right on to another gravel track and follow this until it becomes more grassy and runs down to a river. This river drains Coumfea and can carry a lot of water, but it is generally easy to cross using a series of huge boulders which have been arranged as stepping stones. Turn left along another track, which heads for the River Nire. You cross this using what appears to be a bridge. In fact, if you look underneath you will discover that it is actually the trailer of a lorry – the farmer who placed it across the river is obviously most resourceful! The track rises uphill and joins a minor road at a gateway. Turn right to follow the road straight back to the car park from which the walk started.

## Alternative routes

### ESCAPES

Escapes from the broad, bleak, boggy Comeragh plateau need to be chosen with care. There are some very soft patches of bog where you could lose considerable time floundering in search of a through route. The worst patches are north-west from the highest point on the range, and they are avoided by the route described above. Bear these bogs in mind if you are thinking of an escape in that direction. Elsewhere, if you make an early descent you will need to steer well clear of the rocky coums. All the coums visited on this circuit have cliffs, rocky gullies and potentially difficult bouldery slopes. Generally speaking, the ridges in between neighbouring coums provide the safest routes down, although a descent by way of Coumlara is also possible. In an emergency, it might be preferable to descend via one of the ridges flanking Coumshingaun to reach the R676 road, which could well be quicker than a descent back into the Nire Valley, but this would leave you a long way from any vehicle you might have left at the car park.

*Crotty's Rock, from which Crotty's wife is said to have fallen to her death.*

EXTENSIONS

The Nire Valley is surrounded on all sides by high ground, and extensions to this route are therefore many and varied. Walkers with plenty of energy could climb on to Knockanaffrin directly from the Nire Valley, then walk along the rugged ridge of the mountain to reach The Gap. Anyone who thinks a walk along the central boggy Comeragh plateau will be better than a tour around the rocky coums will be very much mistaken, but the main crest of the range is an option for determined bog-trotters. Rather than descending after circling Coumfea, it is possible to extend the walk to Milk Hill and still be able to drop into the Nire Valley at the end. If you are heading for Seefin and the ridge beyond you should make arrangements to be collected at the top of the Marmar Road below Farbreaga, as you will be walking away from the Nire Valley.

# Route 13: KNOCKMEALDOWN MOUNTAINS

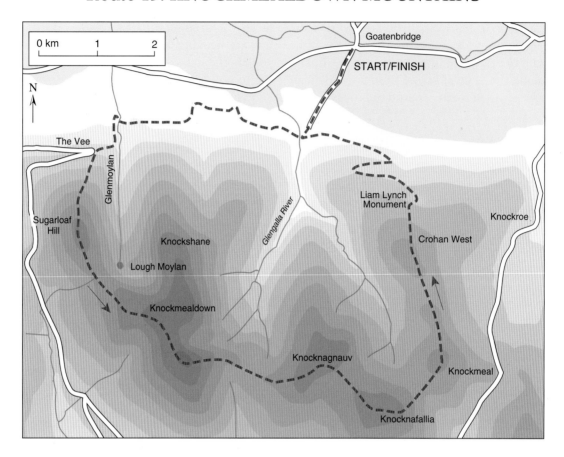

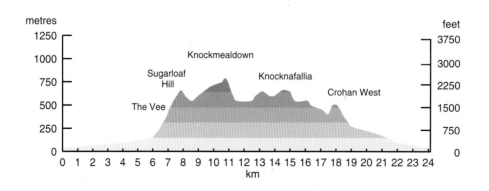

# Route 13: Knockmealdown Mountains

TIME ALLOWANCE 8 hours.

STARTING/FINISHING LOCATION
Goatenbridge.
OSI Discovery 74: GR088136.
Space to park cars at Goatenbridge.
Bus Eireann table number 386 is a limited service.

OVERVIEW/INTEREST
Fine heathery range of mountains, including the
    highest mountain in Co Waterford, with
    splendid views from the summits.
Follows a prominent old boundary marker wall
    and includes a stretch of the waymarked
    Munster Way.
Crosses St Declan's Way, and visits the Liam
    Lynch Monument.

FOOTPATHS
Uses the waymarked Munster Way.
Forest paths can be muddy in places.
Some upland stretches feature trodden paths.

STATISTICS

| | |
|---|---|
| WALKING DISTANCE | 26km (16 miles) |
| TOTAL HEIGHT GAINED | 1,260m (4,135ft) |
| PRINCIPAL HEIGHTS | |
| Sugarloaf Hill | 663m (2,144ft) |
| Knockmealdown | 794m (2,609ft) |
| Knocknagnauv | 655m (2,152ft) |
| Knocknafallia | 668m (2,199ft) |
| Knockmeal | 560m (1,846ft) |
| Crohan West | 521m (1,718ft) |

## The way to Sugarloaf Hill    *Allow 2½ hours*

The Knockmealdown Mountains are a range of
heathery mountains with forested northern flanks.
Although it is possible to enjoy a completely open
prospect all the way along the crest, a complete
circular walk would need to use either roads on the
southern flanks or forest paths on the northern. A
route on the forested northern flanks is provided
by the waymarked Munster Way.

The walk can be started at the crossroads village
of Goatenbridge, between Newcastle and Clog-
heen. A parking space is available here and a
nearby road is signposted for the Liam Lynch
Memorial. You could drive along this road and
hope to find a small space to park at a junction of
forest tracks, where signposts for the Munster Way
and St Declan's Way have been positioned.
Whichever way you arrive, turn right at this point
and follow the course of the Munster Way across
a concrete slab bridge. In wet weather, this is more
likely to be a ford. Follow the forest track onwards,
climbing gently uphill. Do not be tempted to climb
up as far as the two concrete water tanks, but look
out for a vague forest path heading off to the right.
This path follows a forest ride, but it is rather
overgrown and you may not notice it unless you
keep an eye open for it. Some parts of the path
may be muddy, but later it becomes a broad, clear
track running downhill.

While following this track, look out for a
waymark post on the left, which shows the way
along a narrower track. This track is enclosed by
forest at first, but further on there is a glimpse of a
field to the right. Pass straight through a crossroads
of tracks and emerge in a clear-felled and replanted
area with views of the open slopes of the
Knockmealdown Mountains. Cross a stream and
follow a track through more forest, then turn right
along a firmer track. Go straight along this track,
which passes through a crossroads of tracks, and
gradually rises in a clear-felled area with views of
the Galty Mountains. The track reaches a T
junction, where you carry straight on, following a
forest fence to a corner. Cross the fence and use a
stony track in an area of gorse to ford a river, then
climb up a slope. You gain height using a series of
stony zigzags, but then need to head off to the
right to reach a sharp elbow at The Vee on the
R668 road.

*The boundary wall and Sugarloaf Hill, with the Galty Mountains beyond.*

Sugarloaf Hill rises directly above this road and there are two ways to climb it. One is to ascend directly, crossing deep heather at first, before finding easier ground where the heather becomes shorter on the higher slopes. The other is to try to trace old zigzag paths up the slope. Some of them are quite overgrown with heather, while others are easier to locate. Either way, the direction is upwards, and the ground becomes quite steep and stony in places. There is some hummocky ground bearing a scattering of boulders before you reach a large cairn near the summit. The views from this old cairn are rather better than those from the true summit. The summit cairn is also smaller and stands at 663m (2,144ft). Views extending to the Galty Mountains and Comeragh Mountains have been getting better all the way through the ascent.

## The way to Knockmeal        *Allow 3 hours*

Close to the summit of Sugarloaf Hill is the corner of a drystone wall, which marks the county boundary between Co Tipperary and Co Waterford. This wall becomes a heathery embankment on the descent, crossing some bouldery ground before reaching a broad heathery gap. The linear mound becomes a stout wall further uphill, especially where it crosses a gentler shoulder at around 650m (2,130ft). It is more like a line of rubble where it crosses the next broad rise. Continue towards the summit of Knock-mealdown, where there is a perch of rock and a trig point overlooking a steep stony slope at 794m (2,609ft). The views can be quite extensive, as this is the highest point in Co Waterford, and the following features might be spotted:

| | |
|---|---|
| N | Devilsbit Mountain |
| NNE | Slieve Bloom Mountains |
| NE | Slievenamon |
| ENE | Crohan West, Laghtnafrankee, Knockanaffrin |
| E | Knocknagnauv, Comeragh Mountains |
| S | River Blackwater |

WSW  Nagles Mountains
WNW  Knockshannahullion, Temple Hill
NW  Galtymore, Galtybeg, Sugarloaf Hill
NNW  Slieveanard

The rubble mound leads steeply down the heathery slope and then becomes less prominent, although the line is still easy to trace. Cross a slight hump, then walk down across a broad heathery gap at around 515m (1,690ft). Walk up the moorland slope beyond the gap, crossing the very vague remains of the Rian Bó Phádraig, or Track of St Patrick's Cow. The ground rises gently above the gap, and then climbs more steeply on to Knocknagnauv. The heathery boundary mound again becomes a tall and broad drystone wall. As it crosses the summit, an altitude of 655m (2,152ft) is reached. You need to make a decision at this point about how to proceed along the range.

The boundary wall is a clear feature to follow in mist, and it makes a sudden dog-leg turn on the way down from the summit of Knocknagnauv. If you follow it any further, it becomes merely a vague ditch and heathery mound cut across the northern slopes of Knocknafallia. Some walkers might prefer to climb over the top of Knocknafallia, but you should note that this route has no trodden path or feature to follow. A heathery slope bearing patches of stones rises to a small cairn which doesn't quite sit on the 668m (2,199ft) summit. Walking further along the broad crest of the hill, you pass peat hags to reach an ancient burial cairn, where there is a view southwards to Mount Mellerary Monastery.

*The Liam Lynch Memorial takes the form of a round tower in the forest.*

Walk north-eastwards from the burial cairn to descend from Knocknafallia, dropping steeply down a heather slope to land on a gap near a corner of a forest. The heathery boundary mound runs straight uphill on the slopes of Knockmeal, narrowly missing the summit, which is marked by a small cairn at 560m (1,846ft).

## The way back to Goatenbridge

*Allow 2½ hours*

Beyond the summit of Knockmeal, the embankment no longer marks the boundary between Co Tipperary and Co Waterford. Instead, it heads in a straight line towards Crohan West. For some reason, the mound was not constructed along the crest of the ridge, but runs part-way down its western slopes. The ground alongside the mound can be rough underfoot, as the heather is quite long and there are some boulders protruding from the ground. On the ascent the heather bank becomes a stone wall again, and although the ground becomes more bouldery it is easier to walk. There is a dog-leg turn in the wall at the summit cairn on Crohan West, where the altitude is 521m (1,718ft).

Leading straight downhill from the summit cairn to the north is a line of wooden fenceposts. Follow these down the steep, rugged slope, which eases before reaching a forest fence. Cross the fence and walk straight down a narrow, overgrown forest ride. There is a vague path along the ride, but you need to take care as the ground is uneven. Watch for a turning to the right, where you can walk along another narrow, overgrown ride to reach the prominent Liam Lynch Monument. This takes the form of a round tower, raised in memory of the Chief of Staff of the IRA, who was shot nearby in 1923 by Free State troops.

Leave the monument and turn left to follow a clear track down through the forest. This track is also the course taken by the Munster Way, which is marked by yellow arrows on wooden posts. The track passes through a staggered junction and then begins to rise gently for a while, before dropping down further through the forest. There is a sharp turn to the right, and then at a lower level there is a sharp turn to the left. The track eventually levels out in the clear-felled lower parts of the forest. It then runs onwards to reach a signposted junction of tracks which you passed at the start of the walk, where the courses of the Munster Way and St Declan's Way are indicated. A right turn at this point leads along a track and narrow road, which leave the forest and return to the tiny village of Goatenbridge, where there is a shop.

## Alternative routes

ESCAPES
Care is needed on the forested stretches of this walk, as the course of the Munster Way is often poorly marked. Some junctions are missing waymarks, while other waymarks may be faded or hidden. Once the open, heathery crest of the Knockmealdown Mountains is reached, any early descents need to be chosen carefully as all the lower glens are forested. All parts of the forest are served by tracks but again, care needs to be exercised when navigating through it. The easiest early descent is from the lowest gap in the range, following the course of the ancient Rian Bó Phádraig (or modern St Declan's Way) northwards through Glengalla to return to the starting point.

EXTENSIONS
Keen hillwalkers will enjoy following the crest of the Knockmealdown Mountains and may wonder if the walk could be extended further along the range. In fact, it is possible to extend the walk westwards across the Vee Gap to reach the summit of Knockshanahullion. The heathery embankment can be traced almost all the way, although it is of lesser stature where it crosses the mountains to the west of the Vee Gap. Walkers electing to continue even further westwards will find a waymarked route called the Avondhu Way, which is an extension to the course of the Munster Way. This route leads across the open slopes of Farbreaga before running into a network of tracks and roads in the Araglin Valley.

# Route 14: GALTYMORE

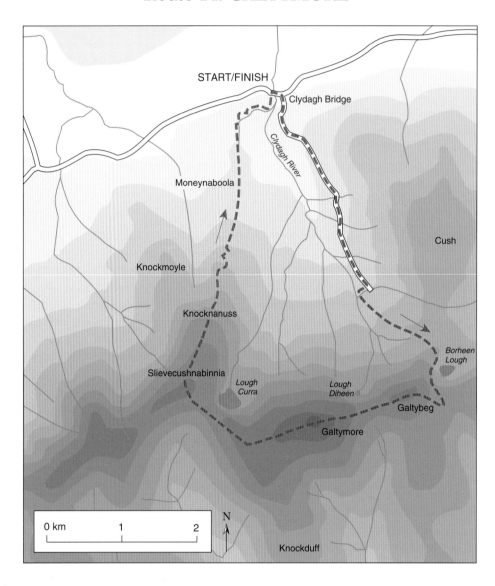

START/FINISH

Clydagh Bridge

Clydagh River

Moneynaboola

Cush

Knockmoyle

Knocknanuss

Borheen
Lough

Slievecushnabinnia

Lough
Curra

Lough
Diheen

Galtybeg

Galtymore

0 km          1          2

N

Knockduff

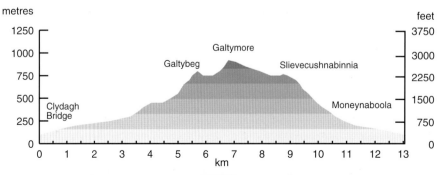

metres                                                                feet

1250                                                                  3750

1000                                    Galtymore                      3000

                          Galtybeg                                     2250
750                                              Slievecushnabinnia

500                                                                    1500
                                                    Moneynaboola
      Clydagh
250   Bridge                                                          750

0                                                                      0

      0   1   2   3   4   5   6   7   8   9   10  11  12  13
                              km

# Route 14: Galtymore

TIME ALLOWANCE 5 hours.

STARTING/FINISHING LOCATION
Clydagh Bridge, near Lisvernane.
OSI Discovery 74: GR874281.
Small parking space near Clydagh Bridge.
No public transport.

OVERVIEW/INTEREST
One of Ireland's highest mountains with
    extensive views from the summit.
Splendid horseshoe route.
Features a series of lovely little loughs, the cliffs
    above providing refuge for arctic/alpine plants.

FOOTPATHS
Easy road access to Glencoshabinnia.
Vaguely trodden paths on the higher ground.
A clear track and road to the finish.

STATISTICS

| | |
|---|---|
| WALKING DISTANCE | 13km (8 miles) |
| TOTAL HEIGHT GAINED | 920m (3,020ft) |
| PRINCIPAL HEIGHTS | |
| Galtybeg | 799m (2,618ft) |
| Galtymore | 919m (3,018ft) |

*Walkers approach a boggy gap and prepare to climb to the summit of Galtymore.*

## The way to Galtymore
*Allow 3 hours*

The Galty Mountains rise in splendid isolation above much lower ground, with several sprawling shoulders raising the prominent peak of Galtymore high above the plains. The main road from Dublin to Cork runs along the foot of the range, and the usual access route from this direction is along the Black Road. Routes from the Glen of Aherlow tend to be steeper and are much more scenic and dramatic. The circuit around Glencoshabinnia offers views of Galtymore from all directions.

The nearest village to the starting point in the Glen of Aherlow is Lisvernane. You need to find the Clydagh Bridge, which is across the glen from the village, and there is a good gravel patch which can be used for parking on the same side of the bridge as Lisvernane. Start the walk by crossing the Clydagh Bridge, continuing along the road for a short way before turning right to follow a minor road serving Glencoshabinnia. Anyone trying to drive up this road runs the risk of meeting another vehicle and having to back out, and parking spaces are extremely limited. The road climbs up through forest and you stay on the tarmac, avoiding forest tracks to left and right. The road climbs past occasional farms, getting narrower and rougher as it proceeds past the higher fields. At the head of the

Clydagh River the road crosses a ford to reach the last farmhouse in a stand of trees.

Keep to the right just beyond the farmhouse, passing through a gate to follow a rough and muddy track out on to the open hillside. You will have noticed signs which state that dogs are not allowed on the mountain. This restriction applies to virtually every access point, and the Galty Mountains are used as a vast, open sheep-grazing range. As height is gained on the grassy moorland slope, you can swing to the left and aim roughly towards the gap between the summits of Cush and Galtybeg. At a higher level, aim more to the right of the gap, climbing over a shoulder of Galtybeg. As you turn around this shoulder you will be able to look down on the lovely Borheen Lough, which is couched in a rugged hollow.

Look around the face of the steep, grassy slope above Borheen Lough to spot the line of a narrow path. This may be nothing more than a sheep path, or it may have served as an occasional path for people for a while. At any rate, it is fairly easy to spot, offers a good line across the steep slope and continues to allow good views of Borheen Lough. The path crosses rockier ground at a higher level, where a series of little rock steps seem to be rather better trodden, and you will emerge on to a broad moorland gap to the east of Galtybeg. There are a couple of wooden posts on this gap, which are the remains of a former fence.

Turn right to walk up the steep upper slopes of Galtybeg, where the grass gives way to areas of short heather and moss. The summit of Galtybeg rises to 799m (2,618ft) and the summit ridge is quite sharply defined with small outcrops of rock. Views stretch across both sides of the Galty Mountains, but the great bulk of Galtymore dominates the western prospect. There is an easy descent to a gap between Galtybeg and Galtymore, overlooking the little Lough Diheen. The lough is frowned upon by very steep slopes and tiers of cliffs, and the water occupies a deep crater with no direct outflow into the Glen of Aherlow. It is dammed by a huge mound of glacial moraine.

From the gap, simply start climbing straight uphill towards Galtymore. The ground gradually gets steeper, but any boggy areas can be avoided by

walking along the abrupt edge overlooking Lough Diheen. The steepest slopes do not support much bog, and the short grass is punctuated by stones and boulders. These are of a very coarse conglomerate, and when the boulders become quite large you will be close to the summit. The summit ridge features a cairn, a broken trig point, the concrete stump of an old cross and a white iron Celtic cross overlooking the Glen of Aherlow. The altitude is 919m (3,018ft), making Galtymore one of the highest mountains in Ireland. In clear weather the views can be remarkably extensive, stretching across the plains to embrace the following features:

| | |
|---|---|
| N | Keeper Hill, Slieve Felim Mountains |
| NNE | Slieve Bloom Mountains |
| NE | Wicklow Mountains |
| ENE | Galtybeg, Slievenamon |
| ESE | Comeragh Mountains |
| SE | Knockmealdown Mountains |
| SSW | Nagles Mountains |
| SW | Mountains of Cork and Kerry |
| WSW | Temple Hill, Ballyhoura Mountains |
| W | Slieveragh |
| NNW | Slievenamuck, Slieve Bearnagh |

## The way back to Clydagh Bridge

*Allow 2 hours*

Walk roughly westwards from the summit of Galtymore, descending on a short, steep, rocky slope before heading towards a slight rise bearing a large cairn. From this point, descend towards an area of level, bare, black bog, where the end of a stout drystone wall can be found. Follow the course of the wall further along the ridge, descending towards a gap offering fine views down into the deep hollow holding Lough Curra. The wall has been reduced to ground level on the steep slope above the lough, no doubt by generations of visitors rolling boulders down into the water. Like Lough Diheen earlier, Lough Curra has a huge dam of bouldery glacial moraine, but it also has a direct outflow into Glencoshabinnia.

The wall runs uphill from the gap, on to a broad shoulder of Slievecushnabinnia. The wall turns sharply left at this point, but you should continue straight onwards, heading roughly northwards down towards the Glen of Aherlow. The ground is heathery, with some boulders in places. As the slope begins to steepen, it is a good idea to drift slightly to the right. Looking down to the right, you will eventually notice the line of a grassy track on the lower part of the hillside. You need to descend towards this track, but a direct descent can be uncomfortably steep in places.    When you reach the track, turn left to follow it downhill at a fairly gentle gradient. There is a point where it features a zigzag, and here you can head more to the right and follow a line of fenceposts along a ditch running down the heathery slope. It is a good idea to cross this old fence at some point and head across the final patch of rugged lower moorland to reach a gate. Once past the gate, a clear track flanked by gorse bushes leads towards a farm access road. Simply follow this road downhill as it twists and turns, before depositing you on a lower road next to the parking space used at the start near the Clydagh Bridge.

## Alternative routes

### ESCAPES

Escapes from this walk need to be chosen with great care, especially in misty weather or in darkness. The very steep northern slopes may start off grassy, but they can quickly lead on to steep, greasy bands of rock and cliffs. Descents northwards from the summit of Galtybeg are steep, but possible. Descents northwards from Galtymore are also steep, but possible. Direct descents from the gaps towards Lough Diheen and Lough Curra should be avoided, as there are sheer cliffs awaiting the unwary. In an emergency situation, a very direct and safe descent might be needed, in which case you should use the course of the Black Road, leading off the southern slopes of Galtybeg. Unfortunately, this does not return into the Glen of Aherlow, but heads for the main road from Caher to Mitchelstown at Skeheenaranky. It is, however, quite easy, clear and safe to follow once it has been located.

### EXTENSIONS

The basic circuit could be extended in a number of ways. The summit of Cush could be included at the start of the walk. There is also a waymarked route rising through forest from the Glen of Aherlow which emerges close to Lough Muskry. This route could be extended across the broad shoulders of Greenane before heading towards Galtybeg and Galtymore. The problem with any extension is that you could be faced with a long road walk back through the Glen of Aherlow to complete a circular route. If transport is available to other points, then strong walkers could consider a walk along the full length of the Galty Mountains. It is possible to start near Caher and finish at Anglesborough after crossing all the summits along the main crest. In this direction, the steep and bouldery cone of Temple Hill is likely to test the stamina of even the strongest. If you are walking in the other direction, the initial climb on to Temple Hill is long and arduous, but at least the walk would end with gentler gradients.

*Looking back to the summit of Galtymore from a point above Lough Curra.*

81

# Route 15: BALLYHOURA MOUNTAINS

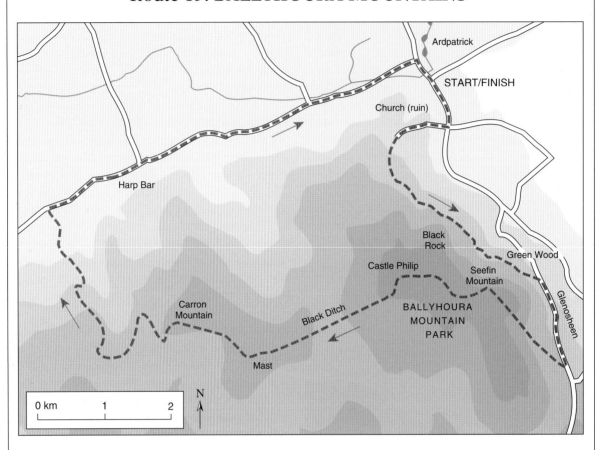

Ardpatrick

START/FINISH

Church (ruin)

Harp Bar

Black Rock

Green Wood

Castle Philip

Seefin Mountain

Glenosheen

Carron Mountain

Black Ditch

BALLYHOURA MOUNTAIN PARK

Mast

N

0 km    1    2

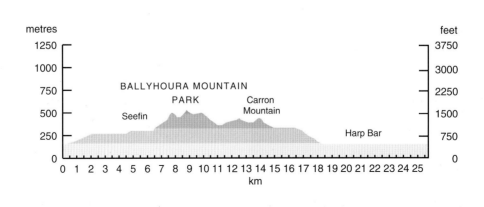

metres                                                          feet

1250                                                            3750

1000                                                            3000

750        BALLYHOURA MOUNTAIN                                  2250
                    PARK
500                            Carron                           1500
                               Mountain
           Seefin
250                                              Harp Bar       750

0                                                              0

0 1 2 3 4 5 6 7 8 9 10 11 12 13 14 15 16 17 18 19 20 21 22 23 24 25
                              km

# Route 15: Ballyhoura Mountains

TIME ALLOWANCE 8 hours.

STARTING/FINISHING LOCATION
Ardpatrick.
OSI Discovery 73: GR644211.
Car parking around Ardpatrick.
Bus Eireann table numbers 329 and 339 run near
    Ardpatrick.

OVERVIEW/INTEREST
Route runs through the Ballyhoura Mountain
    Park and along the high moorland crest of the
    Ballyhoura Mountains, with some stretches on
    forested slopes.
Includes the ancient Black Ditch and rugged
    summits, three pubs linked by a road walk, and
    a number of shorter waymarked walks.
Associations with O'Sullivan Beare and
    Brian Boru.

FOOTPATHS
A number of waymarked trails are linked.
Forest tracks are firm and clear.
Moorland paths are mostly quite clear, although
    some are becoming rather muddy.
Includes a stretch of road walking.

STATISTICS
| | |
|---|---|
| WALKING DISTANCE | 26km (16 miles) |
| TOTAL HEIGHT GAINED | 760m (2,500ft) |
| PRINCIPAL HEIGHTS | |
| Seefin | 519m (1,702ft) |
| Black Rock | 529m (1,736ft) |
| Carron Mountain | 448m (1,469ft) |

## The way to Seefin                    *Allow 3 hours*

Ardpatrick is a small, tidy and pleasant little village
at the foot of the Ballyhoura Mountains. The whole
of Ballyhoura Country abounds in features of
interest. The walk through the Ballyhoura
Mountains makes the most of a broad moorland
strip which has been left free of conifer plantations.
This strip is itself divided by the Black Ditch, which
is a boundary mark in the form of an embankment
of stone and turf. The course of the Black Ditch is
waymarked as part of the long-distance Ballyhoura
Way, although there are a great number of shorter
waymarked walks in the area. The Ballyhoura Way
is part of the longer O'Sullivan Beare Way,
commemorating the bitter march of the O'Sullivan
Beare clan from Dunboy Castle in West Cork to Co
Leitrim in the winter of 1602–3. Of a thousand
people who fled their enemies, only 35 completed
the trek.

Leave the village of Ardpatrick by following the
minor road signposted for Kildorrery. At a
crossroads outside the village there is a turning to
the right, which is signposted as the Scenic
Mountain Drive. Follow this narrow tarmac road
uphill, noting that the surface degenerates to gravel
by the time a clear-felled and replanted forest is
reached. You will reach a crossroads of tracks and
will need to make a decision at this point. Walkers
who wish to complete a shorter walk can continue
straight uphill, zigzagging up through the forest to
reach the open moorland crest above. The dis-
advantage is that the northern part of the range
will be missed, and this features some good views
and pleasant summits.

To enjoy the full walk, turn left at the crossroads
of tracks, following the course of the Ballyhoura Way
through the forest towards Glenosheen. The track
leads into a stand of taller forest, emerging on a bend
with more open views again. Continue along the
track to another junction, where blue and yellow
waymark arrows point straight ahead and downhill.
Walk straight through next junction, following more
blue and yellow arrows, then note a little sign
pointing down a track towards the car park. There
are taller stands of trees now, with a ground cover of
rhododendron. Just as a road comes into view at the
foot of the track, turn right up several steps and
follow a woodland path gently uphill. Turn left along

83

another track, then right to follow a short path to the Green Wood car park. Here there are numerous information boards which illustrate long and short walks from the car park, as well as giving nature trail and orienteering information.

Leave the car park and turn right to follow a minor road. Keep right at a road junction to stay above the small village of Glenosheen, and emerge from the forest to enjoy a more open prospect from the road. Follow the road until you find a stile on the right flanked by blue waymark arrows. Cross the stile and follow a clear track straight towards the moorland dome of Seefin. There are a couple more stiles to be crossed as the track rises across the steep moorland slopes. The surface can be stony, but the gradients are not too steep. As the crest of the track is gained, you could head across an area of short heather to reach the 519m (1,702ft) summit of Seefin. There is the base of a burial cairn to see, as well as fine views of the countryside taking in the following features:

| NNE | Keeper Hill, Slieve Felim Mountains |
| NE | Slievereagh |
| ENE | Temple Hill, Galtymore |
| ESE | Knockmealdown Mountains |
| SE | Coolfree Mountain |
| S | Nagles Mountains |
| W | Black Rock summit |

## The way to Carron Mountain

*Allow 2 hours*

Walk back from the summit of Seefin to the crest of the track, then turn right and walk downhill towards the top side of a forest. There is a blue waymark arrow pointing left, and a rather muddy path to follow up a rough moorland slope. The path is on top of a turf embankment – the Black Ditch – and so is easily traced uphill. Outcrops of rock and a trig point can be seen on the skyline, and in time you will reach these. The trig point stands on an outcrop at 529m (1,736ft), at a place often referred to as the Black Rock. However, the Black Rock is more correctly a feature some distance to the north. This is the highest point in the Ballyhoura

Mountains, although the view is not blessed with the same sense of space as that from nearby Seefin.

Continue along the line of the Black Ditch beyond the summit, following it across moorland where a line of rocky outcrops suddenly appears. The path passes through a gap between two outcrops, then runs down to a gravel car park on the crest of the moors. You are again on the Scenic Mountain Drive, and there is a mapboard explaining the surrounding area of the Ballyhoura Mountain Park. You could follow the track off to the right, then take a boggy track to the left to reach the next summit, Castle Philip, but it makes more sense to remain on the moorland crest and forge straight through the heather to reach this rocky peak.

You may find it slightly easier to pass the rocks on the right-hand side, but you should then turn left to continue following the line of the Black Ditch. Even so, the ditch then swings to the right and begins to run downhill for a while. Looking ahead in clear weather, a Telecom Eireann mast can be seen perched on the next hill, and the Black Ditch runs straight towards this feature. On the way across the rugged moorland you will pass a couple of patches of willow, and then cross an old track on the lowest part of the broad gap. Young forest stands on the slopes to the left of the Black Ditch as it runs up towards the mast. You now join a tarmac road, where a board showing several species of birds is located.

You do not need to follow the road up to the mast, but can instead use a path on the moorland slope which keeps to the right of the mast. Turn right along a clear track running gently downhill, then bear left on to another track to continue downhill. The stony track rises steeply for a while, following the line of a fence. At the top corner of the fence, walk straight onwards along a stony path over the moorland. After crossing a broad dip there is a slight ascent to the summit of Carron Mountain. A huge, hollowed, ancient cairn is situated here, itself surmounted by another cairn, offering views of the surrounding countryside. The cairn has associations with Brian Boru, the last High King of Ireland. There is a tree at this height – 448m (1,469ft) – and a stony hollow which is thought to have been a well.

## The way back to Ardpatrick

*Allow 3 hours*

You will have noticed a waymark post just before reaching the summit cairn on Carron. You can either return a short way along the path, then follow the path waymarked past the cairn, or simply walk straight down the steep, heathery western slope of the summit to land on the path further downhill. When you reach this path, turn left to follow it for a short distance, then turn right to walk down a broader, stonier track. This track runs down from the moorland to enter a forest, proceeding down a rather rugged forest ride. When you land on a track at a lower level, turn left and follow it for a while, until another clear track runs off to the right. At the lower end of this track turn right again, then left to descend from the forest. When the track runs out of the forest and reaches a junction with a minor road, turn right to follow the road. At Effin you will find the Harp Bar, where walking groups can book a cauldron of soup which will be prepared over an open turf fire.

Follow the road onwards to return to Ardpatrick, passing Mona Fitzgibbon's pub which actually draws its water supply from a nearby holy well! The road continues towards Ardpatrick, where the Greenwood Inn is available as a final point of refreshment. This pleasant little village is easily explored at the end of the walk. If you have a few minutes to spare, follow a track uphill from the Greenwood Inn to reach a hilltop graveyard. The base of a round tower can be inspected beside the graveyard, and there are good views of the surrounding countryside.

## Alternative routes

### ESCAPES

It is unlikely that walkers following this route will experience serious difficulties, but there are a couple of obvious escape routes. After crossing Seefin and the Black Rock – the highest parts of the walk – an early descent to Ardpatrick could be made by way of the Scenic Mountain Drive. Simply turn right to follow it off the moorland crest and

*Seefin rises as a moorland dome at the eastern end of the Ballyhoura Mountains.*

return to the village. Later on, there is an old track leading to the right just before the Telecom Eireann mast, and another track could be followed to the right after leaving the mast. Descents via these tracks need a little more care, as they reach junctions with other tracks at a lower level.

### EXTENSIONS

This walk covers most of the heathery crest of the Ballyhoura Mountains, from Seefin to Carron Mountain. The route could be extended a little further along the high moorland crest, but then the surrounding forestry plantations would be reached and the walk back through the forest and along the road to Ardpatrick would be longer. Around either end of this walk – at the Green Wood and Ballinaboola especially, there are networks of colour-coded waymarked loop walks which could be used to boost the total distance covered.

# Route 16: GOUGANE BARRA

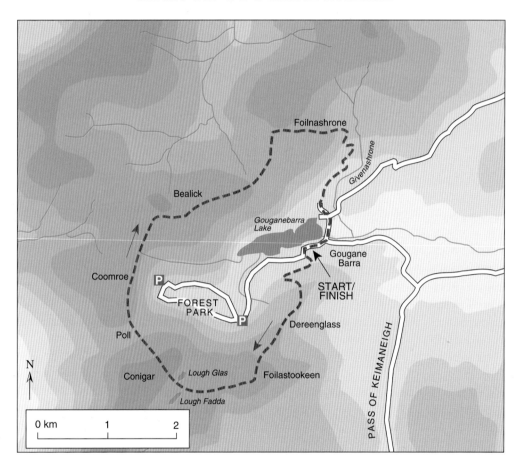

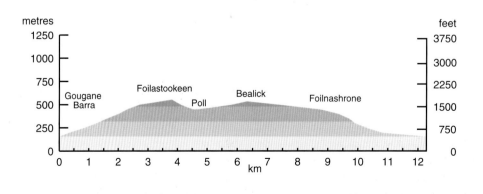

# 6

# WEST CORK

## Route 16: Gougane Barra

TIME ALLOWANCE 4 hours.

STARTING/FINISHING LOCATION
Gougane Barra Hotel.
OSI Discovery 85: GR093660.
Car park close to the hotel.
Bus Eireann table number 255 is a limited
    service.

OVERVIEW/INTEREST
Fine circuit around a rugged glen incorporating
    Gougane Barra Forest Park.
Plenty of interest, including an ancient monastic
    site and echoes of adventure, stories and song.

FOOTPATHS
Clear tracks are used at the start and finish.
Most of the route is pathless, with a few vague
    paths on the mountains.

STATISTICS
| | |
|---|---|
| WALKING DISTANCE | 13km (8 miles) |
| TOTAL HEIGHT GAINED | 500m (1,640ft) |
| PRINCIPAL HEIGHTS | |
| Conigar | 555m (1,828ft) |
| Bealick | 537m (1,764ft) |

### The way to Conigar          *Allow 2 hours*

Gougane Barra is a wild and rocky glen containing a lovely lough, the source of the River Lee, a forest park and a large hotel. St Finbar founded a monastery on a small island nearby which now bears a more recent chapel. There are plenty of short and easy walks around the lower parts of Gougane Barra, but there is also a high-level circuit available around the mountains surrounding the glen. This particular walk should be reserved for a clear day, as the high ground is rough and featureless, with precipitous cliffs falling into the glen from most sides.

In 1921, when General Tom Barry and his Flying Column were on the run, local men guided them under cover of darkness out of Coomhola and down into Gougane Barra via the precipitous gully of Poll. They followed a route which had been used for centuries, but which was notoriously difficult at the best of times. Travelling without light or proper ropes, the men used their rifles to lower each other down the gully to safety.

The walk can be started close to the Gougane Barra Hotel. Residents can of course use the hotel car park, while others may be able to park at a small car park just beyond the hotel, between the island chapel and a small graveyard. There is also an award-winning thatched toilet block alongside. Just next to this is a gate giving access to a track. Follow this gradually uphill and turn right at a junction with another track. This track passes a building, a water tank and a sheep pen, and then runs out on to the open mountainside. The track dips downhill a short way, then turns sharply left and runs uphill a little further.

*OVERLEAF The Gougane Barra Hotel sits by the lough at the mouth of the rugged glen.*

Leave the track and pick a way up the rugged mountainside. There are slopes of tussocky, boggy grass separated by ridges and outcrops of rock. As height is gained you will cross a fence and see a number of small trees clinging to the rock outcrops, but there are none at a higher level. There is no real trodden path, but there are a number of sheep paths which offer easy courses through the rugged terrain. Keep climbing and eventually the top of Foilastookeen will be reached. There is a fine view to be seen along the valley of the River Lee.

A fence can be followed onwards for a while, and this is a useful guide in mist. The fence passes three

*Looking along Gougane Barra Lough to the island chapel of St Finbar's.*

small loughs on the rugged rock and heather crest, ending suddenly at Lough Fadda. There is a summit bearing a small cairn between Lough Glas and a small pool, where the altitude is 555m (1,828ft). This is quite a good viewpoint, taking in mountains on either side of the Cork/Kerry county boundary. The following features are prominent:

N       Bealick, Crohane.
NNE   The Paps, Caherbarnagh.
NE     Mullaghanish, Musheramore.
SE     Shehy Mountains.
W      Knockboy, Caoinkeen.
NW    Carrauntoohil, MacGillycuddy's Reeks.
NNW  Carran, Mangerton Mountain, Stoompa.

## The way back to Gougane Barra

*Allow 2 hours*

Descend north-westwards from Conigar, stepping down past a rocky outcrop before heading across a boggy, grassy, heathery gap. Cross a fence at the head of the steep and rocky gully of Poll, then walk past a small pool sitting just above the gap. A series of rock outcrops rise ahead, but these are easily outflanked. In fact, some of the rocks are tilted at such an easy angle that it is possible to walk up them. There is a slight rise of grass beyond this rocky rise, then a longer stretch of grassy moorland rises ahead.

After crossing a grassy area of Bealick, which rises to 537m (1,764ft), the broad crest continues towards a rough and rocky section. The rocky summit, although slightly lower, is crowned with a cairn. Beyond the cairned summit, ridges of rock lead roughly east-north-east. These ridges are separated by strips of tussocky grass which can be boggy. Great care is needed when walking off the summit of Bealick, as the summit crest ends in rugged prows of rock. However, there is an easy descent to a broad and boggy gap.

The broad gap is mostly grassy and there is a small pool of water sitting on it. There is a slight rise towards the rocky slopes beyond the gap, but you should not actually walk on to the rocky ground. Instead, turn right and start walking downhill from the gap. There are some rocky slabs to cross, and a little stream running downhill, but you need to be careful not to be drawn on to the rocky prow of Foilnashrone. This ridge ends in overhanging cliffs where progress would come to an abrupt halt.

By taking the easiest line downhill, you will pass around the base of the cliffs at Foilnashrone. There is a fence running downhill and a small gap in it just at the foot of the cliffs. Look up the rockface and you will see a host of plant communities and ivy. Follow the fence a short way downhill, then drop down on to a clear track. There are good views here towards the Gougane Barra Hotel and lake.

The track zigzags downhill on a rugged slope and then runs through the lower fields. It passes through gateways before landing on a farm access road. Turn left along the access road, then left again to cross a bridge. Follow the tarmac road past a stone clapper footbridge. It was in a cottage nearby that the book *The Tailor and Ansty* was written – and subsequently banned as 'indecent'. Keep right by road to return to the Gougane Barra Hotel.

## Alternative routes

ESCAPES
As Gougane Barra is completely surrounded by cliffs and steep outcrops of rock, descents from the high ground into the glen are not recommended. There are a couple of places where steep and rocky descents are possible, such as via the gully of Poll, but they are not particularly suitable for foul weather or in darkness. The safest escape from the high-level circuit is either to retrace your steps or continue following the route.

EXTENSIONS
Any extensions to this route would tend to lead the walker away from Gougane Barra, and so would require transport to be available at some other point. Heading westwards from the head of Gougane Barra provides possibly the most satisfying walk. A minor road would be crossed and the route could be continued across the road to reach the summit of Knockboy.

# Route 17: CUMMEENGEERA

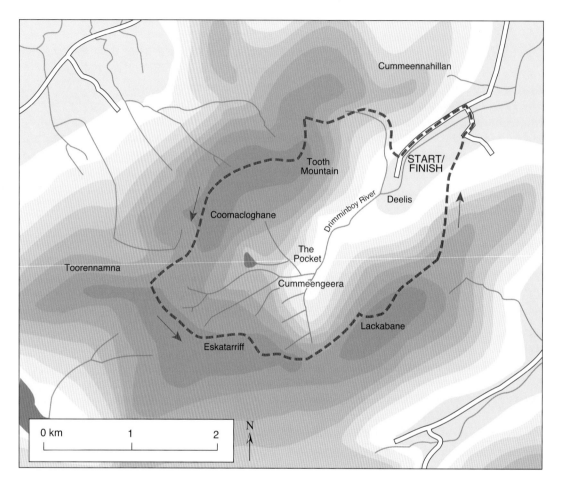

Cummeennahillan

Tooth
Mountain

START/
FINISH

Drimminboy River

Coomacloghane

Deelis

The
Pocket

Toorennamna

Cummeengeera

Lackabane

Eskatarriff

0 km      1      2

N

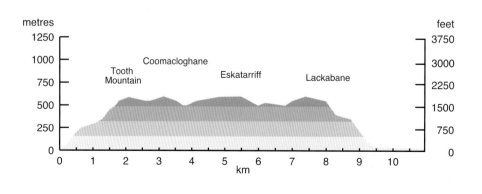

| metres | | | | | | | | | | | feet |

# Route 17: Cummeengeera

TIME ALLOWANCE 5 hours.

STARTING/FINISHING LOCATION
Cummeengeera, at the end of the road.
OSI Discovery 84: GR754554.
Cars can be parked near the end of the road.
No public transport.
Bus Eireann table number 282 serves Lauragh in
summer.

OVERVIEW/INTEREST
Fine horseshoe walk around a rugged glen, with
impressive rock and fine views from the summits.
Prominent stone circle and rath at beginning and
end.
Features the Rabach's Glen.

FOOTPATHS
Most of the route is completely untrodden.
There are vague paths on some of the ridges.

STATISTICS
WALKING DISTANCE          12km (7½ miles)
TOTAL HEIGHT GAINED       890m (2,920ft)
PRINCIPAL HEIGHTS
Tooth Mountain            590m (1,945ft)
Coomacloghane             599m (1,969ft)
Eskatarriff               600m (1,973ft)
Lackabane                 602m (1,970ft)

*Slabs of rock dwarf a farmhouse at the head of Cummeengeera.*

## The way to Tooth Mountain

*Allow 1½ hours*

The Caha Mountains are often broad and bleak, rising to some fine summits. Hungry Hill has some awesomely rocky flanks; the Slieve Miskish Mountains are lower, yet continue to be rough in most parts, and the rugged spine of high ground can be traced even along the length of Dursey Island. There are rough, tough walks all over the Beara Peninsula, but around Cummeengeera there is a fine, natural horsehoe walk with impressive rock scenery and fine views from the summits. Names such as Tooth Mountain conjure up images of great spikes of rock, and although this may be far from the truth, the area is indeed memorable for some of its other rock features.

Buses operate only on a seasonal basis to Lauragh, but motorists can follow a narrow minor road towards the head of Cummeengeera. There is space to park near the buildings at the end of the road, and it would be a good idea to ask for permission. Note the massive slabs of rock above the houses, but do not worry as you won't be grappling with anything like that on the horseshoe walk. You will notice a stone circle near the end of the road, on the right-hand side. Flowing down from the steep slopes above the stone circle is a rushing river, and this is the key to the initial ascent. Follow the river upstream, taking frequent pauses for breath if necessary and enjoying the unfolding vista over the glen. The steep slope seems unremitting, but at a higher level you will be drawn into a rugged hollow where the gradient eases for a while.

Proceed further upstream, following the little river towards its source. Although the gradients have eased, the ground underfoot is rugged. You should notice a notch on the skyline at the head of the hanging valley, then start heading towards it. The ground rears up again, and a steep climb is necessary to reach the top of the notch. Again, a pause for breath would be in order before making a left turn and continuing the ascent. There are outcrops of rock to scramble up, but nothing serious or exposed. The ground then becomes easier to walk and the summit of Tooth Mountain is finally gained at 590m (1,945ft).

## The way to Lackabane *Allow 2 hours*

The horseshoe walk now proceeds from summit to summit all the way around Cummeengeera. Looking at the map, you will see that there is very little difference in height between the summits on this round – only 12m (39ft) from beginning to end – but there are some descents and subsequent reascents which tend to become more severe as the walk progresses. Leaving Tooth Mountain walking westwards and south-westwards, there is a gentle descent towards a broad gap, followed by a fairly gentle climb up to the top of Coomacloghane at 599m (1,969ft). In clear weather this moorland ridge is obvious, but in mist it may be necessary to take a bearing from one summit to another.

Leaving Coomacloghane, there is a more pronounced descent to the next gap, then on the ascent which follows you need to swing from

south-west to south-east as you climb. The blanket bog which covers the first part of the horseshoe has mostly been eroded from the slope of Eskatarriff, leaving a stony surface which is easier to walk on. The broad slope falls away precipitously to the head of Cummeengeera, and the summit of Eskatarriff is rather indeterminate, although it reaches an altitude of 600m (1,973ft). This is a fine perch from which to observe the extensive view, which takes in features such as:

| | |
|---|---|
| NNE | Carrauntoohil, MacGillycuddy's Reeks |
| NE | Mangerton Mountain |
| ENE | Knockowen, Caha Mountains |
| E | Sugarloaf Mountain |
| SE | Hungry Hill |
| S | Mizen Head |
| SW | Maulin |
| WSW | Slieve Miskish Mountains |
| WNW | Hog's Head, Bolus Head |
| NW | Coomcallee |
| NNW | Knockmoyle, Coomacarrea, Brandon Mountain |
| N | Mullaghanattin |

There is a descent from Eskatarriff to a gap. In misty weather, note that there is then a slight rise before the route continues down to a slightly lower gap. From this lower gap there is a long but not excessively steep climb up to the summit of Lackabane, which stands at an altitude of 602m (1,970ft) and is thus the highest point reached on the circuit.

## The way back to Cummeengeera *Allow 1½ hours*

From both Eskatarriff and Lackabane there have been remarkable views deep down to the head of Cummeengeera. Walkers may have been surprised, or even appalled, to note ruined houses dotted around the head of the glen. Steep rock walls and bouldery ground are a feature of what is known as the Rabach's Glen and it is true that families once scraped a living from the wild glen head. The Rabach was a fierce and violent man, who had committed at least two murders before he was caught. He was witnessed each time, but the constabulary were hard-pressed to catch him as he was fleet of foot and had a hideout high on one side of the glen. However, he was ultimately caught when he heard that a child of his was about to be born, and the constabulary had been tipped off that he would make an appearance. One can only wonder at the harshness of life in such forbidding surroundings.

The ridge leaving the summit of Lackabane is quite easy at first, but then it steepens considerably as it heads north-east towards another gap. There is a path along this ridge, and after crossing the gap there is a slight climb on to a minor summit at 406m (1,332ft). Have one last look around at the hills, then take particular note of the lower slopes of the glen, because you will have to cross them in order to return to the road. By heading directly northwards you can cut across the very steep slopes of the glen, aiming for the large, circular rath seen where the ground levels out. This feature is visible almost throughout the descent, but you still need to take care of rocky or boggy areas on the steep slope, where a slip or fall could result in injury. When the ground levels out, it is worth having a look at the rath which is a fine structure, complementing other ancient remains in the glen.

There is a rough sort of track leading through thorny scrub near the rath, and this becomes much clearer as it crosses the Drimminboy River. Turn left along the narrow minor road after crossing the river and you will be led straight back to the parking space beside the houses at the head of the glen. If you are heading on foot for Lauragh, however, you should turn right and follow the road out of the glen.

## Alternative routes

ESCAPES

Escapes from the Cummeengeera Horseshoe need careful thought. Generally, it is inadvisable to try to descend directly to the head of the glen from the surrounding mountains. Even though the ground may sometimes look as if it runs safely downhill, it could still become steep and rocky around the

*Starting the long and steep descent from Lackabane to bring the walk to a close.*

lower parts of the glen. Descents towards Ardgroom Harbour or Glenbeg Lough are safer, but leave you a long way from any vehicle which you may have parked in Cummeengeera. Essentially, escapes are not easy and you would be advised to stick to the route which is described, either retracing your steps or continuing with the route as appropriate.

EXTENSIONS

The Cummeengeera Horseshoe is such a natural circuit that any extension to it is likely to involve a whole extra walk. The only logical extension would be to descend steeply southwards from Eskatarriff, then climb up a rugged, hummocky, boggy, rocky slope to reach the distant summit of Hungry Hill. This hill needs to be treated with care in mist, as there are awkward 'benches' of rock which tend to lead walkers on to dangerous ground. The route could be continued towards the rock-bound Healy Pass, with a descent to Glanmore Lake.

# Route 18: MANGERTON MOUNTAIN

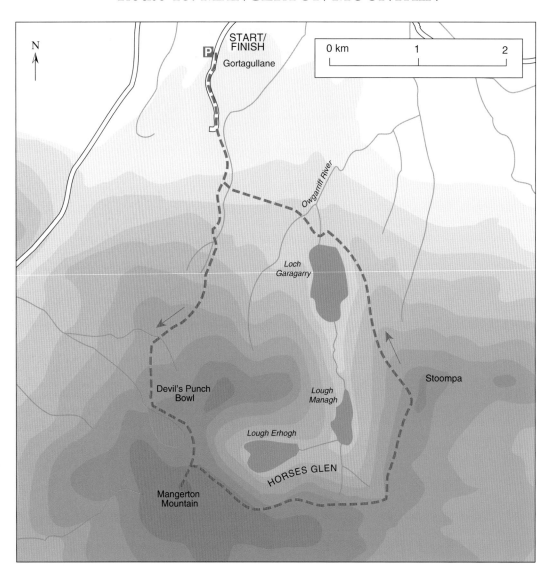

N

START/FINISH
Gortagullane

0 km          1          2

Owgarriff River

Loch Garagarry

Devil's Punch Bowl

Lough Managh

Stoompa

Lough Erhogh

HORSES GLEN

Mangerton Mountain

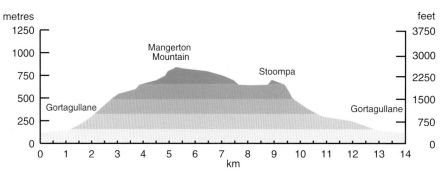

metres                                                        feet
1250                                                          3750

1000                    Mangerton                            3000
                        Mountain
750                                        Stoompa           2250

500                                                          1500

250   Gortagullane                      Gortagullane          750

0                                                             0
      0  1  2  3  4  5  6  7  8  9  10  11  12  13  14
                           km

# 7

# KERRY

## Route 18: Mangerton Mountain

TIME ALLOWANCE 5 hours.

STARTING/FINISHING LOCATION
Gortagullane, above Muckross.
OSI Discovery 78 and 79: GR984857. Also OSI
   1:25,000 Killarney National Park map.
Viewpoint car park beside the road.
Bus Eireann table numbers 44 and 280 serve
   Muckross in the summer.

OVERVIEW/INTEREST
Fine horseshoe walk around the Horses Glen.
Includes a broad-shouldered mountain with
   extensive views from the summit plateau.
Partly within the Killarney National Park.
Views of four fine loughs and the Lakes of
   Killarney.

FOOTPATHS
A clear path leads almost all the way to the
   summit, but is showing signs of erosion
   in places.
A narrower path leads from Mangerton to
   Stoompa.
Some parts on the return route are untrodden.

STATISTICS

| | |
|---|---|
| WALKING DISTANCE | 14km (9 miles) |
| TOTAL HEIGHT GAINED | 825m (2,700ft) |
| PRINCIPAL HEIGHTS | |
| Mangerton Mountain | 839m (2,756ft) |
| Stoompa | 705m (2,281ft) |

## The way to Mangerton Mountain

*Allow 2 hours*

Mangerton Mountain is the only mountain visible from the narrow Main Street in the busy town of Killarney. It rises above the Three Lakes Hotel, when mist doesn't completely shroud the summit. Mangerton is the highest point within the Killarney National Park, although only half of the bleak and boggy mountain is within the park boundary. The broad shoulders of Mangerton extend in all directions, rising to surround the main summit with a host of satellites.

There are buses running from Killarney to Muckross only during the summer, although jarveys and their jaunting cars seem to be available almost throughout the year. From Muckross, minor roads are signposted for Mangerton, leading to a dead-end road at Gortagullane. There is a viewpoint overlooking the Lakes of Killarney, and this is equipped with a small roadside car park. Further along the road, parking is limited to only a couple of roadside spaces.

It is best to use the little car park, then walk further along the road. There is a stand of pines to the right, and masses of gorse to the left. Look out for a turning to the left, where a track crosses a concrete slab bridge over the Finoulagh River and continues towards a sheep pen. Continue onwards, following a grassy path between gorse bushes. This path climbs gradually and can be muddy in places. Pass through a small gate in a fence and leave the gorse bushes behind.

Heather and boulders lie on the next slope. The path crosses a small stream and then heads roughly upstream. There are a couple of iron fenceposts beside the path. After drifting away from stream at a higher level, the path is more deeply entrenched on the mountainside. Further on the path is more stony, and it contours across a heathery slope for a short while before reaching an old gateway. Turn left at this gateway and follow a stone embankment and boggy ditch uphill. Most of the path is on firm ground, but there is a boggy patch half-way along its length. The embankment marks the boundary of the Killarney National Park. The path suddenly reaches a point where the lough known as the Devil's Punch Bowl can be seen. The water occupies a high-level, bouldery coum on the northern side of Mangerton Mountain. Turn left to follow a path which passes an enormous upended slab of rock, and continues past other grotesque rocky features to reach a high gap.

From this gap, you can look down the steep and rugged Horses Glen to see Lough Erhogh. Turn right and follow a path up a blunt ridge towards the top of Mangerton Mountain. The path is becoming quite worn and stays on the slope overlooking the Devil's Punch Bowl rather than on the one overlooking Lough Erhogh, where some walkers might feel less secure. At the top of the slope is a broad area of blanket bog. In clear weather you can head straight towards the summit trig point, which is buried within a cairn at 839m (2,756ft). In mist, you could either take a bearing, or omit the top altogether. In clear weather, the views are extensive and stretch out to include the following:

| | |
|---|---|
| N | Killarney |
| ENE | Stoompa, The Paps, Caherbarnagh |
| E | Mullaghanish |
| SE | Barnastooka |
| S | Knockboy |
| SW | Caha Mountains, Beara Peninsula |
| WSW | Peakeen Mountain, Boughil, Mullaghanattin |
| W | Broaghnabinnia |
| WNW | MacGillycuddy's Reeks, Carrauntoohil |
| NW | Lakes of Killarney, Slieve Mish Mountains |

## The way to Stoompa
*Allow 1 hour*

After visiting the trig point, walk northwards to return to the edge of the broad, boggy, grassy plateau. Turn right to follow a narrow, stony path eastwards. This wanders along a break of slope between the steep drop towards Lough Erhogh and the soggy edge of the blanket bog which occupies the top of Mangerton Mountain. The path offers firm, dry, easy walking with some very good views along the length of the Horses Glen. In turn, Lough Erhogh gives way to a view of Lough Managh, then Lough Garagarry – all surrounded by rugged slopes and walls of rock.

The path gradually falls away from the blanket bog on Mangerton Mountain. In some places the path is grassy, but at others it may be hard to trace. There is more heather, and a small stream to cross before the path drops down through low outcrops of rock. Keep following the path, which keeps off the crest linking Mangerton and Stoompa, and continues to trace a line overlooking the rugged Horses Glen. Simply let the path lead you up a steep, bouldery and heathery slope on to Stoompa. There is a cairn on top of the mountain at 705m (2,281ft), but views are partially obscured by the broad shoulders of Mangerton Mountain.

## The way back to Gortagullane
*Allow 2 hours*

Beyond the summit of Stoompa is another broader, more heathery rise. A path appears to head towards this, but actually drifts off to the left. Soon, all traces of a path will be lost on the heathery, bouldery slope. In mist you should take a compass bearing towards Lough Garagarry, but in clear weather you can simply walk towards it and enjoy the views towards Killarney and its lakes. At the foot of the steep slope, a sort of blunt ridge continues and this bears a faint path. Drop down towards the river which flows out of the lough, crossing boggy ground, heather and small clumps of gorse.

*Lough Managh and Lough Garagarry fill the floor of the Horses Glen.*

There is a footbridge of sorts spanning the river, but it may be in a poor state. If by any chance it has gone, there are plenty of bouldery places allowing an easy crossing. The simplest course now is to head roughly westwards along a moorland shelf. The ground can be boggy, mossy or heathery, but the gradients are gentle. Drifting too far down the slope will bring you into contact with fences, but by aiming straight across you will eventually join the path which you used early on the ascent. Simply follow this path back downhill, passing through the gate in the fence which was also used earlier. The path passes gorse bushes and a sheep pen, and then a clear track leads back to the minor road. Turn right to return to the viewpoint car park.

## Alternative routes

### ESCAPES
All the way to the summit of Mangerton Mountain, the best line of escape is to turn around and retrace your steps. This continues to be true even as you follow the path around the rim of the Horses Glen, as there are no really safe descents leading down into it. However, by the time the gap is reached before Stoompa it is as well to proceed with the route, as there is no easier way to return to the starting point.

### EXTENSIONS
Mangerton Mountain extends its broad and bleak shoulders in all directions, and these could be used to create arduous extensions. By heading south-west from the top of Mangerton, a broad and ill-defined crest can be followed towards the Kerry Way at the Windy Gap. There are rugged hills beyond, stretching to the main road at Moll's Gap. Once the horseshoe walk has been completed to Stoompa, it is also possible to consider a very tough extension towards the peak of Crohane. This needs care, as there is a deep and rugged gap to be crossed where the rocky stump of Bennaunmore presents a significant obstacle. Any extensions towards the shapely peak of Torc Mountain are to be discouraged, as this involves crossing The Wilderness, which is a refuge for native Irish red deer.

# Route 19: MACGILLYCUDDY'S REEKS

A more detailed view of the summits on the Reeks ridge

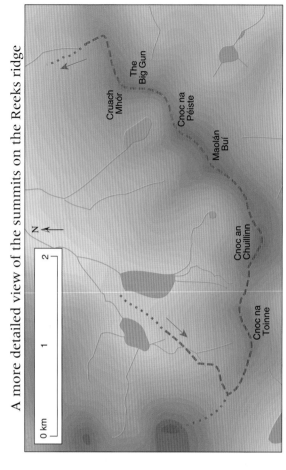

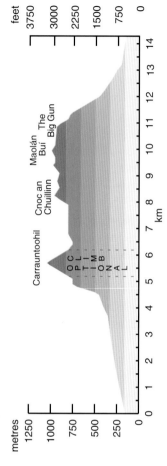

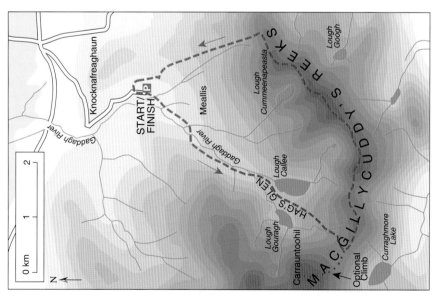

# Route 19: MacGillycuddy's Reeks

TIME ALLOWANCE 6½–8 hours.

STARTING/FINISHING LOCATION
Meallis, near the Hag's Glen.
OSI Discovery 78: GR836874. Also OSI 1:25,000
    MacGillycuddy's Reeks map.
Car park at the end of the road at Meallis.
No public transport.

OVERVIEW/INTEREST
Fine high-level ridge walk across some of
    Ireland's highest mountains.
Exceptionally rugged ridges in some parts, superb
    rock and splendid views from the summits.
Option to climb Ireland's highest mountain.

FOOTPATHS
Clear tracks and paths are used at the start.
Some of the paths on the ridge are quite clear,
    while the descent is untrodden.
Note that this route involves some exposed
    scrambling.

STATISTICS

| | |
|---|---|
| WALKING DISTANCE | 16km (10 miles), not including Carrauntoohil |
| TOTAL HEIGHT GAINED | 1,430m (4,690ft) |
| PRINCIPAL HEIGHTS | |
| Carrauntoohil | 1,039m (3,414ft) |
| Cnoc na Toinne | 845m (2,776ft) |
| Cnoc an Chuillin | 958m (3,141ft) |
| Maolán Buí | 973m (3,190ft) |
| Cnoc na Péiste | 988m (3,240ft) |
| The Big Gun | 939m (3,080ft) |
| Cruach Mhór | 932m (3,062ft) |

## The way to the Devil's Ladder
*Allow 2 hours*

The main crest of MacGillycuddy's Reeks is home to a number of Ireland's highest mountains. Surprisingly, some of the summits are easily walked, while others are ferociously rugged and require the use of hands for extended periods. Be warned in advance that this walk is not for the fainthearted, and a good head for heights is essential. Although Carrauntoohil is covered as part of the tough Coomloughra Horseshoe walk, an ascent can also be made at the start of the walk along MacGillycuddy's Reeks.

The walk can be conveniently started at the end of a minor road at Meallis, where a car park and telephone box are available in a farmyard. There is also a sign outlining routes, and a series of memorial plaques fixed to a wall. Pass through a gate to leave the farmyard and follow a clear track onwards. This is enclosed for a while, and there is a small footbridge where it crosses a little stream. Further on the track crosses an open slope, and a right turn leads down to the Gaddagh River. Ford the river using some of the big boulders which fill its bed, then bear left to follow the track onwards. It runs up to a clearer track, where you turn left and continue onwards.

This track runs roughly parallel to the Gaddagh River and then fords a tributary river. A less well-trodden path continues, which is marked with a couple of cairns and rises across a boggy area of land in between Lough Callee and Lough Gouragh. These two loughs lie at the head of the rugged Hag's Glen, where huge mountains jostle for position and dwarf the humble walker. The path runs into a rock-walled gully where a steep and bouldery scree rises to a notch in the high skyline. This is the Devil's Ladder – the standard route used for the ascent of Carrauntoohil, but one which is not particularly loved by walkers. Take care not to dislodge boulders and the climb is safe enough. Take it steadily and the eroded top of the gully can be reached without too much effort. From this point, at 740m (2,425ft), the climbing is largely accomplished and the shoulders of the mountains have already been gained.

## The way to Carrauntoohil and back
*Allow 1½ hours*

The ascent of Carrauntoohil is an optional extra on this particular walk, and the summit can be gained in a there-and-back walk from the top of the Devil's Ladder. Cross a grassy area at the top of the Devil's Ladder, where cairns lead towards a zigzag path which climbs up the steep and stony slopes of the mountain. Curiously, there are cushions of sea pinks, or thrift, growing amid the stones all the way to the top of the mountain. The summit of Carrauntoohil bears a tall metal cross and a stone wind shelter; the altitude is 1,039m (3,414ft). The views are most extensive in clear weather, and are summarized in the description of the walk to the summit via the Coomloughra Horseshoe (Route 20).

## The way to Cnoc na Péiste
*Allow 2 hours*

The first few summits along the ridge of MacGillycuddy's Reeks are relatively straight-forward and should pose no problem in good weather. From the top of the Devil's Ladder, climb roughly south-eastwards along a path rising from the grassy gap. The ridge is also mostly grassy, and its blunt profile gradually sharpens as height is gained. Continue on to the crest of Cnoc na Toinne, which has two summits with a broad dip between them. The first summit is the highest, at 845m (2,776ft). This is very much the baby of the MacGillycuddy's Reeks, as it is dominated both ways along the range by higher summits.

After passing across the dip on top of Cnoc na Toinne and reaching the slightly lower summit, a grassy descent leads to a stile across a fence and then continues down to a gap. Climb up a slope which is grassy and stony, and which steepens and becomes more rocky towards the top. There is a cairn on the 958m (3,141ft) summit of Cnoc an Chuillin.

A stony path curves along the rocky ridge away from the summit, then there is a long grassy ridge with a few slaty slabs poking out of the ground. There is a minor summit along the way, and then the ridge runs slightly downhill. There are larger slabs of rock on the ascent to the next cairned

summit, which is Maolán Buí. The altitude is 973m (3,190ft) and there is a metal bar firmly fixed into a rock near the summit.

Follow a stony path down from Maolán Buí and then continue along a grassy ridge. Another stony path leads up a slope to reach the summit cairn on Cnoc na Péiste. This is the highest point gained on the walk, unless the even higher Carrauntoohil was included from the top of the Devil's Ladder earlier in the walk. Views are very good in all directions

and are almost entirely mountainous. As this is also the last place where you will be able to stand confidently on two feet alone, it is worth sampling the view. Your mind will be concentrating on other matters beyond this point. Look out for:

| | |
|---|---|
| NE | Cruach Mhór, The Big Gun |
| ENE | Purple Mountain |
| E | Torc Mountain |
| ESE | Mangerton Mountain |
| SE | Peakeen Mountain, Knockanaguish, Knockboy |
| S | Boughil, Caha Mountains |
| SSW | Knocknabreeda, Knocklomena |
| SW | Maolán Buí, Cnoc an Chuillin |
| W | Carrauntoohil |
| WNW | Beenkeragh, Knockbrinnea |

*The first part of the Reeks ridge features relatively easy terrain for walking.*

## The way back to Meallis     *Allow 2½ hours*

The path leaving Cnoc na Péiste runs down a short, steep and rocky slope. Fearsome blades of rock rise up from the ridge, so that walking along it is simply impossible. There is a vague path on the Black Valley side of the sharp ridge, and this should be followed carefully. The golden rule is never to make a move unless you are confident that you can return the same way if necessary. Cross the rocky gap in this fashion, taking as much time as is needed to move safely. Look ahead, then head uphill towards some large rocky slabs and boulders. The way is steep but proves a little easier, with the best-trodden path again being located on the Black Valley side of the mountain. Continue carefully up to the cairned summit of The Big Gun, at an altitude of 939m (3,080ft).

The next part of the ridge has huge lumps of rock projecting from it, and the best path avoiding them is now to be found on the side overlooking Lough Cummeenapeasta. Follow the path carefully, taking care not to dislodge loose rock or boulders, and pass below the lowest part of gap. It is then safe enough to climb upwards and follow the rocky crest onto Cruach Mhór. What appears to be the summit cairn is actually more like a wall with a niche containing a small statue and often a handful of coins. The summit stands at 932m (3062ft) and is the last summit gained on the crest of the MacGillycuddy's Reeks.

Simply continue along the rocky ridge of Cruach Mhór to start the descent. Although there is still plenty of rock and some steep sections leading downhill, the ground is altogether easier to negotiate than the ridges recently covered. Follow the ridge until you reach a fence; this provides the simplest and most effective line off the mountain. Turn left and follow it downhill. It drops down a steep slope of heather and boulders, before bracken and cutaway bog are encountered as the slope begins to ease. Keep following the fence towards a low, green hill, but look out to the left to spot a gateway in a wall.

Pass through the gate and follow a sunken track across a field. The track swings to the right before you need to turn to the left. Another right turn leads towards another gate giving access to a clear, enclosed track. Follow this track gradually downhill; it then turns left and drops a little more steeply to a minor road. Turn left on the minor road to reach the farmyard at Meallis, where the car park used at the start of the walk is located.

## Alternative routes

### ESCAPES

Anyone who loathes the ascent of the scree gully known as the Devil's Ladder should also bear in mind that it provides the most straightforward means of escape from the crest of MacGillycuddy's Reeks. When seen in good light from Carrauntoohil, a green, zigzag path can be seen descending from Cnoc na Toinne to the Hag's Glen. However, this should be used with caution, as it is not very clear when seen at close quarters and ends on a steep and rugged slope. The only practicable descent from any of the summits into the Hag's Glen is from Maolán Buí. Other ridges, and the coums between them, are often too steep and rocky to support safe descents. Once committed to the rocky scramble from Cnoc na Péiste to Cruach Mhór, there is no real option but to continue with the route.

### EXTENSIONS

A mountain range such as MacGillycuddy's Reeks can support all manner of extended routes. Walkers leaving Kate Kearney's Cottage in the Gap of Dunloe could traverse the crest of MacGillycuddy's Reeks and then climb Carrauntoohil, before descending to the Hag's Glen. If a pick-up can be arranged there will be no need to walk back to Kate Kearney's by road. If a pick-up can be arranged at Lough Acoose, then the walk could be continued beyond Carrauntoohil to include Beenkeragh, Caher, or both.

*The Big Gun is flanked by two rocky ridges requiring scrambling skills from walkers.*

# Route 20: CARRAUNTOOHIL

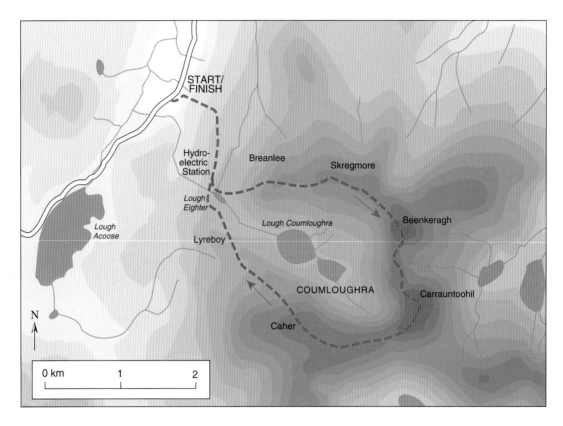

START/
FINISH

Hydro-
electric
Station

Breanlee

Skregmore

Beenkeragh

*Lough
Eighter*

*Lough Coumloughra*

Carrauntoohil

Lyreboy

*Lough
Acoose*

COUMLOUGHRA

Caher

N

0 km      1      2

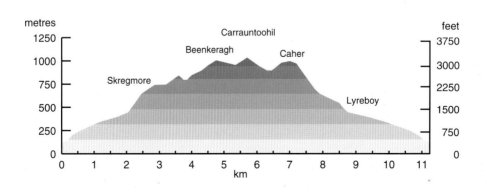

# Route 20: Carrauntoohil

TIME ALLOWANCE 7 hours.

STARTING/FINISHING LOCATION
Near Lough Acoose, Glencar.
OSI Discovery 78: GR772871. Also OSI 1:25,000
    MacGillycuddy's Reeks map.
Parking spaces near Lough Acoose.
No public transport.

OVERVIEW/INTEREST
Classic, rugged horseshoe walk from peak to
    peak, including Ireland's three highest
    mountains.
Exceptional views of mountains and coast.
Climber's Inn nearby.

FOOTPATHS
There is a clear access track but only vague paths
    on some slopes.
The rocky ridges feature well-trodden paths.
Note that some exposed scrambling is necessary.

STATISTICS
WALKING DISTANCE        14km (9 miles)
TOTAL HEIGHT GAINED     1,250m (4,100ft)
PRINCIPAL HEIGHTS
Skregmore               848m (2,790ft)
Beenkeragh              1,010m (3,314ft)
Carrauntoohil           1,039m (3,414ft)
Caher                   1,001m (3,284ft)

## The way to Beenkeragh       *Allow 3 hours*

Carrauntoohil is Ireland's highest mountain, shouldered up by the rocky peaks of Beenkeragh and Caher on one side and the long crest of MacGillycuddy's Reeks on the other. Narrow, rocky ridges between the three highest peaks call for care, as well as a head for heights. The ridge in between Beenkeragh and Carrauntoohil is quite rugged and hands will need to be used while picking a way along it. A relatively recent track to a hydro-electric scheme

offers an easy ascent from the roadside, although cars may need to be parked close to Lough Acoose.

Start from the road running from Lough Acoose towards Killorglin. The track which leads up the lower slopes of the mountain is quite plain to see, and starts from a gateway beside the road. The track is stony and runs straight uphill before turning right and cutting across the rugged flank of the mountain. It ends at an installation beside little Lough Eighter. The high circle of mountains does not seem too rocky from this point, but they will later on.

There is a steep and rugged slope leading straight uphill to the left. This is heathery at first, becoming stony towards the top. The gradient does begin to ease on the final approaches to the summit. A cairn stands at 747m (2,450ft) and there is already a view of a higher summit further to the east. A short descent over bouldery ground leads to a grassy gap, from where the next climb starts. A longer, steeper, bouldery ascent leads to the top of Skregmore. There is another cairn at 848m (2,790ft). A short walk across another gap leads more easily to a slightly higher summit with a cairn at 851m (2,792ft).

If Skregmore's switchback crest proved difficult, then the sight of Beenkeragh's bouldery pyramid rising next in line could reduce some walkers to tears. Blocks of rock litter the steep slope, sometimes appearing decidedly unstable and therefore to be treated with great care. Take pains not to dislodge boulders, for the sake not only of anyone who may be directly below you, but also anyone else who might be out of sight a long way below. After a fairly short but arduous ascent, the bouldery summit of Beenkeragh is gained at a lofty 1,010m (3,314ft).

Now in view is the even higher summit of Carrauntoohil, from which the eye is drawn along the rocky ridge that needs to be traversed to reach it. Anyone who suffers from vertigo should perhaps retreat now, although the ridge is not really difficult for an agile hillwalker. Clear weather is helpful so that you can see well ahead, but in mist there is the advantage of reduced exposure.

## The way to Carrauntoohil   *Allow 1 hour*

The traverse of the rocky arête between Beenkeragh and Carrauntoohil is one of the finest mountaineering experiences an ordinary hillwalker can enjoy in Ireland. First, walk down the steep and rocky slope from Beenkeragh to step on to the ridge. There is plenty of evidence that others have trodden this way, and there is an obvious path most of the way. However, there are steep slopes falling away both into Coomloughra and the Hag's Glen, and some walkers may find this airy position rather unnerving.

Looking ahead along the rocky ridge, a prominent mass of rock is clearly in view. In mist, it tends to appear rather more suddenly. Walkers treading cautiously will be delighted to learn that they do not need to climb over the top of this rock, but even picking a way around the slopes above Coomloughra is likely to involve the use of hands.

There are a couple of trodden routes which can be followed, and the choice is yours. More accomplished scramblers may in fact climb over the rock and add a bit of high adventure to the route! If this jagged rock were to appear anywhere but on the gap in between these two high mountains it would be ranked as a fine peak in its own right. Unfortunately, it is eternally dwarfed by its lofty neighbours.

When the ridge finally runs into the flanks of Carrauntoohil, there is a steep and stony climb towards the summit. A clear path can be followed all the way, with fine views back along the rocky ridge to Beenkeragh. The summit of Carrauntoohil is not in doubt. It bears a huge metal cross in addition to a large shelter cairn. The altitude is 1,039m (3,414ft), making it the highest mountain in Ireland. Often enough the summit will be shrouded in mist, but in clear weather a most extensive panorama can be enjoyed. This is particularly good in relation to the mountains of Kerry, but there may be more distant features also in view. Here is a sample of sights which might be spotted:

| | |
|---|---|
| ENE | The Hag's Glen |
| E | MacGillycuddy's Reeks, Purple Mountain |
| ESE | MacGillycuddy's Reeks, Mangerton Mountain |
| SE | Peakeen, Knockanaguish, Knockboy |
| S | Broaghnabinnia, Caha Mountains |
| SW | Mullaghanattin, Knockmoyle |
| WSW | Caher, Colly |
| W | Coomacarrea, Knocknadobar |
| WNW | Seefin, Mount Eagle, Blasket Islands |
| NW | Brandon Mountain, Beenoskee |
| NNW | Caherconree, Baurtregaum |

## The way back to Lough Acoose   *Allow 3 hours*

In mist, it is easy to leave Carrauntoohil the wrong way – either by being drawn on to steep and rocky slopes, or by accidentally picking up the path leading to the top of the Devil's Ladder. The correct direction to take is roughly south-westwards, along a less well-trodden path. The stony slopes of Carrauntoohil give way to a very narrow and steep-sided rocky ridge. The slopes plunging down towards Coomloughra should be avoided, and the crest of the ridge is often so narrow that walking along it is inadvisable. There are trodden paths on the southern side of the ridge and in the interests of safety these should be followed.

The short, steep ascent towards Caher from the end of the rocky ridge is hard work, but is otherwise free of difficulties. In fact, further on there is a pleasant high-level stroll towards the summit cairn at 1,001m (3,284ft). At this point another summit is revealed at a lower level. Walk downhill a short way to cross a grassy, stony gap where you will notice an old fence, then climb to the second summit cairn at 975m (3,200ft). There is even another cairn further along.

All that remains is the descent, which is consistently downhill all the way from Caher. Head down a bouldery slope roughly north-westwards and look ahead to spot a rather vague path continuing downhill. This path keeps to the broad crest overlooking Coomloughra and its twin lakes. Keep following this crest downhill to the final prow of Lyreboy, before dropping down to the little dam at Lough Eighter. You can now follow the stony track which was used earlier in the day's walk back down to the roadside. If you have parked your car by the roadside near Lough Acoose, then turn left along the road to retrieve it.

Many walkers who have completed the splendid Coumloughra Horseshoe continue along the road, either on foot or by car, to retire at the Climber's Inn. This hostelry has served climbers and walkers for decades and has recently been revamped.

## Alternative routes

### ESCAPES

On a clear day, the Coumloughra Horseshoe is one of the finest mountain walks in Ireland. Unfortunately, the mountains are prone to being blanketed in cloud, and are frequently washed by rain. Competent navigators will have no problem completing the circuit, but others would be advised to walk elsewhere. The ridge route is mostly blessed with some sort of trodden path, so that it often makes more sense to continue than to retreat, but some parts are very rocky and need care. If difficulties are experienced on the rocky parts, things would only get worse by trying to descend early, as there is a lot of rugged, pathless terrain on

the slopes around this circuit. The only other route which might reasonably be used for the descent is the one dropping down the Devil's Ladder into the Hag's Glen. Unfortunately, this leads down to the road a considerable distance from Glencar.

### EXTENSIONS AND ALTERNATIVES

There are all sorts of rough, tough approaches which could be employed to bring the mighty summit of Carrauntoohil underfoot. The usual ascent is via the Hag's Glen and the Devil's Ladder, although this route is usually used simply to scale Carrauntoohil without linking with neighbouring peaks. The Coumloughra Horseshoe is cast in the classic mountain walk mould, and other routes therefore come a poor second. By descending from Caher by way of Curraghmore and the Lack Road, following the Kerry Way to the shores of Lough Acoose, the way down could be made longer and more exciting. One of the steepest ascents of Carrauntoohil can be made from Curraghmore Lough, although the steepest ascent of all, involving plenty of scrambling, is via the Hag's Glen and Eagle's Nest.

*The peak of Caher is the final summit on the rugged Coumloughra Horseshoe.*

# Route 21: COOMASAHARN HORSESHOE

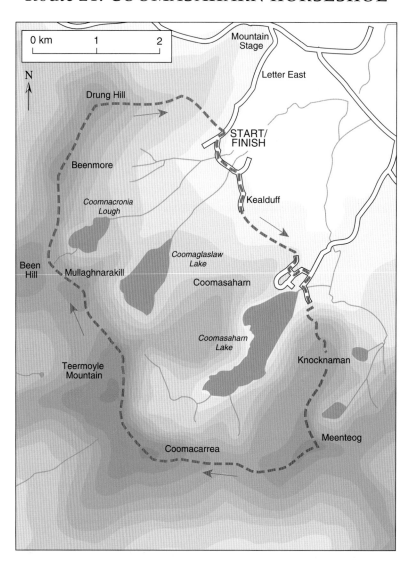

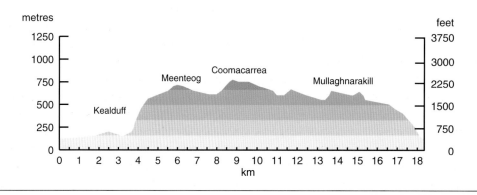

# Route 21: Coomasaharn Horseshoe

TIME ALLOWANCE 8 hours.

STARTING/FINISHING LOCATION
Letter East, Mountain Stage.
OSI Discovery 83: GR623874.
Car parking is very limited beside the road.
Bus Eireann table number 279 serves Mountain
    Stage.

OVERVIEW/INTEREST
Fine high-level circuit around rocky coums, with
    splendid views of four fine mountain loughs.
Starts near the waymarked Kerry Way and
    follows a fairly clear boundary line.
Extensive mountain views from the summits.

FOOTPATHS
A clear bog road is used at the start.
Some parts are steep and pathless.
There are some trodden paths on the mountains.

STATISTICS

| | |
|---|---|
| WALKING DISTANCE | 25km (16 miles) |
| TOTAL HEIGHT GAINED | 1,110m (3,640ft) |
| PRINCIPAL HEIGHTS | |
| Meenteog | 715m (2,350ft) |
| Coomacarrea | 772m (2,541ft) |
| Teermoyle Mountain | 760m (2,442ft) |
| Mullaghnarakill | 665m (2,182ft) |
| Beenmore | 660m (2,199ft) |
| Drung Hill | 640m (2,104ft) |

## The way to Knocknaman

*Allow 2½ hours*

Coomasaharn is an impressively rocky coum in a fairly quiet mountain range on the Iveragh Peninsula. There are a couple of other rugged coums alongside Coomasaharn, and a fine circuit around the surrounding mountains proves to be very scenic. Strange that this walk should be so little known, as it lies just off the popular Ring of Kerry road, as well as the waymarked long-distance trail called the Kerry Way. The walk can be started conveniently from Mountain Stage, where carriages on the road from Glenbeigh to Cahersiveen changed their teams of horses before the arduous journey around Drung Hill and Beenmore. In later years easier roads were constructed, and even a railway was cut around the slopes. When the railway was closed, its trackbed was converted into the main Ring of Kerry road – the N70. There is a crossroads at Mountain Stage, with a small shop and the Mountain View B&B on one side. On the opposite side, an unsignposted minor road runs from Mountain Stage to Letter East. Parking spaces are very limited along this road, and you should take care not to block any access for farm vehicles. If in doubt, you should ask for permission to park.

This is a dead-end road, passing the derelict Letter National School and a handful of farms before the tarmac ends. A gravel track continues beyond the last farm building at Kealduff. There are a couple of gates on this track, which passes old fields. You will encounter a couple more gates beyond Lough Naparka, a little lough which you will see only after you have passed it. The final two gates occur at a right turn on the track, beyond some turf cuttings. When you reach a farm, turn left to walk down a track, then left, right and right again along minor roads. The final stretch of road crosses a bridge over a river, and then proceeds as a track which expires at a gate beyond an old red-roofed building.

Pass through the gate and start following a fence uphill. It ends at the foot of a cliff, but if you turn right you will find another length of fence further uphill. Cross this fence and climb above it on a very steep slope of grass and boulders. Pick the easiest course, either climbing straight uphill or zigzagging around obstacles. The slope is steep, but should not be too difficult if taken steadily a step at a time. Always look ahead and work out how to get around large boulders and outcrops. At a

higher level the gradient eases, but the slope is still steep. There are fewer boulders and more grass, so the walking is easier. The top of Knocknaman is broad and grassy, with slabs of rock lying around. Some of these have been arranged into a small windbreak shelter. The altitude is 501m (1,835ft) and views have been opening up very pleasantly throughout the climb.

## The way to Coomacarea    *Allow 2 hours*

A broad and largely grassy crest runs onwards from Knocknaman. There is a little bog to cross before the slope begins to climb gradually uphill. Some parts of the blanket bog are decayed, and if you follow a line near the edge overlooking Coomeeneragh Lough you will be able to walk on a stony surface from time to time. There is a fence between the open grassy slopes and the steep, rocky cliffs. As you climb further uphill, you will need to cross another fence in order to follow the slope all the way to the summit of Meenteog at 715m (2,350ft). There is nothing to distinguish this point, apart from a couple of stones piled into an apology for a cairn.

Leaving Meenteog, walk roughly south-westwards down a grassy slope. There are some stony patches on the way, and you will reach a fence which leads a short way along the crest more westwards. Do not follow this fence too far, as it heads off to the left and leaves the crest. Instead, look out for traces of a stone embankment and a ditch cut through the blanket bog. This feature can be traced all the way along a series of summits.

Pass through a little gate in another fence and trace the old boundary ditch and embankment across the broad gap between Meenteog and Coomacarrea. A fence accompanies the banking uphill and there are some good views into Coomasaharn. Later the fence turns off to the left, but a line of old fenceposts stands along the line of the ditch and leads to the summit of Coomacarrea at 772m (2,541ft). A small cairn marks the summit on a broad dome of grass. This is the highest point gained on the walk and mountains

*Drung Hill rises above fields and houses to dominate the hamlet of Mountain Stage.*

113

can be viewed in all directions on the Iveragh, Beara and Dingle peninsulas. Look around to spot some of the following:

| | |
|---|---|
| N | Drung Hill, Beenoskee |
| NNE | Caherconree, Baurtregaum |
| NE | Seefin |
| ENE | Knocknaman |
| E | Meenteog, Carrauntoohil, MacGillycuddy's Reeks |
| ESE | Colly, Mullaghanattin |
| SE | Knockmoyle, Knocknagantee, Hungry Hill |
| S | Coomcallee |
| SW | Caunoge, Foilclogh, Bolus |
| WSW | Bentee, Valentia Island |
| W | Castlequin, Killelan Mountain |
| WNW | Knocknadobar |
| NNW | Brandon Peak, Brandon Mountain |

## The way back to Letter East

*Allow 3½ hours*

The boundary ditch leads roughly north-westwards down from the summit of Coomacarrea, and there are upended spikes of rock aligned along it for one stretch. Cross a fence, and then follow another fence around an edge overlooking Coomasaharn. There are cliffs and rugged slopes falling towards the lough, which is itself hemmed in by steep, bouldery slopes. The fence stays near the edge and so misses the 760m (2,442ft) summit of Teermoyle Mountain, but this is only a broad and grassy expanse. Keen summit baggers can of course easily detour and include it as an extra.

*Looking into Coomasaharn from a gap between Coomacarrea and Teermoyle Mountain.*

The fence passes a shoulder of Teermoyle Mountain, rejoins the line of the boundary ditch and then runs more steeply downhill to reach a peaty gap. There are views into the rugged coum occupied by Coomaglaslaw Lough, then the fence climbs up the slopes of Mullaghnarakill. The fence turns left, but the boundary ditch continues straight uphill to reach the summit of the mountain at 665m (2,182ft). There is a curious linear outcrop of shattered slabs at this point.

Follow the line of the boundary ditch onwards. This makes a curious move: instead of following the crest from Mullaghnarakill to Been Hill, it drops slightly off one side of the crest, so that there are views of Coomnacronia Lough. Follow the line of the ditch faithfully, taking care not to be drawn downhill while crossing a couple of small streams which cut the ditch. However, even if you are drawn off-course, a fence will warn you that you are drawing close to precipitous cliffs.

The boundary ditch climbs up towards Been Hill, but as soon as you notice rotting fenceposts, turn right along a less well-defined ditch running roughly northwards. The summit of Been Hill is fairly undistinguished, and might as well be omitted from the walk, but across a gap the more shapely summit of Beenmore can be seen. Follow a ridge down to a gap, then start climbing the heathery slopes of the mountain. You will pass a stone shelter half-way up the slope, and a line of stones leads to the summit cairn at around 660m (2,199ft).

Continue along the crest of the mountain, walking down a slope which is a curious mixture of heather, moss and stones. The ridge narrows and becomes more heathery, then there is a gradual climb to the summit of Drung Hill. There is a trig point and cairn at 640m (2,104ft). As this is the last summit on the walk, it is worth having a final look around at the view before descending.

The descent is best accomlished by heading roughly eastwards down a slope which is almost entirely covered with heather. There is a narrow path in places, and the initial steep slope becomes more gently graded. To return to Letter East, it is useful to identify the old Letter National School from above, which is revealed as a long, grey building near a corner on the narrow tarmac road.

Descending down a steep heather slope towards the building, aim to keep just to its right. A wall marks the upper edge of some fields, but there is a gateway. At the bottom of the field, again to the right of the National School, is another gate and this leads on to the narrow tarmac road. All that remains is to return to wherever your car is parked. If you are staying at Mountain Stage, or catching a bus from that point, turn left and follow the road back in that direction.

## Alternative routes

### ESCAPES

As all the deep coums on this walk are bounded by cliffs, very steep slopes and bouldery slopes, escapes are quite limited. Knocknaman is tough enough climbed from bottom to top, but to climb it from top to bottom could lead to problems as it is not always possible to see a clear run-out on to safe ground. If the weather is likely to be very bad during the day, it would be best to abandon this walk before climbing Knocknaman. There are only a couple of ways to abandon the walk safely once it has started in earnest. The ridge between Coomasaharn and Coomaglaslaw is safe enough for an early descent so long as it can be located accurately in conditions of poor visibility. The ridge between Coomaglaslaw and Coomnacronia should be avoided as it is too steep and rocky. A descent from the gap in between Been Hill and Beenmore, heading into Coomnacronia, is steep but safe. There are bulldozed tracks running south of Coomacarea and west of Teermoyle, but these lead well away from Mountain Stage into a remote glen, and may not be too helpful.

### EXTENSIONS

This is a neat and compact circuit around the mountains, but it could be extended to suit tough walkers. Instead of starting from Mountain Stage, you could start from the village of Glenbeigh and climb to the Windy Gap, Beenreagh and Macklaun before reaching Meenteog. The route could then be extended beyond Drung Hill via the Kerry Way and Glenbeigh Hill and so back to Glenbeigh.

# Route 22: BRANDON MOUNTAIN

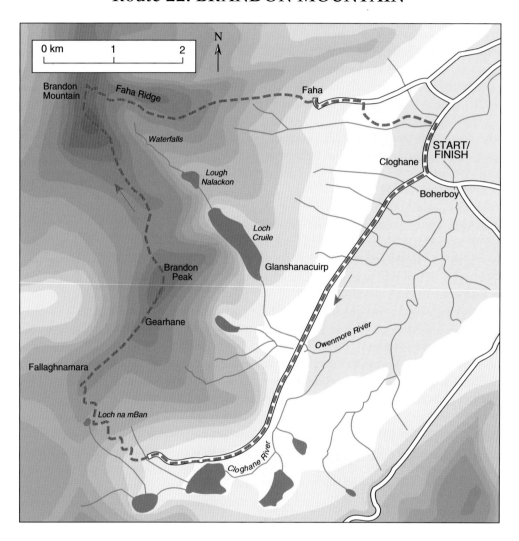

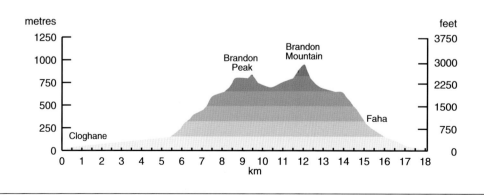

# Route 22: Brandon Mountain

TIME ALLOWANCE 8 hours.

STARTING/FINISHING LOCATION
Cloghane.
OSI Discovery 70: GR509112.
Car parking around the village of Cloghane.
Bus Eireann table number 273 is a limited service.

OVERVIEW/INTEREST
Fine walk to one of Ireland's highest and most
    majestic mountains, with superb mountain and
    lake scenery.
Possibility of extensive coastal and mountain
    views.
Includes an old pilgrim path in rugged
    surroundings.

FOOTPATHS
A road and track are used on the ascent.
Most of the ridge bears a trodden path.
The pilgrim path is well trodden and partly
    waymarked.

STATISTICS

| | |
|---|---|
| WALKING DISTANCE | 24km (15 miles) |
| TOTAL HEIGHT GAINED | 1,200m (3,935ft) |
| PRINCIPAL HEIGHTS | |
| Brandon Peak | 840m (2,764ft) |
| Brandon Mountain | 952m (3,127ft) |

## The way to Brandon Peak          *Allow 4 hours*

Brandon Mountain is one of Ireland's highest and
most revered mountains. Despite often wearing a
woolly cap of cloud, it sometimes clears completely
to present rugged cliffs and buttresses, large and
small loughs, and a line of shapely peaks which are
well served by paths and tracks. Brandon Mountain
dips its feet in the Atlantic Ocean, and most of its
ascent routes start from sea level. Cloghane is a
small village at the head of Brandon Bay. An ascent
from Cloghane takes in a wild glen, the whole of

the summit ridge, and a steep and rocky pilgrim
path. Brandon Mountain would have been the last
piece of Ireland seen by St Brendan the Navigator,
as he set sail from the foot of the mountain on a
fabulous voyage to many wondrous islands. Some
say he even discovered America!

Leave Cloghane by walking along the road past
the church and Information Centre. Turn right
along another minor road signposted for the Lough
Avoonane Walking Trail. The road is flanked by
hedging and appears to head almost directly
towards Brandon Peak. However, it keeps to the
foot of the mountain slope as it heads into a wild
glen. To the right are rugged slopes and fields, while
to the left is a view across the glen taking in a series
of turf cuttings. After passing a prominent split
boulder, the minor road curves gradually to the
right and overlooks a lough. The final farmstead at
the head of the bouldery glen is reached shortly
afterwards. It is possible for walkers to arrange for
a lift to this point from Cloghane, and so omit the
initial road walk.

There is a gate to the right of the farm bearing a
request to close it in four languages. Follow a grassy
track onwards and pass through another gate
bearing a similar sign. At the third gate ahead, do
not pass through, but turn right and pass instead
through another gate alongside. You will find
yourself on a stony track running uphill. As this
track climbs, it zigzags on the rugged grassy and
bouldery slope, and in places the track is itself quite
grassy. You will pass a ruined stone building and
the track climbs on beyond the little mountain pool
of Loch na mBan. A final series of stony zigzags
emerge on to a broad and stony shoulder where
much of the blanket bog has been eroded. Views
are already opening up splendidly.

Brandon Peak rises to the right and seems quite
grassy despite its steep slopes. In mist, the line of a
fence can be followed practically all the way to the
first of its two summits. There is a gate at the top
corner of the fence, and the summit appears quite

117

*Late-evening cloud brushes across the shoulder of Brandon Peak.*

suddenly at an altitude of 803m (2,627ft). This point is called Gearhane, and a fine ridge leads towards the slightly higher summit of Brandon Peak. The ridge is sharp, but not too rocky. It is covered in coarse grass which bears a good trodden path. The path dips slightly downhill to cross a gap and then rises on a slope of grass, boulders and low outcrops. There is a cairn on the highest point of Brandon Peak at 840m (2,764ft), and a dramatic view begins to unfold. Massive buttresses and cliffs fall precipitously into another wild glen and the bulky shape of Brandon Mountain lies ahead.

## The way to Brandon Mountain
*Allow 1 hour*

Descend north-westwards from the top of Brandon Peak, taking care to avoid the cliffs to the right. Walk down a grassy and stony slope to begin following the rugged crest of a ridge towards Brandon Mountain. In clear weather an entertaining walk can be followed along the top of the crest, looking down steep gullies and sideways to monstrous buttresses. Little loughs begin to

appear along the floor of the glen. The ridge even includes a significant peak on its crest which would be a fine mountain in its own right in any other setting, but here it is dwarfed by its taller neighbours.

In mist these views are not available, and the rugged crest could be rather confusing. To be sure of reaching Brandon Mountain in these conditions, follow the course of a ruined wall and a fence which keep just to the western side of the ridge. Further on the wall veers off to the left, but the fence continues straight to the top of Brandon Mountain. The summit bears a trig point at 952m (3,127ft) as well as a large cairn, a metal cross and the low ruins of structures associated with the pilgrimage. In clear weather this is a splendid viewpoint, taking in mountainous and coastal features. The following might be spotted:

| | |
|---|---|
| N | Masatiompan |
| NNE | Mountains of Connemara |
| NE | Kerry Head, Loop Head |
| E | Pilgrim path to Faha |
| ESE | Beenoskee, Baurtregaum |
| SE | Carrauntoohil, MacGillycuddy's Reeks |
| SSE | Brandon Peak, Slievanea, Mullaghanattin |
| S | Ballysitteragh, Knocknadobar |
| SW | Reenconnell, Mount Eagle, Great Blasket |
| WSW | Smerwick Harbour, Sybil Point, Inishtooskert |
| W | Ballydavid Head |

## The way back to Cloghane
*Allow 3 hours*

The best way back down the mountain to Cloghane is to follow the course of the pilgrim path. By looking westwards from the summit its course can be distinguished through a wild and rugged glen, but you cannot walk directly towards it. Leave the summit by following a clearly trodden ridge path northwards. This runs down to a gap where a metal post bears a sign reading 'Down Absteig'. There is a view here along a series of small loughs known as the Paternoster Lakes.

The path descending towards the first of the Paternoster Lakes is steep and rocky in places but also well trodden, and zigzags across the slope. Taken steadily there is no problem, and all you should remember is to keep to the most obvious line. The path actually exploits a bouldery ramp which cuts across an immense cliff face. After running along the foot of the cliff for a while, the path starts to follow a small stream down a very rocky slope strewn with huge boulders. The little loughs which you pass are quite shallow. More experienced scramblers might like the look of the sharp Faha Ridge above, but cautious walkers would be put off at the sight of a peak of rock and broad slab which looks impossible to negotiate.

You will spot a couple of red and white metal posts, and an instruction painted on a rock face says 'Cross Here' (formerly, it read 'Trasna Anseo'). Comply with this instruction and continue following the path. A couple more marker posts ensure that you locate the path which contours across the far slope of this wild glen. It is worth pausing to take in the scenery, which is dominated by great curving slopes and walls of rock, huge boulders and pools of water. It may seem chaotic at first, but there is a symmetry to the place.

The path contours around a steep and rocky slope, but proceeds onwards quite easily. Views ahead begin to open up, and as the path begins to swing to the left the wild glen is suddenly left behind. The path remains clear and is accompanied by several marker posts as it crosses a broad, open slope. The posts show the way through a series of old fields which have recently been reclaimed by fencing. Follow the marked path down to a lovely grotto flanked by trees and containing shrubs, statues and an altar. This grotto was placed on the hillside to facilitate pilgrims who were no longer able to climb the mountain due to old age or infirmity.

The path descends from the grotto and crosses one more field before landing on a clear track. A sign points back towards the mountain, but you should turn left and follow the track to a small car park and information board. Follow a narrow tarmac road downhill from the farmhouses at Faha. Further on you will pass another group of buildings, and beyond these you should look out for a Dingle Way marker post, which is black with a yellow arrow. Follow the Dingle Way to the right down through fields from the minor road, then left alongside a small stream. Cross the stream using a footbridge and walk straight across a field to a gateway made from an old car door. Turn right along a track and follow it back into Cloghane, passing a ruined church on the way. There is food, drink and accommodation readily available in Cloghane, and a bus service limited to Fridays.

## Alternative routes

ESCAPES

Escapes from the rugged ridges around Brandon Mountain are quite limited. Avoid gullies, cliffs and steep, bouldery slopes and you are left with the paths and tracks used for the ascent and descent. In other words, if you need an early exit from the route turn back and retrace your steps, otherwise continue the walk and descend via the pilgrim path. It is also possible to descend using another pilgrim path which heads south-westwards from the summit of Brandon Mountain to the tiny huddle of buildings at Ballybrack. This would leave you on the wrong side of the mountain, but the descent is more gently graded than that leading to Cloghane.

EXTENSIONS

Brandon Mountain could support all sorts of ambitious extensions. Some walkers climb the mountain from the Connor Pass, gradually making height by using each successive mountain as a huge stepping stone to the summit of Brandon Mountain. The route could be continued at a high level to reach the final domed summit of Masatiompan, from where the waymarked Dingle Way offers a descent towards Brandon and Cloghane, or to Brandon Creek. Either way, transport would be required to both ends of the range. Scramblers can extend the route by including the sharp Faha Ridge on the descent. This is a rocky ridge which is quite exposed and narrow in places. It also includes a sharp peak flanked by a sloping slab and sheer cliffs, which need special care to negotiate.

119

# Route 23: CLIFFS OF MOHER

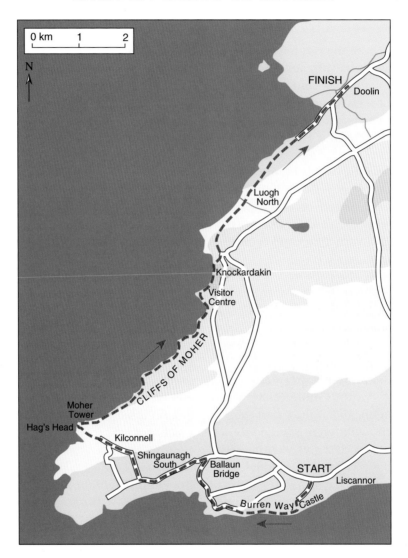

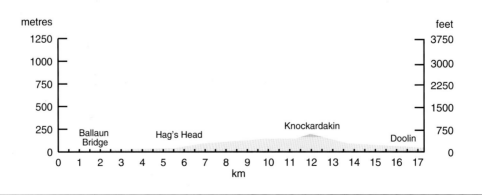

# 8

# THE BURREN

## Route 23: Cliffs of Moher

TIME ALLOWANCE 6 hours.

STARTING LOCATION – Liscannor.
OSI Discovery 57: GR063884.
Car parking in the village.
Bus Eireann table numbers 50 and 337 serve
   Liscannor.

FINISHING LOCATION – Doolin.
OSI Discovery 51: GR071966.
Car parking in the village.
Bus Eireann table numbers 50 and 337 serve
   Doolin.

OVERVIEW/INTEREST
One of Ireland's classic cliff walks, with clifftop
   towers.
Suitable for children.
Includes part of the waymarked Burren Way.
Superb cliff and coastal scenery.
Cliffs of Moher Visitor Centre.

FOOTPATHS
The Burren Way is mostly waymarked.
Cliff paths are generally well trodden.
Some eroded stretches are very near the edge.

STATISTICS
| | |
|---|---|
| WALKING DISTANCE | 18km (11 miles) |
| TOTAL HEIGHT GAINED | 250m (820ft) |
| PRINCIPAL HEIGHT | |
| Knockardakin | 203m (658ft) |

### The way to Moher Tower          *Allow 2½ hours*

The Cliffs of Moher are very well known and well walked, and the highest stretches of the cliff-line are overlooked by O'Brien's Tower and Moher Tower. The waymarked Burren Way takes in the Cliffs of Moher, but the route also includes long stretches of road walking. The walk described here follows the course of the Burren Way out of Liscannor and along low cliffs and roads to reach Moher Tower. The full length of the Cliffs of Moher are walked to O'Brien's Tower and beyond, while a fine old green road can be followed onwards to the lovely scattered village of Doolin.

Liscannor is a pleasant little seaside village offering food, drink and accommodation. It is on the Burren Way, which you will find signposted near the Roman Catholic Church. Follow the minor road beside the church to pass a school, where you will also notice the tottering ruins of a clifftop castle. The Burren Way goes to the end of the road, then keeps just to the right of a farmhouse. Waymark arrows show the course to take across a couple of fields, although these have been earmarked for a housing development.

The path to follow onwards runs along the edge of a cliff at Splink Point. There is only a narrow strip of ground between an adjacent drystone wall and a sheer drop into Liscannor Bay. Worse than that, the cliff may overhang in places and some parts might be close to collapsing. There are profuse growths of thrift and other flowers beside the path. The cliff path passes a house and

121

continues, and you may prefer to lose a bit of height and walk along slabs of rock which lie above the high-tide line.

The Burren Way proceeds along a series of minor roads and is well signposted. The first road hugs the coast, either running along the top of a cliff or curving around a bouldery bay. It passes a number of houses and there are parking spaces marked out beside the road at one point. Further on it heads inland, passing farms and fields before reaching a crossroads at Ballaun Bridge. Turn left as indicated by a Burren Way signpost.

The road runs uphill for a short way, and then proceeds in a straight line flanked by fields. Further on there is a turn slightly to the right, then you need to turn right at a road junction signposted as the Burren Way. The road runs uphill to a group of houses at Kilconnell, where you turn left. The road loses its tarmac surface here and proceeds as a gravel track, with Moher Tower visible in the distance. Pass through a gate and head towards the tower. You will need to pass through another gate at a small flagstone quarry, then you can walk straight towards the tower.

A splendid view of cliffs opens up suddenly at Moher Tower. Although badly holed at its base, the top of the tower seems to be in good repair. It served as a signal tower, and on a clear day a remarkable stretch of coastline can be seen from Connemara to Kerry, also embracing the Aran Islands.

## The way to O'Brien's Tower
*Allow 1½ hours*

Turn right to start following the cliff-line away from Moher Tower. On a clear day O'Brien's Tower can be seen to the north-east. There is a fairly good path close to the edge of the cliff, which is obviously well used by walkers. Strange that the Burren Way should be routed through nearby fields, where it seldom enjoys a decent view of the cliffs, although its course may well be safer, especially in high winds. Walkers will doubtless vote with their feet and choose the path which best suits them.

The path has a precipitous drop into the Atlantic Ocean constantly to the left, while to the right there may be a fence, an earthern bank, or a wall of stout rocky slabs. Views of cliffs and a variety of sea birds ensure that this walk will take longer than you expect; photographers may well be drawn on to precarious perches already worn bare by other photographers. At one point you will pass a small quarry just beyond a broad, unfenced area near the cliff edge.

*O'Brien's Tower, where crowds of visitors tend to spill on to the cliff edge.*

There is an electric fence here, which should of course not be touched, especially as the cliffs are close at hand. You will pass an area of shale where a small quarry once operated, and from this point an attractive wall of large rocky slabs leads onwards towards O'Brien's Tower. There may be a lot more people wandering around on this part of the walk, as there is a large car park just inland beside the Cliffs of Moher Visitor Centre. Teas, snacks and souvenirs can be obtained when the centre is open.

Signs suddenly warn that the cliffs are dangerous, yet people are often seen walking along an overhanging slab of rock beyond the warning signs. A flight of broad steps lead uphill to O'Brien's Tower. Sometimes the tower is open and it is possible to climb to its top and use telescopes to study the extensive coastal panorama. Even without the aid of a telescope, look out for some of the following features:

NE      Slieve Elva
SW      Moher Tower, Loop Head
NW      Inisheer, Inishmaan, Inishmore
NNW     Twelve Bens, Maum Turks, Maumtrasna

## The way to Doolin                *Allow 2 hours*

The Burren Way heads well inland by road to reach Doolin, but walkers are in the habit of proceeding beyond O'Brien's Tower and have worn a path along the top of an embankment. This path passes close to a trig point on Knockardakin at 203m (658ft), and then falls steeply to pass some jagged rocks at the edge of the cliff. Heading inland towards the R478, a track can be joined at a point close to where it leaves the road.

A gate at the end of this short track appears to lead only into fields, but in fact there is the line of an old road here, and this begins to become obvious after you have followed a wall through the field and passed through another gate. The old road has a few low walls or fences strung across its course, but these are easy to step across. Some are electric fences, but they are easily crossed too. As it progresses gradually downhill, the old road becomes easier to trace and

eventually is bounded by either low walls, embankments or fences.

When the green road passes a couple of ruined buildings, there is a stream to cross. You should get some idea of how important the road once was when you spot the stone buttress of what must once have been a substantial bridge. Unfortunately, the bridge has collapsed and you must therefore ford the stream. The grassy green road continues gradually downhill and levels out. There is a slight climb, then the route runs towards an empty house beside a gravel track.

Follow the track straight onwards. It pursues a slightly undulating course and passes through a gate. Further on it is enclosed by walls and joins a minor road at another gateway, close to a B&B. Keep left and follow the minor road onwards and downhill. It runs to Doolin, which offers food, drink, accommodation, Irish music and an occasional bus service back to Liscannor, or onwards to Lisdoonvarna if required.

## Alternative routes

ESCAPES

An escape from this route is hardly likely to be needed. However, in windy weather the proximity of the path to the edge of the cliff should be borne in mind. It is of course possible to arrange to be dropped off and collected at any point along this walk, and the 'classic' section is between Moher Tower and O'Brien's Tower. The car park at the Cliffs of Moher Visitor Centre is the usual starting and finishing point for short cliff walks.

EXTENSIONS

Any extension to this walk is likely to be reliant on the course of the Burren Way. Unfortunately, the route beyond Liscannor and Doolin is largely along roads. A rugged coastal extension beyond Doolin might be considered, but the cliffs are much lower than the Cliffs of Moher. The occasional ferry to the Aran Islands offers a link with some superb cliff walks and ancient clifftop forts and monuments.

# Route 24: GLENINAGH MOUNTAIN

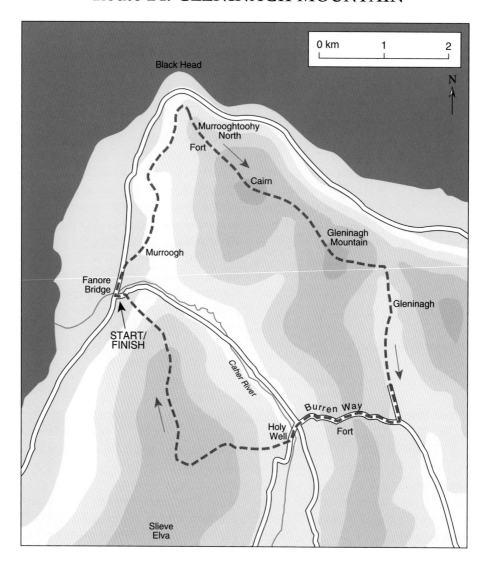

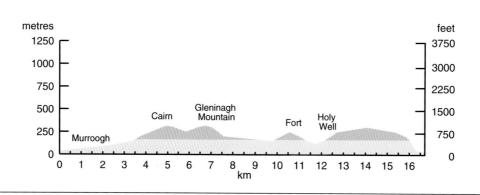

# Route 24: Gleninagh Mountain

TIME ALLOWANCE 6 hours.

STARTING/FINISHING LOCATION
Fanore Bridge.
OSI Discovery 51: GR145089.
Car parking is limited around Fanore Bridge.
Bus Eireann table number 423 serves Fanore Bridge.

OVERVIEW/INTEREST
Combination of green roads and limestone pavements.
Includes part of the waymarked Burren Way.
Exceptional floral delights in May each year.
Intriguing karstic landforms and good views.
Ruins of chapels and ancient hill forts.

FOOTPATHS
Four enclosed green roads are quite clear.
Some upland parts cross pathless limestone pavements.

STATISTICS
WALKING DISTANCE          18km (11 miles)
TOTAL HEIGHT GAINED       650m (2,130ft)
PRINCIPAL HEIGHT
Gleninagh Mountain        317m (1,045ft)

## The way to Gleninagh Mountain

*Allow 2½ hours*

This walk encompasses some of the best countryside and landforms in the Burren. Four green roads can be followed to a reasonably high level and offer fairly easy walking. Two of these form part of the waymarked Burren Way. Other parts of the route bear no trodden path and you need to chart your way across grey limestone pavements and climb up and down terraces of rock. Be warned in advance that this is ankle-twisting terrain and many slabs of limestone are loose, with deep grykes waiting to snare any ill-placed foot. Taken slowly and steadily this type of terrain is not too difficult, but you need to watch where you are putting your feet and tread warily at all times.

The Burren is world-famous for its range of wild flowers, and the best time to see them is on a sunny day in the middle of May each year. This particular walk features an abundance of primroses, daisies, spring gentians, hart's-tongue fern, early purple orchid, mountain avens, creeping juniper, and more. Some of the flowers are so abundant that it is difficult to avoid treading them underfoot, and yet it is important to remember also that they are a product of man's interference with the landscape. The natural vegetation cover for the whole of Ireland should be canopy forest, but early settlers cleared the woods from the Burren, and must have been dismayed to find the soil leaching away.

Parking at the start of the walk is also limited. St Patrick's Roman Catholic Church and the Bridge Hostel both have small car parks, although it would be a good idea to ask permission to use these. Buses do not pass through Fanore every day, but when they do they offer an alternative approach if you are staying elsewhere.

Leave Fanore Bridge as if following the R477 towards Black Head, then turn right on to a clear gravel track. Follow this track uphill until it turns sharply right at a farmhouse. There is a telegraph pole on the left just where the road bends, and if you step over a low wall at this point you can start following an old road which runs around Black Head at a higher level than the R477.

Although the old road is narrow and overgrown at the start, it soon becomes much wider and clearer. It is bounded by low stone walls and mostly has a surface of short green grass. In early summer this track is profusely flowered and it contours around the slope on a terrace between outcrops of limestone. There are some drystone walls which have been built across the old road, but it is generally easy to step across them. Looking uphill and downhill you will see extensive outcrops of limestone, and some large boulders are passed.

Follow the green road until it is flanked by windswept thorn bushes, noting the woodland plants that cower beneath them for shade. When the thorny scrub ends, the old road runs uphill a short way to exploit another limestone terrace, and out of sight below is the lighthouse on Black Head. Leave the green road by turning right and walking straight uphill. Although there is a lot of outcropping limestone, the slope is set at an angle which is fairly easy to walk. Take care, as much of the rock is loose.

When the slope begins to level out, head for the ruins of a circular stone fort, often called Caherdoonfergus. There is a collapsed entrance on the opposite side, but some of the thick walls still stand quite high. Continue beyond the hill fort, crossing a couple of low stone walls beyond a limestone pavement. Cliffs which may look intimidating from afar can actually be climbed with relative ease, as there are several lines of weakness which can be exploited by walkers. You may begin to feel that this is becoming a noisy walk, with loose slabs of limestone make clunking and clattering sounds as you cross them.

When the ground begins to level out, you will see a cairn on the first summit. This large cairn is ancient and vegetated, and it stands at 314m (1,045ft). There is another summit to the south-east which is marginally higher. Do not walk straight towards it, but aim rather more to the left. This avoids some awkward outcrops on the descent towards the gap between the summits. Such a move also brings you close to a curious cairn with a gap through its base.

The gap between the two summits is a level limestone pavement, and off to the right is a deep depression which is completely fringed with cliffs. It is worth descending into this hollow, which has a grassy bottom and a sort of natural plug-hole which prevents it from filling with water. Climbing back uphill, cross a wall beyond the gap and climb uphill towards the summit of Gleninagh Mountain. Although there is plenty of rock to cross on the way, the summit is grassy and, in the appropriate season, flowery too. A squat trig point stands at an altitude of 317m (1,045ft). There are nearby views of the Burren and more distant ones which include:

| | |
|---|---|
| NE | Galway Bay, Galway |
| E | Abbey Hill |
| ESE | Cappanawalla |
| SSW | Slieve Elva |
| WSW | Inisheer, Inishmaan |
| W | Inishmore |
| NW | Twelve Bens, Maum Turk Mountains |
| NNW | Maumtrasna |

## The way back to Fanore Bridge
*Allow 3½ hours*

Descend eastwards from the summit of Gleninagh Mountain, taking care on the steep and rocky slope which leads down to the next gap. Once you reach the gap, turn right and pick up a path which leads down into Gleninagh. This path leads past a hollow full of scrubby woodland at the head of Gleninagh, then crosses a field of grass and heather. The path leads to a wall where a gateway has been filled with a drystone wall, but you can climb over it. Follow the line of tractor wheels towards gaps or gates in a succession of walls. You might notice a ruined farm well away to the right, but you later pass close to an empty farmhouse and follow a gravel track onwards. The track leads to a house, where a right turn is signposted as the Burren Way.

A stony track runs straight uphill and levels out in an area of limestone pavements. Some spikes of rock have been upended, or made into mini-dolmens by passing visitors. Just as the track begins to drop downhill you will see a circular stone fort on the left which contains a couple of ruined buildings. This is Caherandurrish with Chapel and the views look across the Caher River to the next green road above Formoyle. The stony track zigzags downhill and reaches a gateway beside a minor road. There is an obvious way to bring this walk to an early close by following the road back to Fanore Bridge.

To continue the full walk, however, turn right along the road, then immediately left to cross a bridge over a river which may be completely dry. On the right is a wide gravelly area and a signpost reading 'Green Road'. There is a ruined chapel nearby. The track is lined with a few thorny trees at first, but at a higher level it is flanked by stone walls. There are grassy, stony and rocky surfaces, and the track is clear throughout its ascent.

When the wall on the right turns right, follow it for a while to avoid crossing other walls which criss-cross on top of the hill. Cross the wall later and head roughly northwards along the shoulder of the hill. The ground is grassy and heathery but the soil is very thin, overlying limestone pavement where care is needed while walking. As the ground begins to fall away, limestone pavements and rock-steps need to be negotiated, but at first there is no view over the edge to Fanore Bridge.

When the ground begins to fall away more steeply, there are other rock-steps which come in quick succession. Looking down the slope, St Patrick's Church is a good landmark to aim towards. Some of the rock-steps need more care, and by looking along them it is possible to pick fairly easy lines down. The lowest parts of the slope are less steep, but are littered with broken rock. Once you reach the minor road at the bottom, turn left to reach the main road.

## Alternative routes

ESCAPES

The green roads are the easiest parts of this route, and this should be borne in mind if you find the rocky ground beyond them too difficult. Also, if the crossing of Gleninagh Mountain proves difficult or time-consuming, it might be inadvisable to proceed over the next hill. Instead, you could follow the minor road running parallel to the Caher River back to Fanore Bridge.

EXTENSIONS

The only real extension to this route is to continue across Cappanawalla from Gleninagh Mountain. Depending on what route was chosen for the descent, more of the Burren Way could be followed. Another extension could take in the summit of Slieve Elva, but this would be difficult to build into a straightforward circular route.

*Walkers follow a green road uphill from the ruined chapel beside the road at Formoyle.*

# Route 25: GLENCOAGHAN HORSESHOE

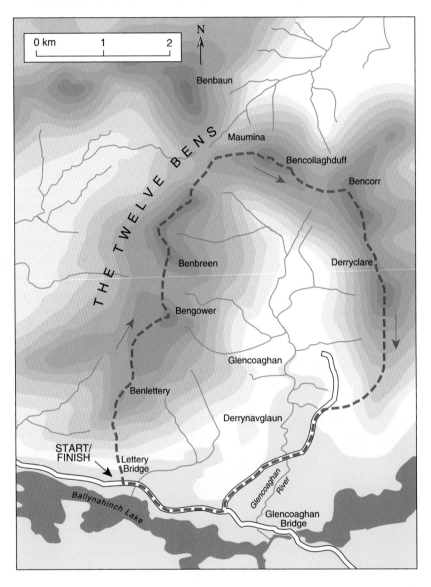

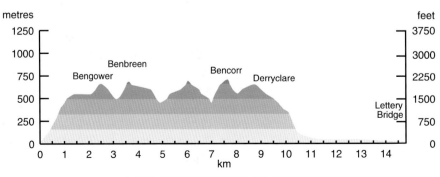

# 9

# CONNEMARA

## Route 25: Glencoaghan Horseshoe

**The way to Benbreen**          *Allow 3 hours*

TIME ALLOWANCE 7 hours.

STARTING/FINISHING LOCATION
Benlettery Youth Hostel.
OSI Discovery 37 and 44: GR777483.
Car parking near the Youth Hostel.
Bus Eireann table numbers 61, 416 and 419 run
   close to the start.

OVERVIEW/INTEREST
One of Ireland's classic mountain walks, over part
   of the Twelve Bens of Connemara.
Extremely steep and rugged terrain, with splendid
   mountain and coastal views.
Adjoins the Connemara National Park.

FOOTPATHS
Paths are often vague over the mountains.
There is plenty of steep rock and scree.
One section requires basic scrambling skills.

STATISTICS
| | |
|---|---|
| WALKING DISTANCE | 16km (10 miles) |
| TOTAL HEIGHT GAINED | 1,570m (5,150ft) |
| PRINCIPAL HEIGHTS | |
| Benlettery | 577m (1,904ft) |
| Bengower | 664m (2,184ft) |
| Benbreen | 691m (2,276ft) |
| Bencollaghduff | 696m (2,290ft) |
| Bencorr | 711m (2,336ft) |
| Derryclare | 677m (2,220ft) |

The Glencoaghan Horseshoe is one of Ireland's classic mountain walks. It is a serious undertaking in foul weather, and challenging even in good conditions. The circuit includes some very steep and rocky ground, varying from outcropping rock to bouldery scree. On one particular section you will need to grapple with the rock on a short scramble downhill; cautious walkers may prefer the security of a rope for this short stretch. Escape routes should be chosen with care and it is not possible to wander downhill in any direction and hope for the best, as there are some fearsome cliffs in places. You will need to keep a careful watch on the time available to complete the circuit, and different walkers will proceed at widely differing rates in this sort of terrain.

Benlettery is a very rugged, steep-sided mountain which completely dominates Benlettery Youth Hostel. Walkers who stay at the hostel can simply walk out of the door and start the climbing in earnest. Anyone arriving by car can park on a loop of tarmac off the main N59 close to the hostel. There are occasional bus services running fairly close to the hostel, though none actually pass it.

Starting from the youth hostel, cross a fence using a stile, then start walking straight uphill and cross another fence on the lower slopes of Benlettery. The direction is straight up, but you will naturally wish to vary the ascent to bypass outcrops of rock at a higher level. In effect, you will zigzag up the slope, finding faint traces of a path from time

129

to time. The steepness of the slope provides the necessary excuses to stop and admire the unfolding view. The slope tends to get steeper with height, but the gradient eases on the final approach to the summit. At an altitude of 577m (1,904ft), the panorama southwards from the summit is amazing. The eye is led across an expanse of lower ground towards the coast, and there are myriad pools of water catching the light in Roundstone Bog.

There is a rugged ridge leading from Benlettery towards Bengower, but the gradients are pitched at an easier angle so that the walk should be rather less arduous. The summit of Bengower rises to 664m (2,184ft) and care is needed when you leave it. The ground begins to fall very steeply towards a deep gap, and it is important to choose the correct route downhill. Look for signs of a trodden path which zigzags down the first part of the slope. Stay on the trodden line and you will be drawn on to bare rock. You will need to scramble a short way down this rocky slope to pick up the next trace of a trodden path, then continue down to the gap. Some walkers might find this short stretch unnerving, but if you can cope with it there is nothing more difficult around the rest of the horseshoe walk. The sight of Benbreen rising on the opposite side of the deep gap is enough to cause some walkers to despair, as they note its flanks are covered in bouldery scree.

Cross the gap and start climbing up the steep, bouldery slopes of Benbreen. Walkers who come in the opposite direction often make rapid progress downhill by 'running' the finely graded scree to reach the gap in a matter of minutes. Going uphill, however, you should keep well away from the fine scree, which offers no great purchase for feet. Instead, keep to the left and climb uphill on more stable boulders. Even then, take care not to send any loose boulders crashing on to people below you. The climb from the gap to the summit is 230m (750ft), but it is worth the effort as there is a fine view around the whole of the horseshoe walk from the summit. If you are taking note of the time, note also that the most arduous and potentially slowest

*Bencullagh, as seen from the deep and rugged gap between Bengower and Benbreen.*

parts of the route are now over. There is still plenty of tough walking to come, but you will probably cover the ground at a greater speed. At this point, perched at 691m (2,276ft) on the summit, it is worth sampling the view which can include:

| | |
|---|---|
| N | Benbaun, Mweelrea |
| NE | Bencollaghduff, Northern Maum Turks |
| ENE | Bencorr |
| E | Derryclare, Southern Maum Turks |
| SE | The Burren |
| SSE | Aran Islands |
| S | Bengower |
| SW | Errisbeg, Roundstone Bog |
| W | Clifden Bay |
| NW | Bencullagh |
| NNW | Muckanaght |

## The way to Bencorr          *Allow 2 hours*

Although the ground remains quite rocky underfoot, the summit crest of Benbreen is fairly gently graded. There are various humps and bumps along the crest which can be omitted in favour of the easiest route. The summit crest makes a pronounced turn to run roughly north-eastwards, and in mist it is important not to follow this course too far. You need to drop off the ridge and descend on steep and rocky ground towards a deep gap near Maumina. The deepest-cut gap in the Twelve Bens is Maumina itself, but walkers on the Glencoaghan Horseshoe need to stay on the gap just above that, so as not to lose height unnecessarily on the way to Bencorr.

The ascent from the gap comes in stages, rather like three enormous steps, so that you are conveyed gradually up towards the summit of Bencollaghduff. The height is 696m (2,290ft) and views westwards begin to show the form of the Maum Turk Mountains much more clearly than from the previous half of the horseshoe walk. The ridge leading down to the next gap falls roughly south-eastwards, but it is rather knobbly and ill-defined. There are traces of a path and the gap itself is quite remarkable, taking the form of a peaty, grassy strip flanked by walls of rock. A brief moment of scrambling might be required just to get across it. There is very little time to adjust from walking down to walking back up again, and you need to scale a very steep and rugged slope to reach the top of Bencorr. The summit crest offers an easier walk, with the summit standing at a height of 711m (2,336ft).

The whole length of the Maum Turk Mountains can be viewed from the top of Bencorr, and by turning around, the whole of the Glencoaghan Horseshoe can be seen too. Anyone who has been checking off the heights of successive peaks will note that so far each summit has been higher than the previous one, with Bencorr being the highest of all.

## The way back to Benlettery          *Allow 2 hours*

Head directly southwards from the summit of Bencorr to follow the ridge steeply downhill for a short way. After crossing a broad gap, there is a short climb up on to Derryclare which comes as a succession of little ascents. This summit stands at 677m (2,220ft) and forms the final 'nail' in the horseshoe. If there is time to spare, pause for as long as is necessary to take in the splendid view. Often enough in Connemara, it is hard to determine which patches of water are bog pools and which are inlets from the sea, or which humps of ground are hills and which islands. The intricacy of the landscape demands that you should study it carefully, but sometimes the details can be overwhelming.

Follow the rugged ridge roughly southwards from the summit cairn on Derryclare, and continue downhill until you have a clear view down towards the minor road in Glencoaghan. You should join this road and turn left to follow it out of the glen. The road runs across Glencoaghan River, twisting and turning until it joins the main N59. Turn right along this road to return alongside Ballynahinch Lake towards Benlettery Youth Hostel.

## Alternative routes

ESCAPES
The Glencoaghan Horseshoe is an extremely rugged circuit and it is not a walk which should be undertaken lightly. In foul weather it is unlikely

that average walkers would be able to complete the course without hardship. Baling out of this walk needs care, as there are many steep and rocky slopes where difficulties could be experienced. In general, do not attempt direct descents from any of the summits into any of the surrounding glens. Safe descents are generally possible from the deepest-cut gaps between the summits. However, even descending from these points you could be facing a long walk down a rugged, boggy glen, with the added difficulty of running into forestry plantations in some parts.

EXTENSIONS

The Glencoaghan Horseshoe forms a natural circuit and therefore any extensions to it are likely to seem unnatural. However, it is possible to combine this circuit with adjacent horseshoe walks. The Twelve Bens are arranged roughly in a sort of cross, with lofty Benbaun at the centre, so there are a possible four ridges bounding four horseshoe walks. The minimum extension to the Glencoaghan Horseshoe would involve an ascent of Benbaun from the low-slung gap of Maumina, and even this miminum extension would add greatly to the difficulty of the circuit. Some walkers have been inspired to dash along the ridges in order to 'bag' the Twelve Bens, but there is some debate about what does and does not constitute a summit. The name Twelve Bens is really one of convenience, given to a group of summits with no particular reference to twelve individual ones. In fact, walkers often argue about what constitutes the Twelve Bens!

*Descending to a rugged gap near Maumina, between Benbreen and Bencollaghduff.*

# Route 26: MAUM TURK MOUNTAINS

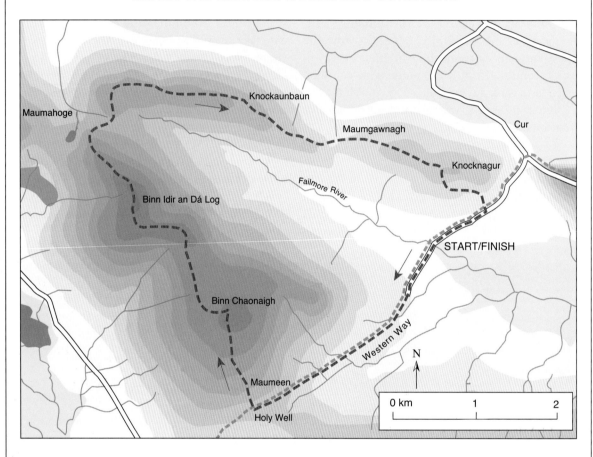

Maumahoge
Knockaunbaun
Maumgawnagh
Cur
Knocknagur
Binn Idir an Dá Log
Failmore River
START/FINISH
Binn Chaonaigh
Western Way
N
Maumeen
Holy Well

0 km     1     2

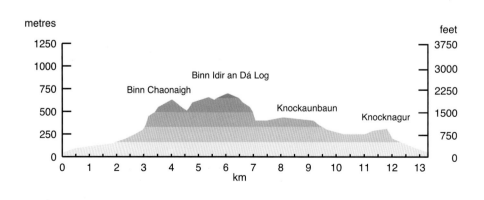

metres                                             feet

1250 — 3750
1000 — 3000
750 — 2250
500 — 1500
250 — 750
0 — 0

Binn Idir an Dá Log
Binn Chaonaigh
Knockaunbaun
Knocknagur

0   1   2   3   4   5   6   7   8   9   10   11   12   13
km

# Route 26: Maum Turk Mountains

TIME ALLOWANCE 6 HOURS

STARTING/FINISHING LOCATION
Failmore River, Cur, near Maam.
OSI Discovery 37 and 38: GR955524.
Small car park near Failmore River.
Bus Eireann table numbers 419 and 420 serve
    nearby Maam.

OVERVIEW/INTEREST
Rugged walk in the middle of the Maum Turk
    Mountains.
Includes a stretch of the Western Way.
Visits a popular pilgrimage site at Maumeen.
Traverses a very rugged mountain range, with
    splendid views from the summits.

FOOTPATHS
A good track is used at the start.
Upland paths can be very vague and some parts
    bear no trodden paths.

STATISTICS
| | |
|---|---|
| WALKING DISTANCE | 18km (11 miles) |
| TOTAL HEIGHT GAINED | 1,020m (3,345ft) |
| PRINCIPAL HEIGHTS | |
| Binn Chaonaigh | 633m (2,076ft) |
| Binn Idir an Dá Log | 702m (2,307ft) |
| Knockaunbaun | 435m (1,436ft) |
| Knocknagur | 310m (971ft) |

## The way to Binn Idir an Dá Log

*Allow 3 hours*

The Maum Turk Mountains form a long and rugged range of summits strung between Maam and Leenaun. Although some walkers traverse the entire range in a day's walk, this is a long and arduous undertaking. One of the finest sections occurs in the middle of the range, where the highest summit – Binn Idir an Dá Log – is located. Maumeen is the site of a popular pilgrimage to St

Patrick's Well and Bed, and the ascent route is also part of the waymarked Western Way. In order to create a circular walk, a return can be made along the lower ridge of Knockaunbaun and Knocknagur.

Follow the roads indicated by Western Way signposts from Maam to Cur, then along a very narrow road which climbs over to the Failmore River. Do not drive across the bridge spanning the river, but park in a space just to the left of the road. Walk across the bridge and follow the road straight uphill. When it bends to the left, keep walking uphill along the track signposted as the Western Way. Initial boggy stretches on this route have been provided with stone causeways or little wooden bridges.

As the track climbs gently uphill, it passes two gateways flanked by ladder stiles and always has a fence off to the right. The grassy slopes crossed by the track are dominated by the Maum Turk Mountains ahead. Look out for a strangely fluted, striated rock beside the track, which bears interesting communities of plants. Further on the track zigzags up a rocky slope and reaches another gate and ladder stile. Beyond is St Patrick's Well and Bed, with a chapel and Stations of the Cross.

Start climbing above this site, either following a fence uphill, or zigzagging between outcrops of rock using grassy strips. Either way, you will gain height on the slopes of Binn Chaonaigh, but the views are more restricted if you follow the fence. Also, the fence does not actually stretch all the way to the summit. After an initial steep start from Maumeen, the gradient eases a little. The upper parts of the mountain are liberally sprinkled with a bright, quartzite scree which crunches loudly underfoot. There are two cairns on top, and the more distant one is the summit cairn at 633m (2,076ft). There is also a small pool nearby.

In mist, it is important to note that the crest of the Maum Turk Mountains zigzags so that short, accurate compass bearings are required to walk from summit to gap, to the next summit and next gap. In clear weather, it is possible to look ahead

135

and plot a good course. There are faint paths trodden on scree, grass or heather in places. Leave the summit of Binn Chaonaigh, following a faint path trodden on the scree which curves towards a gap. Most of the ground is rocky, but there are a few little rugs of heather.

Once you reach the gap, follow a faint path uphill. There is less scree, but still plenty of outcropping rock. The path tends to drift to the left of the true crest of the mountain, and unless you make a detour to the right you will miss a cairned

*A view into the Maam Valley from the lower ridge of Knockaunbaun.*

summit at 659m (2,162ft). Descend a short way to continue across a gap, then start climbing the rugged slopes of Binn Idir an Dá Log. There are a handful of cairned summits along this rugged crest, but the highest stands at 702m (2,307ft). There is a prominent band of white quartz forming a noticeable line just below the summit. The views are extensive and mountainous, including:

| | |
|---|---|
| N | Sheefry Hills, Croagh Patrick, Nephin Beg |
| NNE | Devilsmother, Birreencorragh, Nephin |
| NE | Bunnacunneen, Maumtrasna |
| ENE | Lugnabrick |
| E | Knocknagussy, Mount Gable |

ESE  Lough Corrib, Leckavrea
SE  Binn Chaonaigh, Binn Mhor, Corcog
SSE  The Burren
SW  Cashel, Roundstone
W  Benbaun, Twelve Bens
NW  Letterbreckaun, Mweelrea
NNW  Leenaun Hill

## The way back to Failmore River

*Allow 3 hours*

There is a slightly lower summit to the north of the main summit on Binn Idir an Dá Log, and from that point you should head more to the north-west and descend a rugged slope. There are outcrops of rock and a bouldery scree, then a shoulder of grass which may be boggy. The next descent drops steeply to Maumahoge – a deeply cut gap bearing a small lough. There is no need to descend all the way to the lough, but instead swing sharply to the right as soon as you see it. Drop diagonally across a bouldery scree, then cross steep grassy slopes to reach a peaty gap.

Walk northwards from the peaty gap, rising on a grassy slope, until a fence makes you turn to the right. Follow the fence as it runs eastwards along a crest, which can be rocky in places. Cross a fence and continue onwards, noting that the fence veers off to the left and the crest rises a little to a summit at 435m (1,436ft). There is some blanket bog to cross, then there is a fence to cross too. At the end of the Knockaunbaun ridge there is a descent along the line of a fence and then a shoulder to follow, before a steeper descent leads to the rugged gap of Maumgawnagh.

Cross the gap and start climbing uphill on ground which can be rocky and boggy in places. You need to cross a fence, then another fence leads towards the top of Knocknagur. There are areas of bog where ancient tree stumps have been exposed, and some appear to be Scots pine of a substantial size. The summit of Knocknagur rises to 310m (971ft) and is quite peaty on top. There are good views along the flanks of the higher mountains which you climbed earlier in the day.

Note that there are some cliffs on Knocknagur, and descents should not be made towards any of them. Look for a junction of fences close to the summit, and make a descent from that point. You can walk down a steep slope of short grass and see all the way to the bottom of the slope. There is a stout tree growing from a rock at the foot of the slope, and at this point you turn left to pass through a little valley. There are some 'lazy bed' cultivation ridges here. Also noticeable are outcrops of the fluted, striated rock similar to that seen on the ascent, and again these bear communities of plants safe from grazing sheep. Follow the little valley to a gateway, then turn right to follow a minor road down towards the bridge crossing the Failmore River.

## Alternative routes

ESCAPES

The Maum Turk Mountains are rough and rocky on all sides, and escapes from the main crest of the range are few. If any difficulty is experienced on the ascent of Binn Chaonaigh, then it would be best to retrace your steps to Maumeen and abandon the walk. With care, a steep and rugged descent could be made from the gap following Binn Chaonaigh, dropping into a bouldery coum and later following the Failmore River downstream. The coum on the flank of Binn Idir an Dá Log is rather steeper and rougher. There is a track running roughly northwards from Maumahoge, and by doubling back along another track and road, a low-level escape is available.

EXTENSIONS

The most ambitious extension is to complete the whole length of the Maum Turk Mountains from Maam to Leenaun. This obviously requires transport to both ends of the range, and the journey is best accomplished in clear weather. In fact, in mist and rain it is an arduous treadmill. The horseshoe route described above could be made into a longer circuit by extending the walk over Letterbreckaun and Leenaun Hill, bringing the route down via Derreen to return to Maam.

# Route 27: MWEELREA

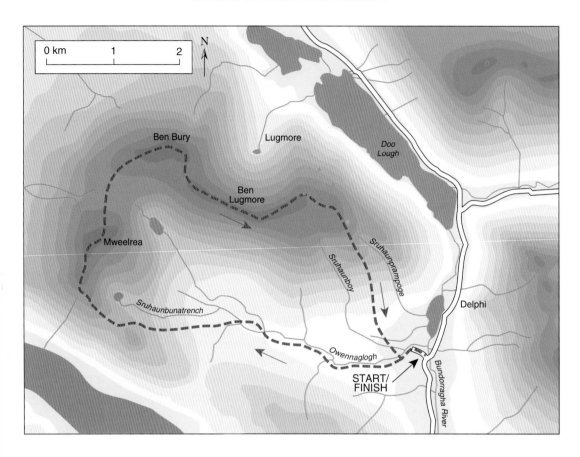

0 km          1          2          N

Ben Bury

Lugmore

*Doo
Lough*

Ben
Lugmore

Mweelrea

*Sruhaunprampoge*

*Sruhaunboy*

Delphi

*Sruhaunbunatrench*

*Owennaglogh*

*Bundorragha River*

START/
FINISH

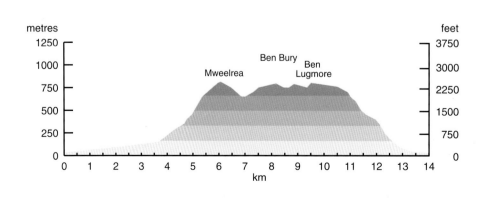

metres                                                                          feet

1250                                                                            3750

1000                        Ben Bury                                            3000
                            Ben
                  Mweelrea  Lugmore

750                                                                             2250

500                                                                             1500

250                                                                             750

0                                                                               0
   0   1   2   3   4   5   6   7   8   9   10   11   12   13   14
                              km

# 10

# SOUTH MAYO

## Route 27: Mweelrea

TIME ALLOWANCE 6 hours.

STARTING/FINISHING LOCATION
Delphi Adventure Centre.
OSI Discovery 37: GR839653.
Small car park by the Adventure Centre.
No public transport.

OVERVIEW/INTEREST
Highest mountain in the Province of Connacht.
All approaches are exceptionally rugged.
Splendid views and impressive rock scenery.
Reminders of the Great Famine and Doo Lough
  Tragedy.

FOOTPATHS
Low-level trodden paths are boggy; high-level
  trodden paths are vague.
Most of the route has no trodden paths at all.

STATISTICS
WALKING DISTANCE      16km (10 miles)
TOTAL HEIGHT GAINED   1,050m (3,445ft)
PRINCIPAL HEIGHTS
Mweelrea              814m (2,688ft)
Ben Bury              795m (2,610ft)
Ben Lugmore           803m (2,635ft)

### The way to Mweelrea        *Allow 3½ hours*

The Delphi Adventure Centre bustles with activity in an area of countryside with very few dwellings. It is approached from either Louisburg or Aasleagh Falls, near Leenaun, by following the R335. This is the Doo Lough Pass road, which has the air of a true mountain pass even though it is hardly above sea level. Do not confuse the Delphi Adventure Centre with the nearby Delphi Lodge. There is no access towards Mweelrea from the latter.

Park near the Adventure Centre and cross the rugged moorland slopes behind the centre to reach the banks of the Owennaglogh. This river flows through a rocky gorge at one point and the watercourse should be studied carefully as you will need to cross it later in the day. There is a path alongside the river, but it is rather boggy and overtrodden in places. A young forest has been planted alongside, and the forest fence prevents walkers getting too far away from the boggy ground beside the river. The grass is often tussocky, which also makes walking difficult.

You will gradually move closer and closer to the towering, bulky mass of Mweelrea, which completely dominates the head of the glen. There is no gradual gaining of height, as level bog fills the head of the glen. The key to the ascent of the mountain is the little stream of Sruhaun-bunatrench, which spills down the mountainside from the hidden little Lough Lugaloughan. Use this watercourse as a general guide only, and pick out any line up the rugged mountainside which seems to offer the least resistance. Do not follow the stream all the way up to the little lough, but branch off to the left to reach a gap on a ridge around 426m (1,400ft).

Follow this ridge steeply uphill roughly north-westwards, with a break of slope where a pause for breath can be enjoyed. There is another short, steep pull uphill, then the gradient eases and the direction to the summit is northwards. There is a clear path on the latter stages of this ascent, leading directly to the summit cairn at 814m (2,688ft). The stones have been heaped on top of a broad area of peat which, surprisingly at this height, has withstood severe gales and heavy rain. The views are remarkably extensive in clear weather, taking in much of Connacht and some more distant features too. A summary of the main ranges is as follows:

| | |
|---|---|
| NE | Ben Bury, Croagh Patrick |
| ENE | Ben Lugmore, Sheefry Hills |
| E | Ben Creggan, Ben Gorm, Maumtrasna |
| ESE | Devilsmother |
| SE | Maum Turk Mountains |
| S | Benbaun, Twelve Bens |
| SSW | Benchoona |
| W | Inishbofin |
| WNW | Inishturk |
| NNW | Achill Island, Croaghaun, Slievemore |
| N | Corraun Hill |
| NNE | Nephin Beg Range |

In mist, of course, there will be no view, and furthermore extreme care will need to be taken with navigation around the rest of the circuit. With rain and gales on these exposed summits mistakes could easily be made, and it is important to bear in mind that there are some very steep and rugged cliffs to the west which must be avoided. On no account try to descend directly to the Doo Lough Pass road.

## The way back to Delphi
*Allow 2½ hours*

To leave the summit of Mweelrea, head roughly north-eastwards down a slope which is both grassy and stony, with some inclined slabs of rock. You will need to cross a broad gap at 650m (2,130ft). The back slopes of Ben Bury are gently

*A view towards Mweelrea and Doo Lough from a point high on Ben Gorm.*

graded, but still rugged underfoot. While ascending them, gradually bear to the right to follow the broad crest of the mountain. As the slope begins to level there are rashes of stones everywhere, as well as a series of cairns which give the impression of being almost at the top. The true summit cairn stands at 795m (2,610ft) in a rather more bouldery area. At this point views are beginning to open up across Doo Lough, a long way down the mountainside.

Proceeding roughly south-eastwards from the summit of Ben Bury, descend a gentle slope to reach a gap, then look down into the awesome dark hollow off to the left. There is a route for scramblers down that way to the foot of Doo Lough, but a descent in that direction would not suit more cautious walkers. There are some very steep and slippery slopes where a fall could prove fatal.

Staying high on the ridge, however, the walking is rather easier. First, climb up from the gap to reach what appears to be a prominent peak. The short ascent quickly reveals that it is in fact the end of a long and fairly narrow ridge. There are two or three distinct summits along this crest, which is known as Ben Lugmore. The highest point is gained in the middle at 803m (2,635ft). At times along this ridge there is a feeling of being on top of the world, but people who suffer from vertigo might occasionally be unnerved at the sight of steep, dark cliffs plummeting northwards.

In mist, take care to alter direction while following this ridge, switching from roughly south-eastwards to north-westwards. The idea on the descent is to come down the steep, blunt ridge dropping roughly south-eastwards in between the streams of Sruhaunboy and Sruhaunprampoge. There is a break of slope between two steep and knee-jarring sections of the descent, then the spur runs out on to a difficult stretch of rugged bog.

Crossing the bog takes you to the banks of the Owennaglogh, which you followed at the start of the walk. You need to cross the river, which is why you were advised to check its course for likely crossing points on the way out. With luck, residents at the Delphi Adventure Centre may still have a makeshift bridge of their own in place, and if you spotted one on the outward journey, use it on the return. If not, choose a rocky place to ford or wade across at a point where the water is fairly shallow.

Accommodation and food can be obtained at the Delphi Adventure Centre, as well as at the nearby Delphi Lodge, although that is a rather more exclusive establishment. A story concerning Delphi is remembered from the dark days of the Great Famine, when Commissioners were in the area to administer some measure of relief. They were staying at Delphi and word reached the population of nearby Louisburg, which was devastated with the famine. Inhabitants walked through the Doo Lough Pass in a rising storm, but on reaching Delphi they were turned away. On the return journey to Louisburg, several of them perished in the storm and some of their frail bodies were actually blown into Doo Lough.

## Alternative routes

### ESCAPES

On a mountain as rugged as Mweelrea, the only sensible escape is to turn around and retrace your steps. This applies even to the summit, where any other lines of escape will be tougher and ultimately lead you far from Delphi. The direct descent towards Doo Lough between Ben Bury and Ben Lugmore is very steep and rugged. While experienced scramblers might enjoy it, the route should not be considered as a line of escape.

### EXTENSIONS

Mweelrea crowns its own mountain range, and stands over a rather compact grouping of summits. Extended walks over this particular range are rather contrived. You could, for example, cross the rugged hill rising to the south-west of Delphi before covering the circuit described above. To get any real distance, you would need to cross the road and climb onto the Sheefry Hills or Ben Gorm, but the extra steep slopes and rugged terrain would lead to a most arduous circuit. These other mountains are best enjoyed in their own right as separate walks. Make no mistake about it: Mweelrea is a rugged mountain and there is no need to add to the difficulties it already presents!

# Route 28: MAUMTRASNA

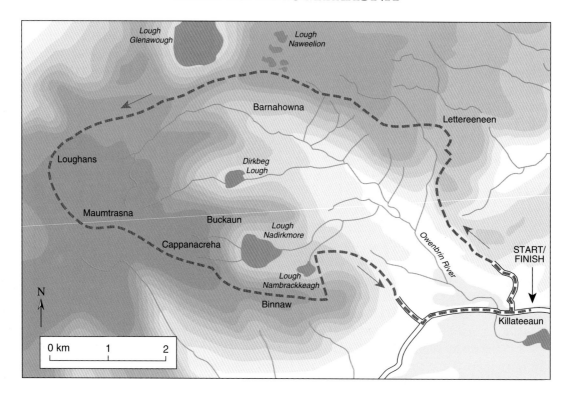

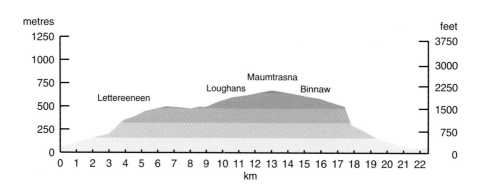

# Route 28: Maumtrasna

TIME ALLOWANCE 7 hours.

STARTING/FINISHING LOCATION
Killateeaun, near Tourmakeady.
OSI Discovery 38: GR046633.
Car parking around the village.
No public transport.

OVERVIEW/INTEREST
Circuit of a broad, bleak and bouldery mountain
   wilderness.
Some good views from the top of steep slopes,
   and interesting little loughs in deep coums.

FOOTPATHS
Clear roads and tracks are used at the start and
   finish.
There are no paths over the rugged plateau.

STATISTICS
WALKING DISTANCE         23km (14 miles)
TOTAL HEIGHT GAINED      750m (2,460ft)
PRINCIPAL HEIGHT
Maumtrasna               673m (2,207ft)

## The way to Maumtrasna          *Allow 4 hours*

Maumtrasna singularly fails to catch the eye in views from many of the neighbouring mountains. In profile it often appears as an immense whaleback rise of high ground, with sprawling shoulders. On closer inspection, the broad plateau is seen to be supported on all sides by exceedingly steep and rugged slopes. These slopes are arranged as massive buttresses and deep coums, and there are some little loughs hidden in these recesses. Maumtrasna is broad, bleak and bouldery. It is not a place for dodgy navigators to travel in poor visibility, but in clear weather it presents a wilderness scene seldom equalled on other mountains in Ireland.

Killateeaun is a handy starting point, where a minor road offers good views across Lough Mask and over towards Maumtrasna. Park your car here and then follow the road down towards the Owenbrin River. Do not go all the way down to the bridge, but turn right where a sign indicates 'Factory'. The road runs uphill for a short way, then you turn right immediately after passing the factory. Follow this other minor road uphill, then turn off to the left along an even narrower road. When this road reaches a hairpin bend, keep left to follow a clear track.

The track contours across the hillside, overlooking the Owenbrin River and taking in a view of a series of massive rocky buttresses and deep coums along the eastern flank of Maumtrasna. It is worth studying the terrain carefully from this vantage point, noting especially a clear line of descent from Binnaw to be used at the end of the day. The track offers an easy line of progress, but the ground will become more and more difficult to cross later in the day. A couple of farms low in the glen stand in contrast to the turf bogs which have been cut higher up the glen.

Follow the track through a gate, then let it lead you up into a side valley, where it climbs to a broad moorland crest at the very head of the valley at Lettereeneen. Turn left to cross some cutaway bog where ancient tree stumps have been exposed. You will notice similar stumps all around this walk, so that in your mind's eye you can reconstruct the woodland scene which must once have been so extensive on this bleak mountain. There are fences ahead, but you need cross only one of them in order to follow the broad moorland crest further uphill. The grass and heather cover is scant due to overgrazing and the blanket bog is in a state of decay, exposing many boulders and low rocky outcrops.

Keep well to the left of the pools of water around Lough Naweelion, and keep moving left to pass between some larger outcrops of rock before dropping down to a gap. There is a cairn sitting on

*PREVIOUS PAGE Cloud brushes the massive buttresses flanking broad-shouldered Maumtrasna.*

this gap, and fine views stretch across Lough Glenawough towards Croagh Patrick and its summit chapel. You will notice a line of rotting fenceposts on the southern side of the gap, where views stretch across parts of Lough Mask and Lough Corrib.

When climbing above the gap, the ridge is broad and rocky, with many boulders embedded in the ground. However, easier walking can be found by following a narrow ribbon of grass which avoids most of the rocky ground, although this can be boggy underfoot. The broad slopes of Maumtrasna's summit plateau lie beyond, and this area can prove most difficult to cross in mist. The direction to take is roughly south-westwards, although a more accurate compass bearing could be taken towards the pools of water at Loughans.

Start veering to the left beyond Loughans, passing a ledge of extremely coarse conglomerate rock. This is quite different to the coarse sandstones crossed on the rest of the walk. On this particular walk, the aim is not to reach the summit cairn on Maumtrasna but to reach a trig point on a separate rise of ground. There is less rock, more decayed blanket bog, and some patches of sand to pass on the final ascent. The last few paces involve weaving between pools of water which almost surround the trig point. The altitude is 673m (2,207ft). The broad plateau stretching in all directions tends to obscure the view, cutting out most of the lower ground and leaving only a few summits protruding in some places. However, the following features might be spotted:

| N | Nephin Beg, Birreencorragh, Nephin Beg Range |
| NNE | Nephin, Croaghmoyle |
| NE | Partry Mountains, Ox Mountains |
| SE | Lough Mask, Mount Gable, Lough Corrib |
| SW | Maum Turk Mountains |
| WSW | Devilsmother, Twelve Bens |
| W | Ben Gorm, Mweelrea |
| WNW | Sheefry Hills |
| NW | Croaghaun, Slievemore, Achill Island |
| NNW | Corraun Hill, Croagh Patrick |

## The way back to Killateeaun   *Allow 3 hours*

The broad moorland top of Maumtrasna is a confusing place in mist, and in such conditions the only way to leave the trig point is to follow a compass bearing. A fairly simple direction off the plateau would be to walk eastwards until you reach the steep slopes dropping into Lough Nadirkmore, then turn right and trace the upper edge of the cliffs towards Binnaw. In clear weather, the broad moorland crest could be followed more east southeast, but even this would be best checked with a compass. The ground is entirely bouldery and covered in the tattered remains of a blanket bog. There is no trodden path.

The gradients downhill from the trig point are fairly gentle, but the ground underfoot is hard going. Towards the end of the high crest, around Binnaw, there is a slight rise, before a very steep and rugged drop in all directions. The easiest descent is to exit to the left before the last rise, taking note of a steep, grassy slope which can be seen from above to be free of rock all the way down to a bog road. This terminates near Lough Nambrackkeagh. Take care on the descent, which could be slippery in wet weather.

When a rash of boulders have been crossed on the more level lower slopes, turn right to follow the bog road gently downhill, away from Lough Nambrakkeagh. The track runs free beside turf cuttings, but later there is a fence to the left. After passing through a gate further downhill, the track is enclosed on both sides and becomes a narrow tarmac road. Follow this road downhill, then turn left along another minor road. This descends gently to cross the Owenbrin River on a narrow bridge. A short climb uphill leads back to the village of Killateeaun.

## Alternative routes

ESCAPES

Any escape from this route should be chosen with care. The steep slopes which surround Maumtrasna on virtually every side are also quite rocky in places. In desperation, many of these slopes might prove negotiable from top to bottom, but they are all a bit too steep and rugged for comfort. A descent southwards from the gap above Lough Glenawough is possible, and even beyond this point it is possible to abandon the route and pick a way downhill using the Owenbrin River as a guide. Descents into the deep coums are not recommended, and the easiest way off the mountain is to stick to the route described towards Lough Nambrackkeagh. Even this route, however, would need care in wet or icy conditions.

*A view across Lough Glenawough leads the eye to the summit of Croagh Patrick.*

EXTENSIONS

This route takes in a portion of the bleak, broad and bouldery plateau of Maumtrasna. In clear weather, this is an extensive wilderness upland which some walkers may wish to explore more thoroughly. Some fine views of deep, steep-sided coums and glens can be enjoyed by traversing around the edge of the plateau, and views of neighbouring summits are also much better from the edges of Maumtrasna. An extended linear walk could stretch all the way from the high road crossing the Partry Mountains to cross Maumtrasna and the Devilsmother on the way to Leenane or Aasleagh Falls.

# Route 29: CROAGH PATRICK

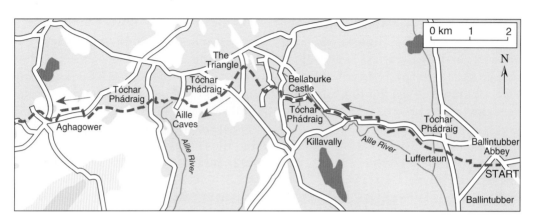

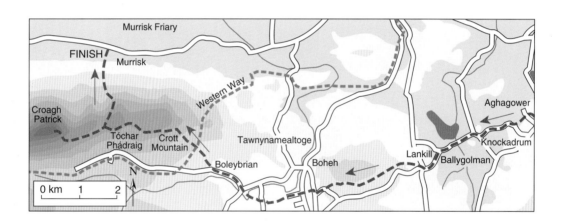

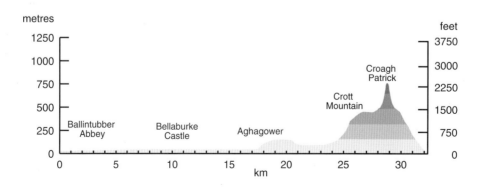

# Route 29: Croagh Patrick

TIME ALLOWANCE 10 hours.

STARTING LOCATION
Ballintubber Abbey.
OSI Discovery 38: GR 155793.
Car park at Ballintubber Abbey.
Bus Eireann table number 456.

FINISHING LOCATION
Murrisk.
OSI Discovery 31: GR 925822.
Car park at the foot of Croagh Patrick at Murrisk.
Bus Eireann table number 450.
Transport back to Ballintubber is provided for pilgrims.

OVERVIEW/INTEREST
An ancient Druidical causeway to a Holy Mountain, christianized and walked by St Patrick.
Route recently reopened as a pilgrim walk.
Several fine views of the pyramidal peak, climbed by thousands of pilgrims on Reek Sunday.
Chapel (and toilets) on the mountain summit.
Superb viewpoint across Connemara and Clew Bay.

FOOTPATHS
The route is to be used only by pilgrims, and guided walks are arranged from Ballintubber Abbey.
Field paths are often vague.
The ancient causeway can be traced in places.
The modern path on Croagh Patrick is severely eroded.

STATISTICS
WALKING DISTANCE           30km (19 miles)
TOTAL HEIGHT GAINED        900m (3,000ft)
PRINCIPAL HEIGHT
Croagh Patrick             764m (2,510ft)

## The way to Aghagower
*Allow 4 hours*

Note from the outset that the route known as the Tóchar Phádraig is not available to the general public as a walking route. After centuries of neglect, a restricted right to use this ancient pilgrimage route was granted to Fr Frank Fahey of Ballintubber Abbey. Pilgrimages along part or all of the route are arranged and publicized through the Abbey Office, and almost anyone is welcome to take part. You will therefore be walking as part of a group, and must obey the instructions given by the leaders.

The Druids held the pyramidal peak of Cruachan Aigle in high regard, and they built a causeway across the lowlands to reach its summit. In the sixth century, St Patrick walked along the causeway prior to enduring a 40-day fast on the top of the mountain. It now bears his name and is known as Croagh Patrick, or more popularly The Reek, and it is Ireland's Holy Mountain. In recent years gold was found in workable quantities on the mountain, but public opinion was against any exploitation of the reserves and mining was expressly forbidden by the government.

As this is essentially a guided walk, detailed route directions are not given here. In any case, the route is often across tiny fields and patches of bogland where directions would be difficult to follow. The guides from Ballintubber are not only familiar with the route, but are also able to relate numerous stories and traditions along the way. Almost every stone, tree and river has a story to tell.

The route starts from Ballintubber Abbey, at a point where pilgrims would have washed their feet and left their shoes behind to walk the causeway barefoot. A short section of the causeway has been reconstructed, and the conical shape of Croagh Patrick can be seen in the distance. The route is marked on Ordnance Survey maps and there is a guidebook available from the Abbey Office which is packed with historical details.

The route is essentially low level, running through fields and crossing minor roads and rivers, with higher rises of ground again featuring a view ahead to The Reek. The Tóchar Phádraig is never too far from the Aille River at first, and also passes the ruins of holy wells, churches and castles. The source of the Aille River is reached at the Aille Caves, where it is believed the crown jewels of Connacht are hidden! There are areas of bog to be crossed on the final approaches to Aghagower.

## The way to Croagh Patrick     *Allow 5 hours*

Lunch is usually taken at Aghagower, where a fine ruined church and round tower can be inspected. It is worth mentioning that a vehicle full of first aid and orange juice generally meets the pilgrims at certain roadside halts, and this is also available to transport tired or wounded walkers back to Ballintubber. It is traditional beyond Aghagower to break for Mass in a well-hidden 'killeen', where a stand of trees obscures an ancient burial place and an altar of stones. Stories are told in these parts of Sean a Saggart, a ruthless man who hunted priests during Penal times. Each of the stones in the killeen has the body of a baby or small unbaptized child buried beneath, and the site has a very sad air about it.

Continuing onwards, the route starts to gain a bit more height, and looking ahead from the slopes of a rugged rise, the peak of Croagh Patrick is definitely beginning to look larger. You cross the main N59 road near Boheh and traverse the final stretch of lowland country. Further on you will cross the course of the waymarked Western Way on the slopes of Crott Mountain, and your ascent of The Reek begins in earnest.

Crott Mountain is really only a low shoulder of Croagh Patrick, but after the long walk-in the ascent seems quite steep. There is a path which cuts across the southern slopes of the mountain, so the little summits just above do not need to be climbed. As the path proceeds, it reaches a gap where it joins a very broad, stony and badly eroded path. This is the 'modern' pilgrimage route up The Reek from Murrisk, which has only been in use for just a few centuries!

The path is relatively easy for a while, and passes a toilet block on the shoulder of the mountain. Looking ahead, however, there is what appears to be a river of boulders on the final steep slopes of the mountain. Choose a route up this slope with care, as it is often unstable. Some walkers prefer to take a more circuitous course and try to outflank this monstrous scree. Take special care not to send boulders crashing down on to people behind.

The bouldery scree continues almost to the very top of the mountain, but at least there is a firm footing after being on such a mobile slope. A white chapel and a toilet block crown the summit of Croagh Patrick. The chapel can in fact be discerned from places well removed from the mountain. On Reek Sunday, which is the second Sunday in July, tens of thousands of pilgrims climb on to the summit; some even complete the ascent in bare feet, and there is almost always a serious accident somewhere along the way.

As Croagh Patrick is such an isolated mountain, and such a steep-sided peak, the views are both extensive and imbued with a great feeling of depth and spaciousness. Clew Bay is reputed to feature one island for every day of the year, and as there are many sandbanks as well as grassy humps, this may well be true. Other more permanent features include:

| | |
|---|---|
| W | Clare Island |
| NW | Achill Island, Croaghaun, Slievemore |
| N | Nephin Beg Range |
| NE | Nephin, Ox Mountains |
| SE | Partry Mountains |
| S | Devilsmother |
| SW | Sheefry Hills, Mweelrea, Twelve Bens |
| WSW | Inishbofin, Inishturk |

## The way to Murrisk     *Allow 1 hour*

To descend to Murrisk, you must unfortunately retrace your steps down the bouldery scree. It is more important than ever to exercise care. Do not attempt the descent at speed and always be considerate of people below. After passing the toilet block on the shoulder of the mountain, the well-

*Following the course of the ancient Tóchar Phádraig towards Croagh Patrick.*

blazed path swings to the left and falls steeply down the heathery flank of the mountainside towards Murrisk.

There is very little at Murrisk – a large car park, a ruined abbey, a few houses, and a pub full of pilgrims and would-be pilgrims. Although the complete course of the Tóchar Phádraig is only available to pilgrims from Ballintubber, the direct ascent from Murrisk can be attempted by anyone at any time of the year. There is likely to be someone on the mountain virtually every day of the year, but be warned once again that on Reek Sunday it is incredibly busy.

Pilgrims from Ballintubber Abbey finish along with everyone else in the pub at Murrisk, and the likelihood is that the final descent will be made with darkness close on your heels. Transport is provided back to Ballintubber, and after a night's rest it is worth exploring the abbey grounds, which boast of two more 'tóchars', which are very short and much more spiritual in style.

## Alternative routes

### ESCAPES

When presented with an opportunity to walk a pilgrimage route which has been in use for two millenia by both Druids and Christians, alternative routes can seem rather pointless. The low-level route which has been negotiated towards Croagh Patrick is the only one available which keeps free of tarmac. The straight-up/straight-down route from Murrisk is of course freely available for use all year round, and that is the ascent most people use. However, make every effort to cover the course of the Tóchar Phádraig from Ballintubber Abbey because it really is a remarkable route. Escapes, incidentally, are available at every road crossing.

### EXTENSIONS

Croagh Patrick is a solitary mountain, and the only possible extension is to cover the length of its crest. This is hardly likely to lead to such a satisfactory conclusion to the walk as ending at Murrisk, and is therefore not recommended.

151

# Route 30: CROAGHAUN AND ACHILL HEAD

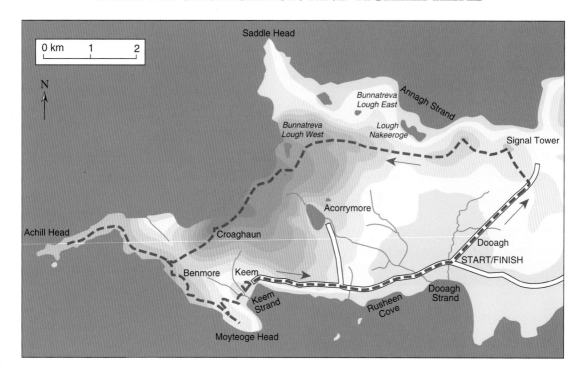

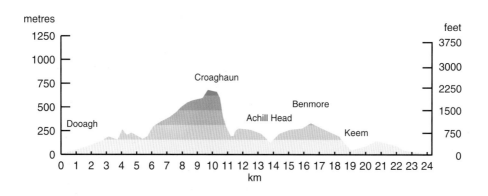

# 11
# NORTH MAYO

## Route 30: Croaghaun and Achill Head

TIME ALLOWANCE 8 hours.

STARTING/FINISHING LOCATION
Dooagh, Achill Island.
OSI Discovery 30: GR605049.
Car park beside the sea at Dooagh.
Bus Eireann table numbers 66, 69 and 440 serve
    Dooagh.

OVERVIEW/INTEREST
Ireland's largest island and highest sea cliffs.
Exceptionally rugged cliff coastline.
Fabulous coastal and mountain views.
Option to scramble out on to Achill Head in the
    Atlantic.

FOOTPATHS
A clear track is used at the start.
Most of the upland stretches are pathless.
Some well-defined ridges bear fairly clear paths.

STATISTICS
WALKING DISTANCE        26km (16 miles)
TOTAL HEIGHT GAINED     1,735m (5,690ft)
PRINCIPAL HEIGHTS
Croaghaun                688m (2,260ft)
Benmore                  332m (1,098ft)

## The way to Croaghaun
*Allow 4 hours*

No ferry is necessary to reach Achill Island, as it is
connected to the mainland by a causeway and
bridge. Most of the island is hilly or mountainous,
but there are also broad boglands which are
extensively worked for turf. Slievemore and
Croaghaun are the two highest mountains on Achill.
Slievemore is rather like an enormous pudding, and
in some profiles Croaghaun seems fairly rounded
too. However, Croaghaun hides an immense cliff
face from view, and reveals it only to walkers who
are prepared to make the effort to see it.

Dooagh is the last village on the R319 road
which runs the length of Achill Island, and it has a
good range of facilities. It is also the terminus of a
Bus Eireann service which starts as far away as
Enniskillen. Cars can be parked overlooking
Dooagh Strand. Start walking from the post office,
and follow the minor road indicated by a sign for
the Atlantic Hotel. The tarmac runs out before the
last building in the village is passed. A pebbly track
continues climbing gently uphill, passing a couple
of fields and numerous turf cuttings.

When you reach the crest of this track, the view
ahead is dominated by the huge shape of
Slievemore, which has the grey ruins of a deserted
village crouched at its foot. Your walk, however, is
in the other direction towards Croaghaun. Turn left
to leave the track, crossing a short stretch of turf
cuttings, then climb up a small, heathery hill. This
hill rises to 194m (645ft) and bears the ruins of an
old signal tower. Head westwards from the tower
across a gentle gap. A short climb up a heathery
slope leads quickly to another summit at 269m
(891ft). The peaty covering has worn off the top to
reveal the schist bedrock. There are good views of
Lough Nakeeroge perched above Annagh Strand.

153

Walk south-westwards for a short way to avoid outcrops of rock, and cross another gentle gap before crossing another little summit. The heather cover gives way to grass on the descent to a broad and boggy gap overlooking Lough Nakeeroge. A steep, heathery slope is bouldery at first, then at a higher level the gradient eases and a broad, grassy, boggy shoulder leads more gently uphill. There are a few pools of water along the way, but at a higher level the ground is more stony. You then make a left turn around a steep and rocky edge, where there are fine views into a coum holding Bunnatreva Lough West.

After passing the head of the coum, the route reaches the steep and rugged cliffs falling from Croaghaun into the Atlantic Ocean. Keep following the edge onwards, but beware of deeply fissured ground where immense piles of tottering, fractured rock must surely fall one day. A final steep, heathery, boulder-strewn slope leads to the top of Croaghaun. A cairn stands on the summit at 688m (2,260ft). Given that the sea surrounds the summit closely on three sides, views are still remarkably extensive, although the westwards sector is largely an empty quarter. Look for the following features:

| | |
|---|---|
| N | Inishkea South, Inishkea North |
| NNE | Belmullet Peninsula |
| NE | Slieve Fyagh |
| ENE | Slievemore, Corslieve |
| E | Glennamong, Birreencorragh, Nephin |
| ESE | Minaun Heights, Corraun Hill |
| SE | Croagh Patrick, Partry Mountains |
| SSE | Clare Island, Mweelrea |
| S | Inishturk, Inishbofin |
| W | Achill Head |

## The way back to Dooagh          *Allow 4 hours*

Getting on to Croaghaun by the route described above is simply a matter of gaining height gradually, but leaving the summit involves losing height dramatically. First, however, there is a relatively easy stretch along a sharp summit ridge. A fairly well-trodden path follows this rocky edge, with a steep slope falling southwards and a steeper,

rocky slope falling northwards. After crossing a broad gap there is a slight climb on to a subsidiary summit of Croaghaun at 664m (2,192ft). Enjoy the airy perch for a while, as there is a punishingly steep descent to come.

Leave the summit and drop south-westwards down the slope. The ground steepens rapidly, but if it is taken slowly and carefully there should be no difficulty. The ground is heathery and bouldery; the latter parts best avoided by zigzagging on the heather. On the lower reaches of this steep slope there are fewer boulders and more grass. The slope runs out on to a boggy area to the right of a couple of small loughs.

Rising immediately above the boggy area is a jagged ridge, and you should climb straight uphill to reach the summit of Benmore at 332m (1,098ft). There are two options at this point. One is to turn left and head for Keem Strand; the other is to turn right and walk towards Achill Head. You will be able to see most of the way to Achill Head in clear weather and appreciate that the route is something of a switchback. Although there is plenty of short, green grass, there are also some exposed rocky stretches. If the Achill Head option is chosen, walk as far as you want and then retrace your steps towards the Benmore ridge.

Walkers who are in a hurry to bring the walk to a close can bypass most of the jagged summits on the Benmore ridge, as the line of little summits has the appearance of a mountain range in miniature. Anyone covering the whole ridge will find some impressively rugged slopes and overhanging rocks. The final little summit is crowned with a ruined lookout tower, and this point is known as Moyteoge Head. You would need to retrace your steps a little from here, but it is also possible to head off downhill before Moyteoge Head. A path runs down the steep, grassy slope to land at a little car park beside Keem Strand. There is an information board overlooking the strand.

All that remains is to follow the road back from Keem Strand to the village of Dooagh. The road zigzags uphill from the strand, passing a toilet block

*Looking down on Bunnatreva Lough West, Saddle Head and the Atlantic Ocean.*

and an upper car park. It then slices across a steep and rugged slope, and has been partly cut into the rock and partly buttressed from below. There are fine coastal views from the road, which climbs and then starts to descend. Off to the right the word 'EIRE' is spelt out in stone on a coastal heath – a device used to warn warplanes not to land in neutral Ireland during the Second World War. Pilots landing even in an emergency were interned.

As you enter Dooagh, the scattered white buildings begin to offer food and drink. There is even a cottage selling chunks of local amethyst. Look out on the right for a commemorative stone recording the arrival of Don Allum, the only man ever to have rowed a boat both ways across the Atlantic Ocean. The pub across the road has photographs and further information about the event. A short distance further on is the post office and car park where the walk started.

*The rocky ridge of Achill Head points far west across the ocean.*

## Alternative routes

ESCAPES

This route starts by using a clear track, then crosses a handful of small hills. The best escape in the early stages is simply to retrace your steps. Once you have reached the summit of Croaghaun, it is also possible to descend early by walking roughly southwards towards Keem Strand, but the ground is very steep and needs to be taken slowly and carefully. Once Achill Head or Benmore have been reached, the route should be followed as described above to reach Keem Strand. Walkers who can arrange to be collected by car at this point can save themselves the road walk back to Dooagh.

EXTENSIONS

The track used at the start of the walk heads towards Slievemore, and this huge hump of a mountain could also be included as part of the route. To make the most of it, however, it is best climbed from sea level at Doogort, and the whole route would be best left open-ended with transport arranged to both ends. The spectacular line of cliffs at Minaun Heights beckons the walker to make further explorations, but the cliffs can only be reached after enduring a long walk along the road and so are not easily incorporated into an extended route.

# Route 31: GLENDAHURK HORSESHOE

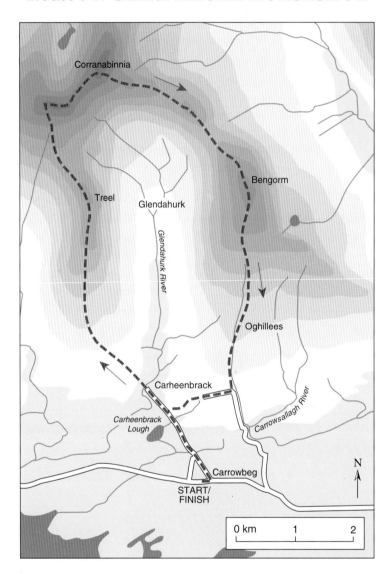

Corranabinnia

Bengorm

Treel

Glendahurk

*Glendahurk River*

Oghillees

Carheenbrack

*Carheenbrack Lough*

*Carrowsallagh River*

Carrowbeg

START/
FINISH

N

| 0 km | 1 | 2 |

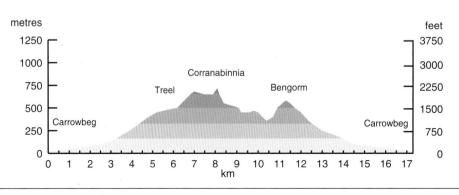

metres — feet

| 1250 | | 3750 |
| 1000 | | 3000 |
| 750 | | 2250 |
| 500 | | 1500 |
| 250 | | 750 |
| 0 | | 0 |

Corranabinnia

Treel

Bengorm

Carrowbeg

Carrowbeg

0  1  2  3  4  5  6  7  8  9  10  11  12  13  14  15  16  17
km

# Route 31: Glendahurk Horseshoe

TIME ALLOWANCE 6 hours.

STARTING/FINISHING LOCATION
Carheenbrack.
OSI Discovery 30 and 31: GR923963.
Car parking is very limited on the approach.
Bus Eireann table numbers 66, 69 and 440 pass
  Carheenbrack.

OVERVIEW/INTEREST
Fine horseshoe walk in the Nephin Mountains,
  within a proposed national park.
Relatively undiscovered walking country.
Fine views of remote mountains.

FOOTPATHS
A couple of clear tracks are used on low ground.
There are only vague paths on the mountains.
Many parts of the route are untrodden.

STATISTICS
| WALKING DISTANCE | 19km (12 miles) |
| TOTAL HEIGHT GAINED | 950m (3,115ft) |

PRINCIPAL HEIGHTS
| Treel | 478m (1,574ft) |
| Nameless summit | 681m (2,240ft) |
| Corranabinnia | 716m (2,343ft) |
| Bengorm | 582m (1,912ft) |

## The way to Corranabinnia   *Allow 3 hours*

The bleak and remote Nephin Mountains are relatively untrodden even in Irish terms. Access to the high mountains can be difficult and often involves long walks across bog or through forest. There is, however, a fine horseshoe walk which has easy access from the main N59 road between Newport and Achill Island. A road and track at Carheenbrack give access to Glendahurk. The glen is mostly boggy and has been planted with forest, but the mountains are completely open and form a horseshoe around the glen.

Spotting the access road into Glendahurk can be difficult. When travelling from Newport towards Achill Island on the N59, look out for a little yellow sign reading N59 0840. Just beyond this is a narrow minor road on the right where a small sign reads 'Carheenbrack'. This is probably easier to spot from the bus than from a faster car. Note that parking is very tight at the start of this walk, and it might be an idea to ask for permission from one of the houses along the way. Follow the tarmac road over a rise as it passes a handful of houses. At the end of the tarmac, a gravel track continues over another rise and passes close to Carheenbrack Lough. The track enjoys a view of the mountains around the Glendahurk Horseshoe, and descends slightly to pass a ruined farmstead in a clump of trees. Apart from a few small fields, the rest of the scene is wild and rugged moorland and mountain.

Cross an arched bridge over the Glendahurk River and pass through a gate. The track runs up a bouldery moorland slope and you should avoid any turnings to left or right as you climb. At a higher level there are turf cuttings, and you need to leave the track and start climbing more directly uphill at some point: there are no paths on the moorland slope, and it is in your interest to leave the track at a point where turf cutting is of limited extent.

The grass covering the bog on the lower slopes has been grazed extensively, but as you gain height there is more grass cover. You will pass a couple of rocky outcrops, but the ground is generally easy to cover and is set at a reasonable gradient. The broad slopes give way to a fairly clear, blunt ridge, and a vague path can be followed where walkers have begun to use one particular line. The summit at Treel rises to 478m (1,574ft). It is unmarked and is covered in short grass, heather, moss and bilberry.

There is a slight descent to cross a gap marked by a long black gash through the blanket bog. Once across the gap, you need to climb a fairly steep slope and pass around outcrops of rock. These outcrops later give way to a clearly defined edge, which can be followed further uphill. There is a summit off to the left towards the end of the climb, which rises to 681m (2,240ft). It is covered in blanket bog, but bears no cairn or other marker. It overlooks a steep slope dropping to Corranabinnia Lough.

There is a narrow ridge running north-eastwards and you should follow this next. It descends easily for a short while, then grows immense fangs of rock which are threaded by a trodden path. Any difficulties along this ridge can be passed by keeping always to the Glendahurk side of the rocky edge. You will need to use your hands in a couple of places, but there is nothing too awkward to be negotiated with care. After crossing the bottom of the gap, there are a couple of rocky outcrops on the ascent, but these are easily avoided. After crossing a blunt shoulder, there is a final steep climb on short grass and moss, passing scattered slabs of rock.

The summit of Corranabinnia is marked by a trig point at 716m (2,343ft) which stands in an area of boulders. There is a very low, crude stone shelter. The view takes in the whole of the Nephin Beg Range and stretches away to embrace other ranges of mountains. The following features should be spotted in clear weather:

NNE    Glennamong, Corslieve
ENE    Birreencorragh, Nephin
ESE    Buckoogh, Croaghmoyle
SE     Bengorm
SSE    Partry Mountains, Maumtrasna
S      Croagh Patrick
SSW    Mweelrea
WSW    Corraun Hill
W      Minaun Heights, Achill Island
WNW    Slievemore, Croaghaun, Achill Island
NW     Belmullet Peninsula
NNW    Slieve Alp

## The way back to Carheenbrack    *Allow 3 hours*

A steep and bouldery slope falls eastwards from the summit of Corranabinnia. The ground is not too difficult to negotiate, and there are signs of a trodden path in places. The boulders become smaller as the descent progresses, then there is a gentle gap to cross. A slight ascent leads across a hump on the ridge, then there is a steep descent to a gap. Care is needed on this descent in mist, as there are slabs of rock which become more difficult the further left you stray. Keeping more to the right, you will find a slope of steep heather and

*Looking along the track at Carheenbrack which leads towards Glendahurk.*

stones. There is a trodden path of sorts steering a course partly on rock and partly on heather to reach the gap.

Cross the gap and climb up a gentle slope for a short while. There is a crest of heather, grass and boulders before the ground falls away to another gap. The slope is heathery, with a few low outcrops of rock, while the gap is covered in low peat hags which do not impede progress. Climb up a steep slope of heather and rocky outcrops, zigzagging to choose the easiest way uphill. The gradient eases a little on the upper part of Bengorm, then the summit appears, crowned by a cairn at 582m (1,912ft). There is time for one last good look around at the view before the final descent. The island-studded Clew Bay backed by Croagh Patrick looks particularly good.

There is easy ground to cross as you leave the summit cairn, but you quickly move on to a more rugged moorland slope. The slope is pitched at a fairly gentle gradient, but looking ahead you will be able to distinguish extensive turf cuttings. To avoid these, look for a prominent green line slashed through the blanket bog, and aim towards it. A ribbon of green grass runs along a channel which may have been cut through the bog by hand, or it may be a natural feature. A small stream often runs this way too.

Whatever the origins of the channel, it offers an easy way off the moorland slope and does not get involved with any turf cuttings. Towards the end, you can step to the right and walk along a gravelly bog road. When you reach a junction with another bog road, turn right to follow a clearer track onwards. This track runs into the one you used at the start of the walk, on a rise between the Glendahurk River and Carheenbrack. You can take one last look around the high-level horseshoe, then turn left and walk back towards the main road at Carheenbrack.

## Alternative routes

ESCAPES

It may seem that the obvious line of escape from this walk simply involves descending into Glendahurk. Although this is possible from many parts of the route, there are steep and rugged slopes in places and some lines of cliffs. Furthermore, there is a lot of boggy ground and forestry to be negotiated, which could mean slow progress. In view of all this, the best early escape would involve retracing your steps to Carheenbrack. Later on in the walk, Bengorm could be omitted in favour of an early descent into Glendahurk, but it might be just as easy to continue over the mountain and complete the whole walk as described.

EXTENSIONS

Glenthomas lies just to the west of Glendahurk, and it would be possible to combine two horseshoe walks into one. A much longer and tougher alternative would involve walking along the entire crest of the Nephin Beg Range. The mountains are still mostly pathless and free from extensive fencing. A large portion of this mountain range is due to be designated as a national park.

*The domed summit of Bengorm is the last 'nail' in the Glendahurk Horseshoe.*

# Route 32: BANGOR TRAIL

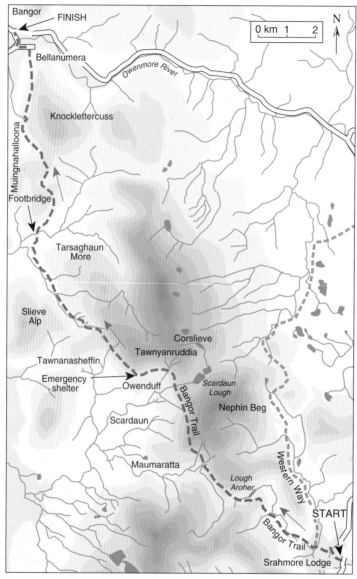

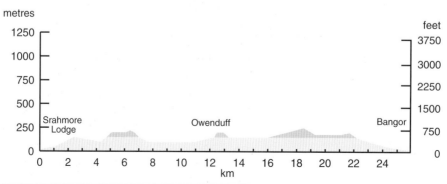

# Route 32: Bangor Trail

TIME ALLOWANCE 8 hours.

STARTING LOCATION
Srahmore Lodge.
OSI Discovery 23: GR974045.
Cars can be parked beyond Srahmore Lodge in a
    forest.
No public transport.

FINISHING LOCATION
Bangor Erris.
OSI Discovery 23: GR863232.
Cars can be parked around the village.
Bus Eireann table number 446.

OVERVIEW/INTEREST
An ancient drove road through the Nephin
    Mountains, passing through bleak and remote
    wilderness.
The route is walked by local people each
    midsummer.
Offers splendid views in clear weather.

FOOTPATHS
The Bangor Trail is rough and boggy throughout.
Waymark posts are numbered for convenience.
There are only a couple of junctions with other
    paths.

STATISTICS
WALKING DISTANCE        26km (16 miles)
TOTAL HEIGHT GAINED     590m (1,935ft)
PRINCIPAL HEIGHT
Waymark post 20 on Nephin Beg at 260m (850ft)

## The way to Owenduff

*Allow 4 hours*

The full extent of the Bangor Trail is from Newport to Bangor Erris, and it is marked throughout with waymark posts bearing green arrows and numbers. The route-marking system is designed to be used in conjunction with a guidebook produced by Mayo County Council, which features maps and a commentary to tie in with the numbered waymarks. Although the route is waymarked between Newport and Bangor Erris, the early stages are mostly along roads. Beyond Srahmore Lodge the route crosses the Nephin Beg Range and wanders around the edge of a bleak and barren bogland.

As a through route, the Bangor Trail has been in existence for over two centuries, and possibly much longer. In its time the trail has obviously been maintained, and there is plenty of evidence of construction and surfacing work along the way. However, it has been overwhelmed by bog in some places, and other parts are completely waterlogged. The surface has been reduced to uneven boulders in some parts, making walking difficult. Note that this is a rough and tough walk, with no easy escape routes; in poor weather it would be a treadmill. Note also that the only shelter along the way is a very basic cabin which was flown in by helicopter and deposited inside an existing ruin. This structure is for emergency use only.

Leaving Srahmore Lodge, follow the narrow road onwards to reach Waymark 13, where a left turn leads into a forest at Letterkeen. Motorists who leave their car at a nearby forest car park can easily return to this point to start the walk. At Waymark 14, turn left again to reach the Altaconey River, and cross over it using a footbridge which was installed specifically for walkers following the trail. Another river is followed upstream and normally this will be easy to ford, but in wet weather it may prove difficult. If the water is high and yet the river is passable, rest assured that there are no more difficult river crossings ahead. Follow the Bangor Trail uphill alongside Letterkeen Wood, then cross a shoulder of a hill at 200m (650ft). A short descent leads back alongside another part of Letterkeen Wood, then the route continues alongside the Bawnduff River, which carves a significant gap through the Nephin Beg Range.

You now cross a series of small streams on a green slope, where the ruins of an old farm building can be seen. Take note of the oak tree nearby, which is one of the few trees surviving in this broad, bleak and boggy wilderness. The Bangor Trail climbs up a rugged slope to reach a shoulder of Nephin Beg at Waymark 20. The height of this shoulder is 260m (850ft) and the view stretches across a huge boggy bowl around Scardaun. This point should be treated as significant if weather or time are against you, because there should still be time to turn around and retreat to Srahmore Lodge if you know you are unlikely to complete the walk to Bangor Erris.

If you decide to continue with the walk, cut across the rugged slopes of Nephin Beg. At Waymark 21 there is a track heading off to the left which ultimately leads to Sraduggaun, but it is probably too long to be considered as an escape option. Cross over the stream which gushes as a waterfall from the unseen pool of Scardaun Lough. If you continued the walk in the face of adversity and are beginning to regret the decision, the emergency shelter mentioned earlier is available at Owenduff. This is the only shelter of any type available along the length of the Bangor Trail. A night spent here is unlikely to be relished, but it is a safer option than a bivouac on the open mountainside. At Owenduff the Bangor Trail can be considered half completed, but it is galling to note that it gets no easier as it proceeds.

## The way to Bangor Erris          *Allow 4 hours*

Leaving Owenduff, the Bangor Trail contours around the rugged slopes of Tawnyanruddia, then climbs up on to a shoulder of the mountain. Waymark 24 is reached on this shoulder, and there are views ahead across the final stretches of the route. Although Bangor Erris cannot actually be seen, at least its position can be determined from the map. This shoulder is a fine place to make a study of the wider view in clear weather. Owing to

*Looking back across bleak bogs towards the mountain of Glennamong.*

the proximity of the Nephin Beg Range, the views are necessarily restricted to the western prospect. Look out for some of the following features:

SSE  Glennamong
SSW  Claggan Mountain, Corraun Hill
SW  Knockmore, Achill Island
WSW  Minaun Heights, Achill Island
W  Slievemore, Croaghaun, Achill Island
NW  Belmullet
NNW  Knocklettercuss, Benwee Head

The Bangor Trail drops from the shoulder of the mountain and begins to follow a river downstream. The route generally keeps to the brow of the small valley through which the river runs, but you will need to cross a couple of inflowing streams on the way. Looking ahead, you may notice a footbridge spanning the Tarsaghaunmore River and you should aim for this feature. The bridge is long and narrow, and it was constructed specially to aid walkers on the Bangor Trail; in the past, anyone arriving beside this river to find it flowing fast and furious, with no hope of being able to ford it, would have despaired at this point. In an emergency, you could abandon the walk by following the river downstream and linking with a road which proceeds directly towards the main N59. The Bangor Trail, however, continues on its rugged course towards Bangor Erris.

Follow the route uphill, as it cuts across the slopes of a hill called Mamakleta. The old track avoids the summits of Mamakleta and nearby Croaghaun Mountain, and slips through a boggy gap between Croaghaun Mountain and Knock-lettercuss, reaching an altitude of nearly 220m (720ft) in this final cluster of little hills. The route then falls, before contouring and falling more gently across the slopes of Knocklettercuss. Bangor can be seen ahead, but the Bangor Trail maintains a rough surface throughout the descent. The first firm and dry footing since leaving Srahmore Lodge is gained beside a football field, where you turn left towards the main N59 road. Turn right to cross the Owenmore River and continue into the centre of the village. There are shops, pubs and a few places to stay. Bus services are also available, but if you

left your car parked near Srahmore Lodge you will need to organize some other form of transport to collect it again.

## Alternative routes

ESCAPES
The important thing to remember about the Bangor Trail is that it runs straight through one of the last big wilderness areas in Ireland, and consequently escape routes are very few. In fact, if the going is too rough or you are aware of losing too much time, the simplest course of action is to turn around and abandon the walk while there is still time. The only feasible escape routes which might be considered include the old track running from Scardaun to Sraduggaun, which has little to commend it, and the track and road leaving the Tarsaghaunmore River to reach the main N59 road. These are both mentioned in the route description. If time is lost during the walk and you have not chosen an escape route, there is a danger of running on into darkness in this bleak bogland. Take heed of the fact that the only shelter available is the cabin at Owenduff mentioned in the route description.

EXTENSIONS
The full course of the Bangor Trail is from Newport to Bangor, with the numbered waymark posts counting upwards from 1 to 34. The early stretch involves a lot of road walking. Once a year, on the Saturday nearest to midsummer, a hundred local walkers cover the full length of the trail. Numbers are limited in the interests of preserving the environment. If you have plenty of energy, then the Bangor Trail could be used as a way of getting on to the remote Nephin Beg Range, and a high-level walk could be attempted. It is also possible to enjoy an extended weekend walk by combining the course of the Bangor Trail with the Western Way. Yellow arrows are used to mark the Western Way, which is routed along the opposite side of the Nephin Beg Range to the Bangor Trail. The two routes are joined together at Srahmore Lodge, but the only link between Bangor Erris and the Western Way at Bellacorick is the main N59 road.

# Route 33: OX MOUNTAINS

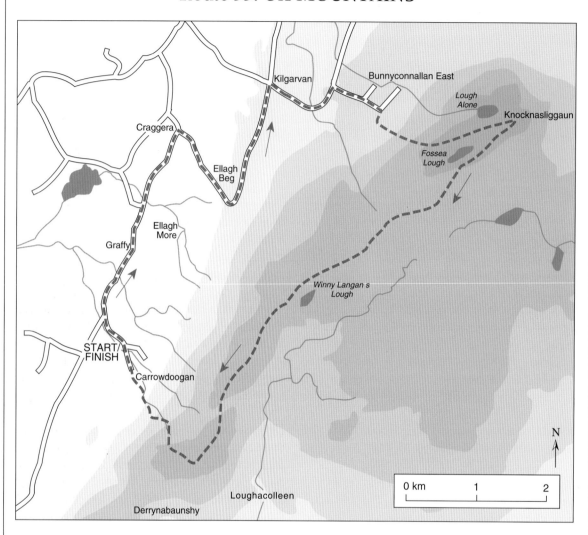

Craggera

Kilgarvan

Bunnyconnallan East

*Lough Alone*

Knocknasliggaun

Ellagh Beg

*Fossea Lough*

Ellagh More

Graffy

*Winny Langan s Lough*

START/ FINISH

Carrowdoogan

Loughacolleen

Derrynabaunshy

N

| 0 km | 1 | 2 |

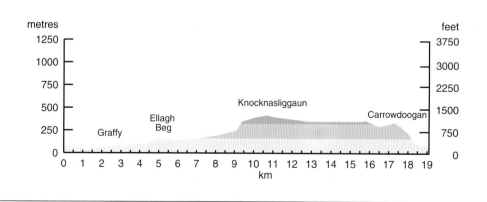

| metres | | | | | | | | | feet |
|---|---|---|---|---|---|---|---|---|---|
| 1250 | | | | | | | | | 3750 |
| 1000 | | | | | | | | | 3000 |
| 750 | | | | | | | | | 2250 |
| 500 | | | Knocknasliggaun | | | | | | 1500 |
| 250 | Ellagh Beg | | | | | | Carrowdoogan | | 750 |
| | Graffy | | | | | | | | |
| 0 | | | | | | | | | 0 |

0 1 2 3 4 5 6 7 8 9 10 11 12 13 14 15 16 17 18 19
km

# Route 33: Ox Mountains

TIME ALLOWANCE 6 hours.

STARTING/FINISHING LOCATION
Carrowdoogan, near Attymass.
OSI Discovery 24: GR316125.
Car parking is limited to a small roadside space.
No public transport nearer than Foxford.

OVERVIEW/INTEREST
Broad, undulating, relatively unfrequented
  moorlands and small loughs.
Includes parts of the Western and Foxford Ways.

FOOTPATHS
Minor roads and tracks are used at the start and
  finish.
The upland parts are largely pathless.
The descent includes an interesting 'staighre'
  path.

STATISTICS
WALKING DISTANCE        19km (12 miles)
TOTAL HEIGHT GAINED     560m (1,835ft)
PRINCIPAL HEIGHT
Knocknasliggaun          417m (1,364ft)

## The way to Knocknasliggaun    *Allow 3 hours*

The Ox Mountains are of no great height, but they are broad, bleak and quite rugged in places. In recent years both the Western Way and Foxford Way have been routed on to the slopes of the mountains. The Foxford Way enjoys a high-level course between Bonniconlon and Foxford, and forms the basis for this walk on the Ox Mountains.

Finding the start of the walk is not easy, and you will have to negotiate your way carefully through a network of minor roads where signposts are rare. If you are travelling from Foxford to Bonniconlon, you will pass a junction signposted for Attymass. Keep to the right, and do not go into the village.

Instead, look out for an unsignposted turning on the right for Carrowdoogan. There is a white house at this junction with two white buildings alongside, both with red roofs. Follow a narrow road onwards, keeping right at the next junction, then park beside a forest using a space flanked by boulders which would accommodate a couple of cars. There is a sign fixed to a tree reading 'Attymass Gun Club'.

There are some minor roads and bog roads which you may as well walk first. Leave the parking space at Carrowdoogan and walk back along the narrow road you have already driven along. Turn right at the road junction beside the white buildings, and pass a ruined house. Avoid all road and track junctions to left and right and pass fields, wooded areas, bouldery areas and a couple of stands of forestry. Eventually, at Craggera, you will see a Western Way marker post with a yellow arrow beside the road. Turn right at this point to follow a narrow tarmac road.

The road quickly becomes a track, passing a stand of forestry and a couple of old farm buildings. At a junction of tracks, head off to the left, climbing up past a water tank to reach a rugged moorland slope at Ellagh Beg. Keep following the track to pass a forested area. There are young trees to the right and older trees, fringed with birch, to the left. After another rugged moorland interlude, the track passes another small stand of forest and some fields, and then reaches a crossroads of tracks at Kilgarvan.

Leave the course of the Western Way by turning right at the crossroads. A track climbs above the fields, swinging left to cross a couple of streams on a rugged moorland which has been extensively given over to turf cutting. Turn right along another track. Although there is a sign reading 'No Dumping' quite an amount of rubbish has been dumped beside the bog road. The track heads straight towards the rugged slopes of the Ox Mountains, offering easy access through an area which would otherwise be quite difficult underfoot. Turn right at the end of the track, and follow it until it almost expires. A Foxford Way marker post stands here, bearing a red arrow which has faded to pink.

The Foxford Way climbs up a rugged, pathless slope of bog and heather, with some exposed rock. You could either follow the direction indicated by the markers to reach Fossea Lough, or begin to drift more to the left and gain the high, heathery crest with a view to reaching the summit of Knocknasliggaun. The crest has some boggy patches, as well as one huge boulder and a number of smaller ones. There is a trig point rooted in an old cairn at 417m (1,364ft). The views are reasonably extensive but, apart from the Nephin Mountains, they are not particularly impressive. The following features might be noticed in clear weather:

| | |
|---|---|
| N | Carrick Peninsula, Donegal |
| NE | Benalta, Ox Mountains |
| E | Arigna Mountains, Slieve Anierin |
| S | Letterbrone, Ox Mountains |
| SW | Ox Mountains, Croaghmoyle, Croagh Patrick |
| WSW | Lough Conn, Nephin |
| W | Nephin Beg, Corslieve, Knocklettercuss |
| NW | Maumykeogh |

### The way back to Carrowdoogan

*Allow 3 hours*

Walk south-westwards from the summit of Knocknasliggaun to pass the southern shore of Fossea Lough. There are all sorts of lonely moorland pools which might be spotted around the Ox Mountains. You will pass a couple more on this walk, but others are in view from time to time. The Foxford Way makes some attempt to follow the crest of the Ox Mountains in a south-westwards direction. The crest, however, is ill-defined and the route steers a course which avoids unnecessarily difficult ground.

*Bouldery mountainsides give way to fields at the end of the walk near Carrowdoogan.*

Leaving Fossea Lough, walk along a broad crest where there is little heather and an abundance of boggy grass and moss. Further on there is a slight rise which is more heathery. Cross a broad gap which is grassy and boggy, then aim to cross ground which can be heathery, boggy, or sprinkled with a few large boulders. Look out for Winny Langan's Lough and pass it on its northern side. There is a heathery crest beyond, where old turf cuttings will be encountered and the going is decidedly difficult. There are also some patches of boulders.

Looking ahead, you will see a broad dome of heather and boulders, and this is a useful feature to aim towards. The top of the hill is covered in large boulders, although the highest point is a peat hag covered in heather. Views across to the Nephin Mountains also include a series of low-level loughs and fields. A descent from the hill leads across a grassy, boggy gap, then there is a climb over another heathery rise before little Loughacolleen is found on a narrow gap. Cross boggy ground to the right of this lough, then climb up on to the next broad rise.

Descend roughly north-westwards towards a broad, mossy bowl beyond which some old turf cuttings can be seen. Walk out of the mossy bowl to find a small stream draining away. Suddenly, you will find a slab of rock spanning the stream, and a pathway paved in stone leads down the rugged slopes of the Ox Mountains. This path is one of a number of 'staighre' routes – or 'stairs' – which were used by people climbing up and down the mountainside. Follow this path faithfully, noting how it zigzags around boggy and rocky obstacles. If it becomes unclear in places, look more carefully to spot it.

The slopes of the Ox Mountains are broad, bleak, heathery and bouldery. The boulders seem to be even larger on the lower slopes. The staighre path reaches a gateway at the lower fields, and a grassy track flanked by low walls leads towards another gate near a farmhouse. Follow the access road away from the farm at Carrowdoogan, passing a huddle of whitewashed buildings. A short distance further on you will reach the little parking space where the walk started, bringing this circuit to a close.

## Alternative routes

### ESCAPES

The Ox Mountains are broad, bleak and rugged, despite their modest height. In clear weather walking can be pleasant, but in foul weather they are best left alone, and anyone inclined to walk across them needs to be a good navigator. Escapes from the rugged crest are not obvious, and are largely dependent on locating other staighre paths similar to the one used at the end of the route described above.

### EXTENSIONS

The Foxford Way is largely a low-level route, but its highest stretch is that which runs through the Ox Mountains. The route could be followed from a point near Bonniconlon to take in a good stretch of the Ox Mountains before descending to Glendaduff. In fact, from that point it would be worth crossing Roosky Mountain too, but either way the route is linear and requires transport.

# Route 34: BENBULBIN AND KINGS MOUNTAIN

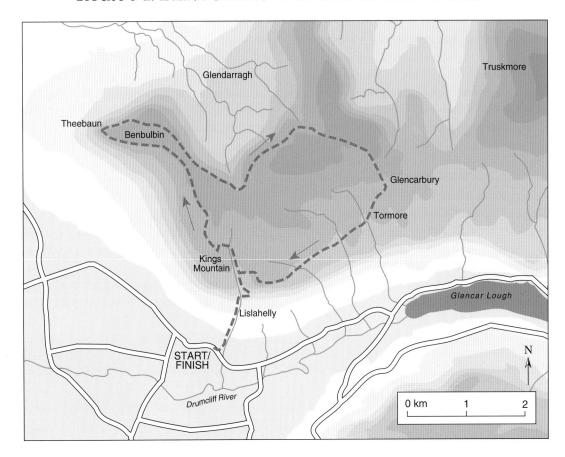

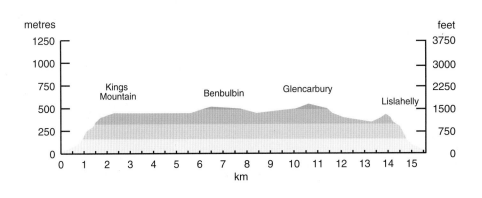

# 12

# SLIGO LEITRIM

HIGH-LEVEL ROUTE

## Route 34: Benbulbin and Kings Mountain

TIME ALLOWANCE 6 hours.

STARTING/FINISHING LOCATION
Lislahelly, near Drumcliffe.
OSI Discovery 16: GR703426.
Car parking is limited beside the road.
Bus services run along nearby main roads.

OVERVIEW/INTEREST
Circuit around a plateau fringed with limestone
cliffs, overlooking Glencar.
Fine cliff scenery and rugged upland walking.
Benbulbin – a remarkably prominent mountain
with extensive views from the summit.

FOOTPATHS
A good path is used at the start and finish.
There are very few paths on the uplands.
A length of mining track is used at Glencarbury.

STATISTICS
| | |
|---|---|
| WALKING DISTANCE | 19km (12 miles) |
| TOTAL HEIGHT GAINED | 700m (2,300ft) |
| PRINCIPAL HEIGHTS | |
| Kings Mountain (west) | 462m (1,527ft) |
| Benbulbin | 526m (1,730ft) |
| Kings Mountain (east) | 436m (1,435ft) |

### The way to Benbulbin
*Allow 2 hours*

Benbulbin has a striking profile when seen from
the main road running between Sligo and Donegal.
Its layers of limestone and steep grassy slopes rise so
precipitously from the lowlands that the mountain
has the appearance of an enormous slice of cake.
From Cashelgarron, on the main road, Benbulbin
appears as a sharp, rocky peak, but anyone
climbing the mountain from the side finds that its
summit is a broad, grassy moorland. The cliffs
which fringe the summit of Benbulbin bar any
direct ascents, but there are ways on to the top
from the shoulders of neighbouring mountains.

This route combines an ascent of Benbulbin with
Kings Mountain, whose impressive limestone cliffs
overlook Glencar. Kings Mountain has two
summits which are separated by a steep-sided
valley above Lislahelly. A zigzag path in this valley
is the key to the ascent and descent to and from
the cliff-fringed uplands. The circuit described
below mostly traces the edges of several cliffs in
preference to crossing rugged moorlands.

Start on a minor road between Drumcliff and
Glencar, where a short, narrow road leaves the
minor road at a bend. This bend has an attractive
rockery at the junction of the two roads, but parking
is rather limited. There are a couple of roadside
spaces, but they are close to houses and it might be
a good idea to ask for permission to park a car.

Walk along the short, narrow road, which ends
with two gates. Pass through the gate on the right
and keep to the left of the field, following a line of
trees towards an old farmhouse. Turn left around
the farmhouse, then walk straight towards Kings
Mountain. There is a long field leading towards the
foot of the mountain, and this is divided only by a
low, ruined wall. At the top end of the field you

173

will need to cross a fence in order to reach the steeper mountainside. Look carefully for the line of a zigzag path on the steep and grassy slope. This path eases the ascent considerably, and eventually conveys walkers from the open slope into the recesses of the steep-sided valley.

Follow the path into the valley, but leave it when it starts zigzagging uphill to the right. Aim to walk straight up through the valley and you will find a useful, narrow, stony path heading towards the top of the valley. Follow this path until you can see a shallow valley heading off to the left. You will need to cross a fence, as well as a small stream, before being able to follow the shallow valley uphill. Rising to the left is the highest of the summits of Kings Mountain. It appears as a limestone peak rising above a heathery moorland. A short but steep ascent leads to the top, where the altitude is 462m (1,527ft). The views are already opening up very well, but are largely restricted to the south and west.

Descend from the limestone peak back on to the heather moorland, then look ahead to chart an easy course around the edge of the mountain. Overall, you will be heading north-westwards towards the steep end of Benbulbin, but there is no definite path or direction. Aim to walk on the easier slopes above the lines of cliffs, but off the more rugged upper moorlands. There are some stony surfaces, or areas with short vegetation. You will need to cross a stream in a crumbling gully, then it is a good idea to gain height gradually while continuing across the heathery moorland.

Cross a fence, and if you can pick up a good sheep path across the moorland slope you may be able to avoid the more rugged areas of peat and heather. Further on you need to cross another fence, then you may need to climb a little higher to keep above the steep southern slopes of Benbulbin. The break of slope between the upper moorland and the fringe of cliffs becomes more definite as the walk proceeds. The end of the mountain, at Theebaun, is a prominent prow with a grand view along the coast.

Turn completely around the end of Benbulbin and follow the northern cliff-line onwards. There are a series of dramatic gullies and buttresses along here, and in early summer there may be many

flowers sprouting from the rock, safe from grazing sheep. To visit the summit of Benbulbin, veer uphill away from the cliffs, crossing a grassy moorland until the trig point can be seen and gained. It stands at an altitude of 526m (1,730ft). The views are restricted in the direction of Truskmore, but are quite extensive in other directions and include the following features:

| | |
|---|---|
| NNE | Blue Stack Mountains |
| NE | Benwhiskin |
| E | Truskmore |
| ESE | Cuilcagh |
| SE | Cope's Mountain, Castlegal Range, Slieve Anierin |
| S | Slieve Daeane, Bricklieve Mountains |
| SSW | Knocknarea |
| SW | Ox Mountains, Nephin |
| WSW | Nephin Beg, Corslieve |
| W | Downpatrick Head, Benwee Head |
| NNW | Slieve League, Carrick Peninsula |

### The way back to Lislahelly            *Allow 4 hours*

Head roughly south-eastwards from the summit of Benbulbin. You could either walk along the top of the cliff-line, or keep above the steep slopes looking towards Benwhiskin, or aim to follow the moorland crest onwards. There is a faint path along the crest, but it runs out while crossing another rise on the moorland. Keep to the less steep upper slopes of the plateau, making a pronounced turn around the head of a valley. From walking south-eastwards on a limestone slope, after crossing a boggy area the direction changes so that you climb more northwards on another limestone slope.

Keep to the break of slope near the edge of the plateau, walking more to the north-east and crossing a few rises and dips along the way. There is a more pronounced valley, which should be followed to its head. There are some little swallow holes and boggy areas in this valley, while at the very head of it there is a stony gap on the broad

*Benbulbin's classic profile, as seen from a point above Cashelgarron near the main road.*

174

moorland. This gap rises to 560m (1,835ft) and so is the highest point reached on the walk.

Do not walk straight down the next valley, but head across the moorland slope to the left to reach an area of mining spoil. There is a clear track which can be followed downhill alongside a pronounced gash in the limestone. The spoil includes a heavy, white mineral called barytes. Keep away from holes and fissures, as the ground is liable to subsidence. Follow the track downhill until you reach an electricity transmission line. Standing on a limestone knoll just to the left is a small, concrete cross which was erected in Marian Year – 1954. If you walk up to the cross, return to the track afterwards.

It is possible to head from the old mine across country to Kings Mountain without having to gain or lose much height. First, you cross a limestone area, and ford a small stream. A rugged stretch of bog and heather comes next, followed by another slope of limestone. The rock is fairly broken, so do not trust it to be firm underfoot. The eastern summit of Kings Mountain lies just beyond, but first it is worth heading towards the cliffs at the edge of the plateau to enjoy splendid views through Glencar.

Keep to the edge of Kings Mountain, walking on short heather and stones, with a series of precipitous gullies and buttresses falling into Glencar. There is an almost aerial view of the fields at the foot of the mountain. The summit of this part of Kings Mountain rises to 436m (1,435ft), so it is a little lower than the nearby summit which you climbed earlier in the walk.

Descend away from the cliffs to reach a gap which is entirely stony, then turn left to start following a path downhill. There is a small stone cross perched just above the path, marking the spot where IRA volunteers were shot dead during the Civil War of 1922. Continue walking down the path, which zigzags into a steep-sided valley, joining the path which was used on the ascent. It is now simply a matter of retracing your earlier steps, zigzagging downhill, crossing a fence and walking down the long field to reach the old farmhouse. Turn right around it and walk to the gate which gives access back to the road where the walk started.

*Looking towards Glencar Lough from the cliffs near the summit of Kings Mountain.*

## Alternative routes

### ESCAPES

As the plateau is largely fringed with cliffs, any early descents need to be chosen with care. Descents from Benbulbin and Kings Mountain should be avoided, but between them there are steep slopes which run safely down to fields. You would need to look for gates and tracks continuing down to the road. After

climbing Benbulbin and following the moorland crest, it is possible to head back to Kings Mountain across the moorland, cutting the walk short by avoiding the loop to Glencarbury.

EXTENSIONS

The highest mountain in this area is Truskmore, a sprawling summit crowned by a tall and very obvious TV mast. This mast is served by a road, which is also quite obvious in the view. Anyone making an ascent of Truskmore could use the road, but if an alternative route is required, the slopes are largely bleak and pathless. However, there are some bog roads on the Glencar side which could be useful. Including Truskmore in a circular walk from Lislahelly could be difficult, but if a descent was made to Glencar Lough, with transport arranged to suit, this would make a satisfying walk.

# Route 35: CASTLEGAL RANGE

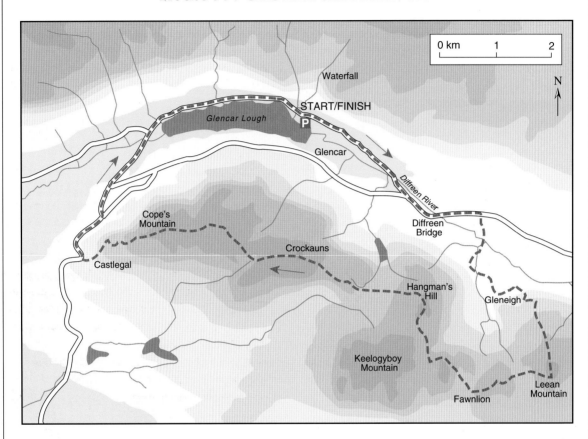

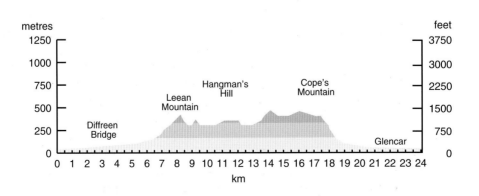

# Route 35: Castlegal Range

TIME ALLOWANCE 8 hours.

STARTING/FINISHING LOCATION
Glencar Waterfall, Glencar
OSI Discovery 16: GR760434.
Car park near the waterfall.
Bus Eireann table numbers 66, 67 and 470 use
the main road.

OVERVIEW/INTEREST
Rugged range of limestone hills.
Fine views around Glencar.

FOOTPATHS
Roads and tracks are used at a low level.
Upland parts have few tracks and paths.

STATISTICS

| | | |
|---|---|---|
| WALKING DISTANCE | 27km (17 miles) | |
| TOTAL HEIGHT GAINED | 990m (2,350ft) | |
| PRINCIPAL HEIGHTS | | |
| Leean Mountain | 417m (1,373ft) | |
| Fawnlion | 364m (1,200ft) | |
| Hangman's Hill | 400m (1,310ft) | |
| Crockauns | 463m (1,527ft) | |
| Cope's Mountain | 452m (1,487ft) | |

## The way to Leean Mountain

*Allow 2½ hours*

The Castlegal Range is a name of convenience for the rugged limestone hills on the south side of Glencar. This is a convoluted range with knobbly hills and boggy gaps arranged in a chaotic order. A keen walker could try to climb every hill in the range, but this route climbs only a handful of them, missing out some of the summits. Because the range is linear – after a fashion – a decent circular walk is difficult to arrange. Roads in Glencar can be used at the start and finish of the walk to make a circuit, but it is also possible to arrange transport to either end of the range, or even to use the occasional bus services.

Anyone using bus services could start at Diffreen on the main N16 road, but cars should be driven along a loop of minor road in Glencar, where a good car park is available at the entrance to Glencar Waterfall. There are also smaller car parks beside Glencar Lough, which are used mainly by fishermen. There are a couple of B&Bs near Glencar Lough, and anyone using these could start the walk without the need for transport.

Leaving the Glencar Waterfall car park, follow the minor road away from Glencar Lough, passing Glencar Post Office and following the road straight onwards to cross Diffreen River. The minor road runs up to join the main N16, where you should turn left. The road veers left and crosses Diffreen Bridge, passing Diffreen National School and the new Diffreen Cemetery beside the road. Turn right at the cemetery to follow a narrow farm road. This road, like the previous ones on this walk, crosses Diffreen River yet again.

After crossing the river, the road becomes a patchy tarmac and gravel track, and by turning left and left again you will be led into a forest at Gleneigh. The track climbs a little, then descends a little to pass a stone building with a corrugated iron roof. The track climbs again to reach a crossroads of tracks, where a left turn leads out of the forest and along a hill track. Pass through a gate on the right and through a sheep pen, to start climbing up the slopes of Leean Mountain. Aim to follow the edge of the forest uphill, crossing remarkably varied ground. Grass gives way to profuse growths of rushes and remnants of turf cuttings. After crossing a fence there is more short grass, with plenty of limestone poking through.

Simply keep climbing up the grass and limestone slopes on Leean Mountain. There is a trig point at 417m (1,373ft) on the summit, but this will be seen only at the last moment. Views westwards take in the rugged crest, where there are summits large and small, smooth and knobbly, grassy and heathery, dry and boggy. In clear weather

179

navigation is mostly simple enough, but in mist you need to be very good at reading convoluted contours from the map and applying them to shapes on the ground.

## The way to Crockauns        *Allow 3 hours*

Descend a short way north-westwards down a steep slope of grass and limestone. There is a splendid grassy track running across the slopes of Leean Mountain, but all you do is cross over it. Keep well to the right of a sheep pen to avoid a short cliff face on the far side of a little hill. Continue along a short length of stony path to cross a broad and boggy area. There is a fence to cross on the gap, then you climb straight uphill on a short, steep, grassy slope at Fawnlion. There are two summits and two low stone walls to cross. The highest summit is at 364m (1,200ft).

Continue over the hill and reach a junction of fences. Follow a fence which runs downhill alongside a forest. A wall continues downhill away from the forest, and there is a track alongside it. The track leads down from the hills off your route, so pass through a gate on the right to continue. There are two hills ahead, and you could either climb both of them or pass between them. To pass between them, cross a wall and fence and walk up through a dry valley between the two hills. There is another wall and fence running up through the little valley, and you can cross these on the narrow gap between the two hills.

To continue towards Hangman's Hill, contour around the steep slopes of the hill overlooking Gleneigh. The steep slopes are mostly grassy, but there are small outcrops of limestone too. Contour around the hillside to enter another small valley and cross a stream. There is a grassy track on the opposite side of the stream, and this leads up to a gateway in a fence. Beyond the gateway, turn right and cross a rugged, boggy, heathery area, walking towards Hangman's Hill.

*The rugged slopes of Cope's Mountain as seen from the valley bottom in Glencar.*

You cross a fence before the slope steepens, and you will reach the summit of Hangman's Hill at about 400m (1,310ft). Looking back, the broad shoulders of Keelogyboy Mountain can be studied. This knobbly mountain could have been included, but an ascent puts an awkward dog-leg bend in the route. The summit crest of Hangman's Hill is curved and

covered in heather. Take care on the descent at the end of the crest, as there are outcrops of shattered rock; there are a couple of places where a right turn leads easily between outcrops.

Head westwards across a broad, heathery, boggy gap, crossing a fence on the way. Looking ahead, there are two hills side by side, both with lines of cliffs which, although quite short, are impassable to walkers. Aim straight towards the little valley between the two hills, where you need to cross a fence near a small stream. Start to drift uphill to the right on a grassy slope, crossing a wall and fence on the way towards the summit of Crockauns. There are small outcrops of limestone

on the grassy mountain, as well as traces of low walls. The highest point on Crockauns bears a cairn at 463m (1,527ft). The views are a bit limited owing to lack of height, but look out for the following:

| | |
|---|---|
| N | Truskmore |
| NE | Arroo, Dartry Mountains |
| E | Dough Mountain |
| ESE | Hangman's Hill, Leean Mountain |
| SE | Keelogyboy Mountain, Slieve Anierin |
| S | Bricklieve Mountains |
| WSW | Knocknarea, Ox Mountains, Nephin |
| W | Downpatrick Head, Benwee Head |
| NW | Kings Mountain |

## The way back to Glencar          *Allow 2½ hours*

Leaving Crockauns by heading westwards, a slope of grass and limestone outcrops leads to a broad, boggy, heathery gap. As you cross this gap, you might be inclined to follow a fence simply for the sake of having a line to trace. The fence runs uphill and along the rugged moorland top of Cope's Mountain, but it is not always aligned to the broad crest and you will need to make a slight detour to visit the 452m (1,487ft) summit of the mountain.

Leaving Cope's Mountain in clear weather should not present a problem, but care should be taken in mist. The western slopes of the mountain are heathery and hummocky, with some small crumbly cliffs. Do not descend towards Glencar Lough, as there are some dangerous cliffs tucked out of sight. Keep walking westwards, staying on the rugged crest, until you can follow a path through the heather. The path drops from the heather slopes on to a steep slope of grass. However, it now becomes a good, clear track which zigzags to ease the gradient. Follow the zigzags faithfully; they become much broader as the foot of the slope is approached. The last stretches are

*Looking across Glencar to Cope's Mountain from the cliffs of Kings Mountain.*

lined with trees, then finally a gateway leads on to the main N16 road.

Turn right to follow the main road, but only a short way along you can turn left and follow a minor road signposted for Glencar. The road runs gradually downhill, crossing Drumcliff River before reaching the shore of Glencar Lough near a B&B. There is no lakeshore path, so you must follow the road onwards. There is often a screen of trees between the road and the waters of the lake. As soon as the road pulls away from the lakeshore, you will reach the car park for Glencar Waterfall and the walk is brought to a close. After the final stretch of road walking, you might like to end by visiting the foot of the waterfall in the nearby woods.

## Alternative routes

ESCAPES

There are some paths and tracks crossing gaps in the Castlegal Range. Any paths or tracks leading northwards can be used to make an early exit from the route, but taking paths or tracks southwards will leave you far away from your car or the bus route. It is best not to descend into Glencar without the aid of a clear path, as you will run into fields or forest which could be difficult to negotiate. Do not descend into Glencar from Cope's Mountain, except by the path described in the route, as there are long lines of cliffs barring the way. There are a couple of points where zigzag paths exploit breaches in the cliff-line, but it is difficult to find the start of these paths in mist, so they are best left alone. In any case, they are not well trodden and still leave you having to find a way through lower fields.

EXTENSIONS

The full length of the Castlegal Range from Leean Mountain to Cope's Mountain is covered on this walk, but not every summit is climbed. One way of extending the route is to climb every summit; another – and this is best done as a linear walk – is to include the prominent summit of Benbo, nearer to Manorhamilton.

# Route 36: DARTRY MOUNTAINS

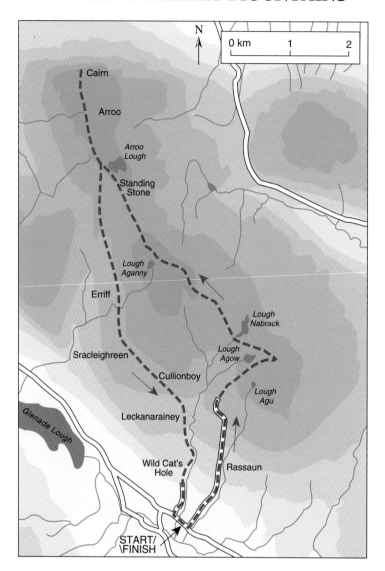

Cairn

Arroo

Arroo Lough

Standing Stone

Lough Aganny

Erriff

Lough Nabrack

Sracleighreen

Lough Agow

Cullionboy

Lough Agu

Leckanarainey

Glenade Lough

Wild Cat's Hole

Rassaun

START/ FINISH

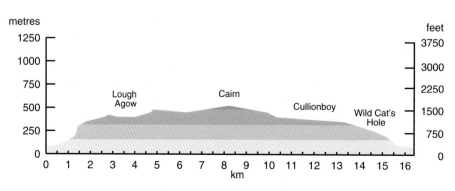

metres

1250

1000

750

500

250

0

feet

3750

3000

2250

1500

750

0

Lough Agow

Cairn

Cullionboy

Wild Cat's Hole

0  1  2  3  4  5  6  7  8  9  10  11  12  13  14  15  16

km

# Route 36: Dartry Mountains

TIME ALLOWANCE 7 hours.

STARTING/FINISHING LOCATION
Rassaun, in Glenade
OSI Discovery 16: GR850445.
With permission, cars could be parked in a
  farmyard.
No public transport.

OVERVIEW/INTEREST
Extensive moorlands with lovely little loughs.
Standing stone and marooned millstones.
Extensive views from the higher ground.
Wild Cat's Hole and waterfall.

FOOTPATHS
Good tracks at the start and finish.
The high moorlands are virtually pathless.

STATISTICS
WALKING DISTANCE           21km (13 miles)
TOTAL HEIGHT GAINED        550m (1,800ft)
PRINCIPAL HEIGHT
Arroo                      523m (1,720ft)

## The way to Arroo                    *Allow 4 hours*

The Dartry Mountains are broad, bleak and extensive heather moorlands broken by lonely moorland loughs and outcrops of gritstone. In clear weather, they offer good walking, but in foul weather the entire walk would need to be completed by following compass bearings. The walk which is suggested here wanders along the broad moorland crest of the mountains and then returns along a sort of natural moorland shelf to make a circuit. While other lines of descent are possible, these would result in lengthy road walks to return to the start.

The R280 road runs from Manorhamilton to Glenade Lough, but you should travel along the minor road which runs parallel to it, passing the church at Mullies before reaching Rassaun. There is

a farmyard near the start of this walk, where a polite request for a parking space might be favourably received. There is a clear, enclosed track running north-east uphill from the minor road, and this is your access route to the higher moorlands. Simply follow the track uphill, passing beneath two electricity transmission lines. The track twists and turns on the slope, but keeps climbing until it expires in an area of turf cuttings.

Head north-eastwards across the moorland slopes, crossing rugged heather and boulders in places, to reach a broad and vague summit at 423m (1,390ft). There are two little pools – Lough Agu and Lough Agow – but you should head north-westwards to the larger Lough Nabrack, which sits on a broad gap on the moorland crest. The ground can be boggy, and the best footing is available just beyond the outflow of the lough. Continue walking along the moorland crest, very gradually gaining height as you walk across the heathery, bouldery slope. In clear weather you will be able to distinguish a cairn far ahead, and you can aim straight towards it. There are plenty of cairns along this crest, and some of them make fine viewpoints. There is a slight gap on the crest, where a walk more due westwards leads to a summit at 482m (1,609ft) near Lough Aganny.

Continuing along the crest, views to east and west are opening up very well, but the broad slopes of Arroo still block some of the northward vista. There are slight rises and falls along the crest, but generally the trend is downwards. Look carefully around the sides of any rocky outcrops and you may be lucky enough to spot huge millstones lying abandoned in the heather. These great disks were hewn from the rock, but for some reason were never taken down from the moors. Perhaps the mill for which they were made suddenly closed. When crossing the broad gap, you will pass a prominent standing stone. This is a useful reference point in mist and it is unlikely to be confused with any other lumps of rock.

The moorland crest rises gradually towards Arroo Lough, and by continuing roughly northwards across rather more difficult moorland terrain, the summit trig point on Arroo itself can be gained at 523m (1,720ft). Despite its relatively modest height this can be a fine viewpoint, and the panorama includes the following:

| | |
|---|---|
| NW | Slieve League, Crownarad, Carrick Peninsula |
| NNE | Blue Stack Mountains |
| NE | Breesy Hill |
| ENE | Cliffs of Magho |
| E | Lough Navar and Big Dog Forests |
| ESE | Belmore Mountain |
| SE | Saddle Hill, Dough Mountain, Cuilcagh |
| S | Benbo, Arigna Mountains |
| SSW | Castlegal Range |
| SW | Truskmore |
| WSW | Tievebaun |
| WNW | Mullaghmore Head |

## The way back to Rassaun
*Allow 3 hours*

There is a natural moorland shelf running all the way along the western slopes of the Dartry Mountains. It is helpful if this has been noticed on the outward journey, because it is used on the return journey. Although you could descend westwards from the summit of Arroo and pick up the course of the shelf, it may be better to retrace your steps to Arroo Lough, then continue southwards to join the line of the shelf. Keep on the gentle moorland slopes between slightly steeper slopes above and below. By maintaining this line, you will need to cross a couple of little streams, and there is also some boggy ground and areas of peat hags. Despite occasional difficulties, follow the shelf onwards as far as Cullionboy. You may find a small, circular stone sheepfold perched on the edge of the shelf, offering a view across Rassaun where the walk started. There is also a better view of the Castlegal Range.

*A walking group treks across the heathery flanks of the Dartry Mountains.*

Descend rather steeper slopes towards a river. This is the one shown on the map as flowing out of Lough Nabrack, crossed at a higher level earlier in the day. Follow the river downstream, without crossing it, and look out for traces of a path which leads towards a clearer track on the lower slopes. The river itself is drawn into a rocky gorge, ending in a sudden waterfall, so you cannot follow it too closely in any case. However, once the track zigzags down through enclosed fields, it is worth making a short diversion back into the rocky, wooded gorge to take a close look at the waterfall from below. Note also the course of the river, which is flowing on limestone and is suddenly swallowed into subterranean passageways. The modern maps are mute about this spot, but older maps refer to it as Wild Cat's Hole. After exploring, follow the track onwards, passing beneath two

electricity transmission lines, to proceed past derelict houses on the way back to the minor road. Turn left along the minor road, passing attractive farm cottages on the way back to the starting point.

## Alternative routes

### ESCAPES

There are lines of cliffs around some parts of the Dartry Mountains, but in general terms it is safe to descend in almost any direction. However, simply walking in any direction may leave you having to hurdle walls and fences in order to reach the road, so it is best to refer to the map and chart a course towards one of the clear access tracks. If the walk commences in poor weather, the best thing to do is abandon it by retracing your steps, although the walk could be half-completed and a decision made to switch on to the course of the return route, which would at least put a bit of variety into the walk. The waterfall at Wild Cat's Hole would look much better after a spell of heavy rain.

### EXTENSIONS

Any extension to the route is limited only by the area of the Dartry Mountains. Sprawling shoulders spread in most directions and it is possible to walk with a fair amount of freedom across the heathery moors. However, any descents far away from Rassaun are likely to result in a long road walk back to the starting point. The only way to avoid this would be to arrange a lift from another finishing point in advance.

# Appendix:
# Useful addresses and information

## General Tourist Information

Bord Failte (Irish Tourist Board), Baggot Street Bridge, Dublin, Ireland. Tel: (01) 2844768.

## Local Tourist Information

Local tourist information is available from Tourist Information Offices at the following locations:

Jocelyn Street, Dundalk, Co Louth. (042) 35484
Fitzwilliam Square, Wicklow, Co Wicklow.
  (0404) 69117
Crescent Quay, Wexford, Co Wexford. (053) 23111
Williams Street Centre, Tullamore, Co Offaly.
  (0506) 52141
Chamber Buildings, Clonmel, Co Tipperary. (052) 22960
Main Street, Kilfinane, Co Limerick. (063) 91300
Aras Failte, Grand Parade, Cork, Co Cork.
  (021) 273251
Main Street, Kenmare, Co Kerry. (064) 41233
Town Hall, Killarney, Co Kerry. (064) 31633
Main Street, Dingle, Co Kerry. (066) 51188
Clare Road, Ennis, Co Clare. (065) 28366
Aras Failte, Eyre Square, Galway, Co Galway.
  (091) 63081
Market Street, Clifden, Co Galway. (095) 21163
The Mall, Westport, Co Mayo. (098) 25711
Achill Sound, Achill Island, Co Mayo. (098) 45384
Aras Reddan, Temple Street, Sligo, Co Sligo. (071) 61201

## Accommodation

The above Tourist Information Offices can usually book your accommodation for you. However, there is also a central accommodation reservation service, which operates on an all-Ireland basis, for which you need a credit card and access to a telephone. The number is Freefone (0800) 317153.

## Getting to Ireland

Ferries, flights and car hire are all easily arranged. It is possible to catch ferries and flights as simply as you catch a bus or train, but if you can plan ahead you can take advantage of special fares.

You can reach Ireland by flying into Dublin Airport, or a flight to one of the regional airports. These include Waterford, Cork, Kerry, Shannon, Galway, Knock and Sligo, but there will be fewer flights to the minor airports. Fast ferries are available between Holyhead and Dublin or Dun Laoghaire, with other services from Fishguard or Pembroke to Rosslare. There is also a longer ferry journey from Swansea to Cork. You could, of course, arrive in Ireland via Belfast or Larne, then drive southwards, or catch frequent trains or buses. Cars can generally be hired from the major airports and ferryports but enquire in advance, and make sure that you carry the appropriate documentation.

Travel between Britain and Ireland has always been a passport-free affair, and this is now becoming the case for travellers from all around Europe. If you are travelling from further afield, you may wish to check in advance to see if you will require a passport and/or visa to gain entry.

## Public Transport

Bus Eireann, Dublin. Tel: (01) 836 6111.
Dublin Bus, Dublin. Tel: (01) 873 4222.

## Mountain Rescue

Get to the nearest telephone and dial 999. Ask for the Mountain Rescue. This may well be co-ordinated through the Gardai (Police). Do not waste time trying to contact Mountain Rescue Teams direct. Follow any instructions you are given.

# INDEX